DICTIONARY OF GRAPHIC ARTS TERMS

A Communication Tool for
People Who Buy Type and Printing

DICTIONARY OF GRAPHIC ARTS TERMS

A Communication Tool for People Who Buy Type and Printing

Patrica Barnes Mintz

VAN NOSTRAND REINHOLD COMPANY
NEW YORK CINCINNATI ATLANTA DALLAS SAN FRANCISCO
LONDON TORONTO MELBOURNE

Van Nostrand Reinhold Company Regional Offices:
New York Cincinnati Atlanta Dallas San Francisco

Van Nostrand Reinhold Company International Offices:
London Toronto Melbourne

Library of Congress Catalog Card Number: 80-25236
ISBN: 0-442-26711-8

Manufactured in the United States of America

Published by Van Nostrand Reinhold Company
135 West 50th Street, New York, N.Y. 10020

Published simultaneously in Canada by Van Nostrand Reinhold Ltd.

15 14 13 12 11 10 9 8 7 6 5 4 3 2 1

Library of Congress Cataloging in Publication Data

Mintz, Patricia Barnes.
Dictionary of graphic arts terms.

1. Printing—Dictionaries. 2. Graphic arts—
Dictionaries. I. Title.
Z118.M56 686.2'03 80-25236
ISBN 0-442-26711-8

Introduction

This book is for people who have to buy type, printing, or other graphic arts services. It defines the most common terminology from six industries: printing, typography, binding, publishing, papermaking, and design. It does not cover each industry comprehensively, but rather, it is written to resolve confusions between people in the different industries, and it is a reference to enable them to communicate with other people within those industries. The most important terms are presented here, so that the reader can quickly look up the basics of these trades.

The *Dictionary of Graphic Arts Terms* is for anyone whose business it is to communicate with producers of the printed word, be it preparation of advertising, business forms, or bound books. The book also offers suggestions for saving costs while obtaining the desired results. It is for editors who must deal with production and distribution. It is for new production supervisors who don't want to overspend through lack of thorough knowledge of printing and typesetting processes. It is for all those who have been confused by modern technological advances in the graphic arts.

Changing times are more evident in the graphic arts industries than in almost any other. Trends toward the use of offset lithography, phototypesetting, video display, color reproduction by scanners, and the laser have represented revolutionary changes. Within the industry, newspapers and large commercial printers have been the first to use the new technology because they have had the capital to cover the expense, and because almost all stages of the graphic arts processes are included within their organizations, they have direct control of them.

Eastman Kodak Company's Graphics Markets Division says, "We don't foresee altogether new technologies in the next five to ten years. What we do see ahead is development and broader application of existing technologies—all directed toward minimizing or eliminating steps within the basic reproduction process."[1] It is therefore imperative for those involved with the published word to know what is going on in the graphic arts and how to communicate with suppliers.

[1] Frank E. Benham of Eastman Kodak's Graphics Markets Division, "We're Not Just Printers Anymore," *Book Production Industry,* September, 1978, p. 28.

In the A to Z section of the dictionary you will find concise, specific definitions of terms concerning processes, techniques, and materials that are basic in printing and associated fields. You will:

1. Quickly find answers to specific questions.
2. Make sure no information has been overlooked in a production process.
3. Consider related fields of information.
4. Refresh your memory in areas that contain too many details to remember all at once.

For example, if you want to know more about paper, you can refer to the entries on *paper* and on *paper basis weights.* If you are selecting type, the section on *typeface styles* will be helpful. If the various printing processes seem confusing, look up *printing* for brief definitions, then read about one or more in detail under its own listing. One reference may answer your question, but often two or three will serve the purpose. Cross-references will refer to alternatives and suggested materials to use. *If any of the terms within an entry are not understood, look up those terms themselves.*

Readers of this dictionary need quick information for practical purposes. Some entries include suggestions as to where to get more information and what to ask your supplier. Prices are not listed and should be obtained by asking for an estimate from the supplier, agency, or free-lancer providing the particular service in question.

Acknowledgments

Special thanks go to those whose invaluable help and availability for answering questions rendered this book possible. They are Jeff Barrie of University Graphics, Inc.; Marianne Gladych of M. Gladych Design Inc.; L. Ron Hubbard, educator and photographer; Jemet Inc.; J. M. Post Graphics; Steve Romano of Halliday Lithograph; Andrew Steigmeier, freelance designer; James Drew Werner, typesetter and layout artist; William B. Woody of Arcata Book Group; and many other enthusiastic people who willingly provided information about their respective fields.

DICTIONARY OF GRAPHIC ARTS TERMS

A Communication Tool for
People Who Buy Type and Printing

A

a.a. Author's alteration. Any correction in a proof not caused by a printer's error. Such corrections must be paid for by the client, whereas cost for a p.e. is absorbed by the printer or typesetter. A.a.'s are not included in any estimate, and when they are caused by an author as opposed to a designer or an editor, the publisher may charge the author for costs above a certain percentage of the total composition bill. Author's alterations are charged by the typesetter on a per line basis which may include resetting the rest of the paragraph for fit. A printer may charge for a.a's on a time basis. Some a.a.'s may be inevitable, but many are a result of careless editing or spec'ing of the manuscript. *See also* copy preparation, proof, and proofread.

abrasion resistance. The ability of ink or paper to withstand treatment such as rubbing or scuffing.

absorption. 1. The property of paper which allows it to take up liquids or vapors. 2. The partial suppression of light through a transparent or translucent material. An absorbent material takes in light rather than letting it pass.

accordian fold. A series of two or more parallel folds which open opposite to each other like an accordian.

acetate. 1. A cellulose sheet. The sheet can carry type matter and be placed over a mechanical which is to be shot. Or it can contain light-blocking material to indicate color breaks for printing in which more than one color will be used. 2. Clear film on which positive type is set in photocomposition. It is used when stripping a working positive flat, and is now often used by designers in-house to paste up positive art and type in final form to send to the printer for shooting. If pasted-up in-house, it saves steps usually done by the stripper when a conventional mechanical is provided.

acetate proof. *See* color key.

across the grain. *See* against the grain.

adapting fonts. Blowing up fonts and adapting certain letters on specially designed cameras in either Linofilm or VIP systems. This service is sometimes required by educational standards for letter forms in texts for lower grades, or to satisfy a designer's whim. Not all compositors provide this service.

adcut. *See* logotype.

additive color. Color produced by combining light rays of various colors on the spectrum. The additive primary colors are blue, red, and green. If three film projectors are set up to project the additive primary colors, blue, red, and green, the three colors will overlap to form the subtractive primary colors, magenta, yellow, and cyan. Where the blue light overlaps the red light, magenta is produced. Where red light and green light overlap, yellow is produced. Where green light and blue light overlap, cyan is produced. Magenta is the complementary color of green, yellow of blue, and cyan of red. That is to say, when each color is mixed with its complementary color, white is formed, i.e., the mixture will be neutralized. And this is the basis for process color separation. When magenta, yellow, and cyan ink are printed, they overlap to form red, green, and blue, and this is how halftone dots are printed to form the illusion of continuous tones of a full-color illustration. *See also* color, color separation, and halftone dot.

adhesive binding. An in-line high-speed method of binding soft-cover or hard-cover books or magazines, allowing a publication to lie open flat. Adhesive bind-

Adhesive binding getting hot-melt. (*Courtesy Kingsport Press*)

ing also allows more last-minute inserts and use of special stock for certain signatures than any other method except mechanical spiral binding. Pages are tested at the bindery to see that page pull and page flex hold up according to specifications. If not well prepared, pages can fall out of an adhesive binding.

Adhesive binding is less expensive than sewn binding, but in some cases not as sturdy. It can have a stronger page pull test, but in a tumbler test, sewn bindings last longer.

Signatures are either handfed or delivered in sequence from a gathering machine or conveyor and placed in a bookclamp. Vibrators jog the book to fit the clamps. As the book or magazine passes through the machine, the backbone is trimmed, roughened, brushed, and dust is extracted with toothed saw blades and roughing discs. Applicator wheels apply animal glue, polyvinyl acetate, or hot melt, then covers are fed from a pile on continuous feeders. Clamps are opened and adhesive-bound volumes are released onto a stacker or conveyer where they must be handled carefully to maintain an even square.

Uncoated papers are good for adhesive binding, but enamel-coated papers which are necessary for high-quality illustrations create problems because the glue sticks to the coating of the paper instead of to the paper. However, the use of adhesive bindings is increasing in hard-cover books. Also called perfect binding. *See also* binding, binding tests.

aerial composition. *See* computer assisted makeup.

against the grain. At right angles to the direction of the grain of the paper in feeding the press or in folding. The grain direction is formed by the fibers aligning themselves along the wire of the papermaking machine. *See also* papermaking.

agate line. Originally the name of a 5½-pt. type, now a unit of measure for newspaper or advertising space. Fourteen agate lines equal one column inch. One agate line is one standard newspaper column wide by 1/14-in. deep. It does not matter what size of type is printed in that space. Cost of advertising per agate line per million of circulation is called a milline rate. Cost per agate line per billion dollars of retail sales in the market area covered is called the marline rate.

Agate line ruler.

air. *See* white space.

airbrush. A small pressure gun that sprays paint, or a film of color, by means of compressed air. It is used to retouch photographs and to correct or obtain graduated tones and soft effects that cannot otherwise be achieved. Also used in platemaking to remove spots or unwanted areas of image.

airbrush shaded contour. A halftone shaded effect done by airbrushing around the contours of letters. The effect can also be made photographically from the negative of the plain letters and used as a special effect of lettering.

airbrush shaded effect. A shading that gives lettering a dimension of depth, as if the letters are floating in the air. It is done with the letters and a halftone screen, photographically, or by hand with an airbrush.

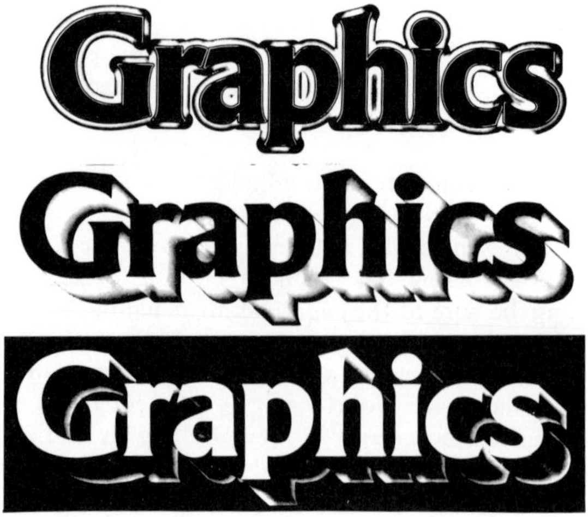

Airbrush shaded lettering. (*Courtesy Graphics Modifier, Byers Corporation*)

albertype. *See* collotype.

albumin glazing dyes. Dyes which are transparent and easily mixed. They are often used to tone or dye a matte or glossy black-and-white photograph. Separate areas can be colored individually, and the whole image can be dyed to achieve a result that has no resemblance to a conventional color enlargement.

albumin plate. A surface offset plate onto which the printing image is chemically baked. These plates have been developed to the point where they now have a longer life and are competing with deep-etch plates which were formerly used for longer runs. *See also* deep-etch and presensitized plate.

align. To arrange type or illustrations so that vertical and horizontal lines appear even on the page.

alphabet length. The horizontal measurement, in points, of the lowercase alphabet set in a particular typeface and size. It is a measure of the type style's compactness and can be converted into characters per pica for copyfitting. *See also* copyfitting.

alphanumeric. Any system of letters and numerals combined. For example, AM 640. Alphanumeric data is the keyboarded copy of a manuscript to be typeset.

alteration. A correction in copy or art after it has been typeset or shot. *See also* a.a.

aluminum plates. Sheet of aluminum used in offset lithography to carry the image.

Amberlith. Trade name for a red- or orange-coated acetate sheet used on a mechanical to indicate areas of color, tints, etc. It can be cut or stripped to form outlines and silhouettes.

ampersand. The character "&," used for the word "and."

aniline printing. *See* flexo or flexography.

annotate. To include explanatory or critical notes or comments either at the foot of a page, in the margins, or in an appendix.

antique finish. Paper with a rough surface similar to the old handmade papers. It is off-white in color, has no shine, and bulks thicker than paper with a smoothly calendered finish. Halftones do not reproduce well on antique wove or antique laid paper. *See also* finish.

appendix. Material added to the end of a book including notes, tables, etc.

arabic. Common way of numbering 1, 2, 3 as opposed to Roman i, ii, iii.

arranging lines of type. There are five ways to arrange type on a page: (1) Justified, in which all the lines align both on left and right sides; (2) unjustified, or flush left, ragged right, in which lines align on the left and are left as they fall at the end of each line; (3) flush right, ragged left, similar to the above, but in reverse; (4) centered, with both sides ragged, but the lines centered on the page; (5) asymmetrical, with no predictable pattern in the placement.

Justified	There are five basic ways to arrange lines of type on a page; the style you choose is dictated by esthetics, legibility, and the amount of copy to be set.
Flush left, ragged right	There are five basic ways to arrange lines of type on a page; the style you choose is dictated by esthetics, legibility, and the amount of copy to be set.
Flush right, ragged left	There are five basic ways to arrange lines of type on a page; the style you choose is dictated by esthetics, legibility, and the amount of copy to be set.
Centered	There are five basic ways to arrange lines of type on a page; the style you choose is dictated by esthetics, legibility, and the amount of copy to be set.
Asymmetrical	There are five basic ways to arrange lines of type on a page; the style you choose is dictated by esthetics, legibility, and the amount of copy to be set.

Arranging lines of type.

art. Any reproducible copy such as mechanicals, photographs, transparencies, line work, etc., to be photographed for a printing plate. Artwork together with manuscript and layout are necessary to complete a printing job. Artwork must not be damaged or laid against anything that will leave marks on it. It is wise to protect artwork by a tissue overlay and to wrap it in cardboard. For the artwork to be prepared, the size, the method of reproduction, and the paper to be used should be known to the artist. Instructions for reproduction should be clear for the printer. *See also* halftone, line photography, mechanical, photography.

art director. The person who directs the production of all art for a publication or agency. He or she makes final decisions regarding the art and processes to be used, but usually does not do actual paste-up. *See also* design.

artotype. *See* collotype.

art services. A studio that provides such services as photography, retouching, typesetting, making photostats, layout, and pasteup of mechanicals. An art service usually charges more than an individual free-lance artist.[2]

artwork. *See* art.

Artype. *See* pressure-sensitive lettering.

ascender. The upperstroke of a lowercase letter that extends above the x-height, or body of the type such as in h, b, d, l, and f. Likewise, a descender is the lowerstroke of a letter that descends below the line as in p, q, and y. The type size is measured from the top of the tallest ascender to a point below the bottom of the lowest descender, called the shoulder.

assembly. All elements which are stripped together according to a layout for color separation, duplicating, or platemaking.

asterisk. Used for reference to footnotes where the use of superior numbers might look confusing. Looks like * . For entire series *see also* footnote.

asymmetrical type. Lines of type with no pattern of placement. *See also* arranging lines of type.

ATF. American Type Founders. They have been the leading makers of foundry or hand-set type since the days when letterpress was the principal printing method used.

author's alteration. *See* a.a.

automatic typewriter. *See* word processing.

Autonegative film. Special duplicating film used to contact negative to negative without going to a positive as is usually done. The film has already been exposed by the manufacturer. It is very high-speed film requiring more light at higher intensity than normal films. Autonegative film was formerly required for the Cameron belt-press because of the emulsion being up on right-reading film, and it was used to make the necessary flexible plates. Now flexible plates can be made from emulsion down film.

Autopositive film. A negative piece of film that converts into a positive during the development process, thus creating a positive directly from a positive.

Autoscreen film. A screened film with which halftones can be made without the use of a ruled screen or contact screen. This process saves time in making halftone negatives.

[2]Two useful guides to artists and art services are *The Literary Market Place,* R. R. Bowker Company, an annual publication, and *Printers Buying Guide,* Printing Industries of Metropolitan New York.

B

baby dummy. A grid representing all the pages and spreads in a publication. The editor, art director, and production manager can mark or pin page layouts on the baby dummy for planning an issue. It can be made from paper, cork board, acetate, or any substrate on which changes can be made.

backbone. 1. The back of a bound book connecting the front and back covers. 2. The spine of folded and gathered signatures when they receive covers in adhesive binding. *See also* spine.

backbone. The back of a bound book connecting the front and back covers. *See also* spine.

backing. The part of the bindery process which spreads the back edge of the gathered signatures to make a shoulder against which the book cover will fit and can be hinged. The indented hinge makes the book stay in its cover twice as long as a flatback book. The backed book is lined with pieces of crash and cased-in, or fit, into the cover by paste, pressure, and heat. *See also* binding, bookblock, crash, gather, round backing or rounding.

backing up. Printing the reverse side of a sheet that has already been printed on one side. This is either done after the ink has dried, or in one operation on a perfecting press.

back lining. Paper or fabric that adheres to the spine of a hardcover book. *See also* crash.

back matter. *See* end matter.

bad break. 1. The setting of a hyphenated line as the first line on a page, starting the page with a widow. 2. Incorrect hyphenation at the end of the line.

bag paper. Kraft paper used for making paper bags. It comes in various weights. *See also* kraft paper.

bankers flap envelope. *See* envelope styles.

Baby dummy. Note odd numbered pages are on the right-hand side. Even numbered pages are on the left-hand side. These are always facing pages.

baronial envelope. *See* envelope styles.

base. 1. All the metal below the shoulder of a piece of metal type. *See* type for illustration. 2. The metal or wood block on which letterpress printing plates are mounted to make them type high.

base color. The first color printed, over which other colors are laid down. In four-color process printing, this is usually yellow. *See also* process color.

baseline. 1. Horizontal line upon which all the characters in a line of type stand, and below which the descenders fall. 2. A point of reference at the bottom of a piece of art for purposes of register or cropping.

base-to-base. Measurement in points from the bottom of the base line of a given line to the bottom of the base line of the line immediately following. Abbreviated B/B. For example:

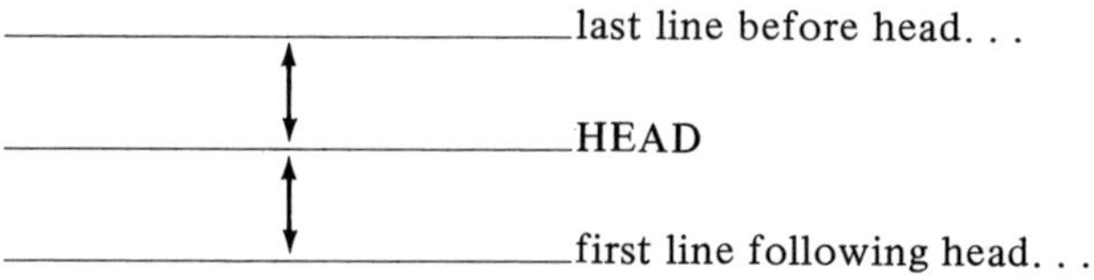

Base to base.

basis weight or **basic weight.** Weight in pounds of a ream (500 sheets) of paper cut in a standard size for each grade of paper. For example, standard size of book papers is 25″ × 38″; for cover papers, 20″ × 26″. The basic size is not the same for all grades of paper. Thus 50-lb book paper means that 500 sheets of 25″ × 38″ weighs 50 lbs. The basic weight is determined by the pulp and additives at the headbox of the papermaking machine. Weight is sometimes referred to per thousand sheets in which case "substance 50" would be written "100/M." Also called substance. *See also* paper grades and papermaking.

bastard progressives. *See* progressive proofs.

bastard size. A nonstandard size of any material used in the graphic arts.

bastard title. The title of a book printed on the right-hand page preceding the title page. Sometimes called half title although the half title is really the title of the book printed on a page immediately preceding the first page of text.

batter. Damaged type. A press batter refers to damaged cuts or type on the letterpress.

bed. The flat part of the press that holds the type form during letterpress printing. A job that is ready for printing is said to be "put to bed."

bellows. The part of the camera which extends from the lens to the film board behind and keeps the light from entering the camera. It looks like an accordian and is expandable.

belt-press book production system. A printing unit developed in the late sixties on a one-color web press which also folds, trims, and glues binding. Individual flexible page plates are mounted in imposition on variable length belts. The press prints both sides of the web, slits the web, folds the slit ribbons into signatures, collates the signatures and perfect binds them into finished books. It is being improved to permit better quality halftone reproduction. *See also* Cameron book production system and Letterflex.

Benday process. A method, invented by Benjamin Day, of laying a screen of dots, lines, or other patterns on line plates for letterpress by the use of gelatin films to give the printed image an appearance of tone. The process has been superseded in offset printing by the use of transparent, adhesive, printed screens such as Zip-a-Tone, or acetate overlays, with which the artist works directly on the original artwork or mechanical.

bf. *See* boldface and proofreader's marks.

bible paper. A thin, opaque, high-tensile strength book paper used where low bulk is necessary such as in bibles and dictionaries. Basic weights are from about 14 to 30 pounds.

bibliography. **1.** A list of writings relating to a given subject or author. **2.** The science of describing books and recording their histories.

bimetal plates. Plates used for long runs of a million or more. The base for the printing image is copper or brass, grease-accepting metals. The nonprinting area is aluminum, stainless steel, or chromium, water-receptive metals. Bimetal plates last longer than deep-etch plates.

bimonthly. A publication which comes out every two months.

binder. **1.** A device with metal rings for holding loose-leaf sheets. **2.** Also, a substance which binds ink to a substrate. **3.** Person who works at a bindery.

binder's board. High-quality, single-ply, solid pulp pasteboard over which cloth, paper, or leather is applied for a stiff book cover. It is compressed under heat and steam, and has no grain direction. For quality books, binder's board should be used rather than pasted oak, which warps.

bindery. An establishment that finishes and covers books, pamphlets, magazines, etc. The printer must know who is binding a job, since the printer's imposition must suit the binder's equipment. Some binderies handle only book manufacture, and some only offer soft cover, or adhesive binding, subcontracting

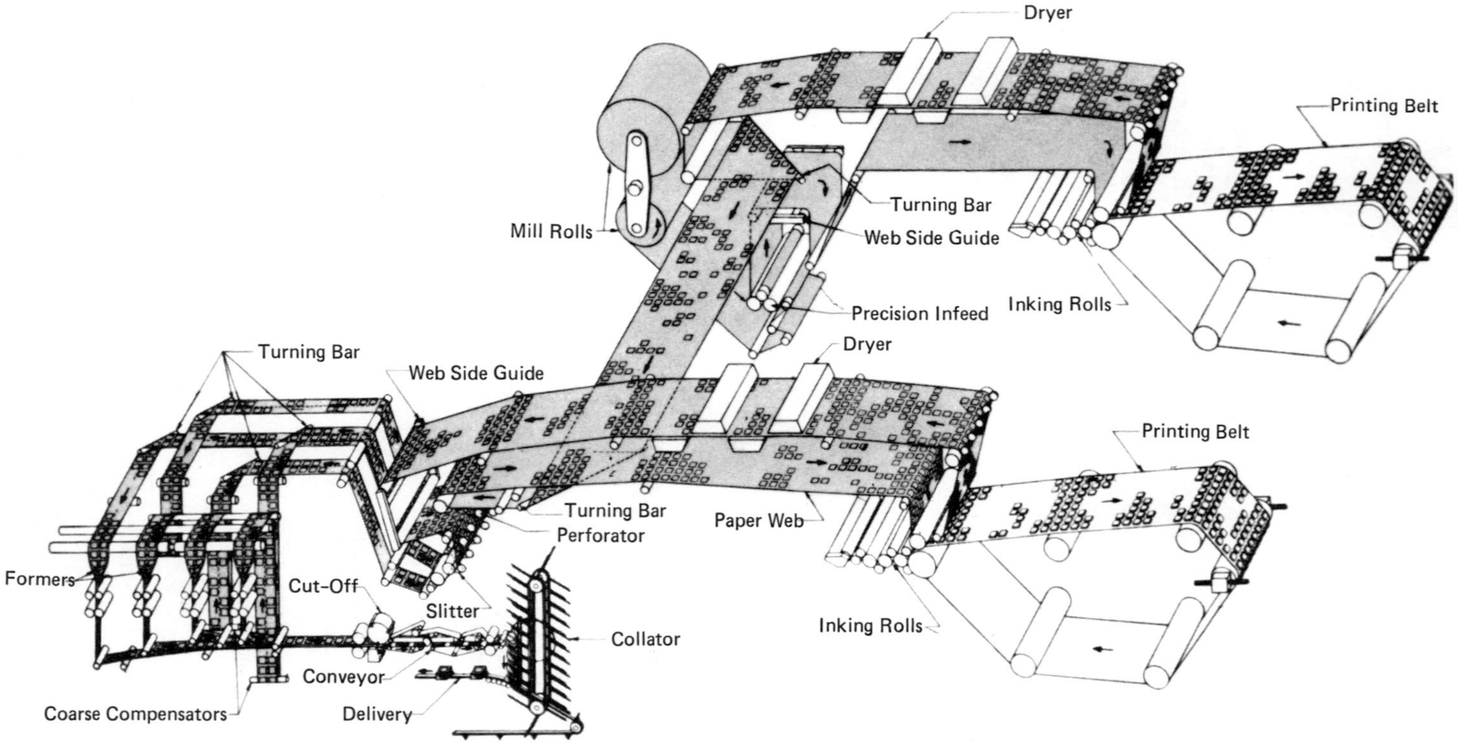

Belt press. (*Courtesy of Kingsport Press*)

Benday tints.

hard-cover work. Others offer additional finishing services, such as perforating, round-cornering, tabbing, creasing, or varnishing.

binding. Binding includes folding, trimming, gathering, stitching, glueing, inserting, and casing-in, after the sheets have been printed.

A one- or two-page brochure that is finished when it comes off the press has no binding. A piece folded either on press or on a folding machine is the next simplest. Some folding machinery will do rough trimming, or make serrated edges. Trimming the signatures opens the pages and evens up uneven edges produced in folding. Special folds, inserts or cancels are very expensive, because they require handwork.

Types of binding. A *self-cover* pamphlet is one with the cover printed with the text on the same kind of paper as the text.

Books are usually printed in 16- or 32-page signatures, gathered, sewn, or the spine cut for glue, smashed, given end papers, trimmed on three sides, rounded, backed, and cased in. In *case binding,* or *edition binding,* sewn signatures plus end papers are enclosed in a rigid cover. *Smyth sewing* is made with a thread passing through the fold of each signature and knotted at the back. In a *side-sewn* book, the thread passes through the side of the signature. This is the strongest possible binding. A *side-wire* is the same and makes use of a wire instead of thread.

Bindery processes. Signatures are collated on conveyor. (*Courtesy Kingsport Press*)

Signatures are sewn. (*Courtesy Kingsport Press*)

Book blocks are inspected. (*Courtesy Kingsport Press*)

Books have been cased-in. (*Courtesy Kingsport Press*)

Hand tooling a leather binding. (*Courtesy Kingsport Press*)

In *saddle stitching,* wire staples are inserted through the fold at the spine of a publication and clinched at the center spread.

Perfect binding, or *adhesive binding,* holds together the pages without sewing. The backs of the signatures are cut off or notched, and an adhesive of animal glue, polyvinyl acetate or hot melt is applied. The book is then cased in or given a paper cover. Adhesive binding is much faster than sewn binding, but in some cases not as strong. It is not practical with enamel-coated papers because the glue sticks to the coating rather than to the paper.

Notch binding and *burst binding* use less paper than adhesive binding. Notches are perforated or cut into the signatures, and the book is glued together. This is stronger than adhesive binding, but cheaper than sewn binding.

In *mechanical binding,* the pages and cover are held together by metal or plastic coils such as in a loose-leaf notebook.

There are also new systems for office binding in which a document or report can be individually heated, glued, or otherwise fastened into a permanent covering.

Now in experimental stages is *welding* which requires a specially coated paper, and *thread sealing,* which fuses thread and paper. Binding wire coated with hot-melt adhesive is being developed.

Web presses are also being adapted so that a thread-stitched signature can come off the press in line with the printing operations.

See also adhesive binding, Bindery Usages of the Trade—Appendix Six, book covering materials, cerlox binding, perfect binding, saddle stitch, or saddle wire, side-sewing, Smyth sewn, spiral binding, and wire-o binding.

binding tests. *See* page flex and page pull.

bite. **1.** The time required for the etching solution on an engraved plate to wash away a relief below the desired image. Also called take. **2.** A surface characteristic of paper which determines the degree of the ink's acceptance.

biweekly. A publication appearing every two weeks.

black and white. Originals or reproductions in a single color, as opposed to multicolor. Abbreviated bw.

blackface. *See* boldface.

black letter type. Old English or text typeface with pointed Gothic letterforms that look like a style of handwriting from the fifteenth century. Fraktur is a lighter version. *See also* typeface styles.

blackline. *See* blue or blueline.

black printer. The black plate or negative in color printing, made to give proper emphasis to neutral tones and detail, and to add density to the illustrations.

Cloister Black

Black letter type.

blanket. The rubber-surfaced material clamped around the cylinder in offset lithography which transfers the ink from plate to paper. It is made of several plys of cotton fabric laminated and coated with natural or synthetic rubber.

blanket-to-blanket-press. A perfecting press in which the web runs between two blanket cylinders, each of which acts as the impression cylinder for the other. *See also* offset lithography.

blanks. Pages on which nothing is to be printed. Blank pages in a book should be designated when material is given to the compositor or stripper so that nothing will be misplaced during imposition.

bleed. A printed image that extends off the page when the edge of the paper has been trimmed. The bleed can be seen on the edge of the page. The bleed image must extend from 1/8-in. to 1/4-in. beyond the trim size for trimming. The printer uses a larger sheet size to accommodate bleeds than for a job that has no bleeds, and this must be considered when ordering paper.

bleed marks. Marks on either a proof or on a mechanical that indicate to the printer where the trim of the paper will be. If an image is to bleed it must extend beyond the trim by 1/8- to 1/4-inch. It is necessary for the stripper to know which pages of a job bleed and which do not so that he strips them into the flat properly.

blind embossing. A bas-relief design that is stamped with a regular stamping die except that no ink or foil is used. Also called blind stamping.

blind folio. A page number which is counted but not actually shown on the printed page.

blind keyboard. A tape-producing keyboard in a typesetting unit which has no visual display and which produces no hard copy. Thus the keyboard operator cannot see what he or she has typed.

blind-stamping. A blank impression made under heat and pressure without ink, foil, or leaf. A substrate is often blind stamped before stamping in ink or foil. *See also* blind embossing.

blistering. A condition on a press sheet where the surface of the sheet has been sealed tightly by ink or varnish and the moisture within the sheet is higher than normal. This can occur where extreme amounts of heat are used to dry ink. The moisture within begins to boil, creating a vapor which expands and cannot escape through the surface, thus creating a bubble on the surface of the sheet.

block. 1. A group of words, characters, or digits in one section of an input/output medium, handled as a unit. 2. A cut or engraving that is mounted on a wood or metal base.

block letter. Sans serif type-face style.

block quotation. *See* extract.

blocking. 1. Mounting an engraving on a block of wood or metal to make it type-high so it can be locked up in a letterpress form to be printed. 2. The sticking together of printed sheets when piled too high before the ink has dried.

blow-up. An enlargement of the size of copy or an illustration. This is usually indicated by the percentage to which the illustration is to be enlarged or reduced. Thus, twice the size of the original would be 200%, and three-quarters the size of the original would be a reduction to 75%. A camera is limited to enlargements of 400% but a laser scanner will enlarge to 1600%. *See also* proportion scale and scanner.

Screened artwork cannot be enlarged without some treatment of the dot pattern in the screen in order to retain the look of continuous tone. *See also* copy dot.

When typefaces are blown up there is a distortion of the contours of the characters. A computer can redesign blown up-letters for optimum shape. *See also* display type.

blue or blueline. A photoprint made on paper contacted to a stripped-up negative, used as a proof to check position of negative assembly of images and copy before the printing plate is made. The name comes from the color used when the process was invented, but many colors are now used to make the proof. Except for the light-sensitive chemical on the surface of the paper, bluelines, brownlines, and vandykes are identical.

Many people have difficulty reading blues, and the following points should be considered when checking them:
(1) Although a blueline is one color, usually blue, brown, or gray on a yellow or gray paper, color variations will show up as a different intensity of the color being used on the blueline, if all the negatives have been burned into the same blueline. When checking against the original illustration or a dummy, check for register where more than one color is laid down. A fuzzy line will show if the colors are not perfectly in register. If a separate blue has been made for each color used, then the intensity of the negative for each color will show up on each blue. (2) Screens can be checked for proper percentage by the use of a screen

determiner. (3) If the printer has cut a window and dropped in illustrations, e.g., when the compositor has provided a mechanical and stat for position of halftones, blues should be checked against the dummy or mechanicals for proper cropping and positioning of illustrations. All alignments should be checked against corner marks and trim marks on the blues. (4) Corrections marked on the previous proofs must be checked to see if they were made. Blues also offer the last chance to check for broken letters and hickies before plates are made. Unless it is a printer's error, corrections at this stage are extremely expensive and time consuming because they involve setting new type, shooting, stripping, and recontacting, so blues are mainly used to check as to whether or not all previous instructions have been carried out.

blue pencil. **1.** Nonreproducible pencil used for editing and proofreading. Camera reproduction is designed so that it is not sensitive to the blue pencil. **2.** To edit a manuscript. Traditionally, editors use a blue pencil to correct, or cut a manuscript.

blueprint. **1.** The Photoprint method used to duplicate mechanical and architectural drawings in the same size, showing white lines on a blue background. The paper may stretch or shrink a little in the process. During contact exposure, the photoprint paper turns blue wherever light hits it and remains white where light is not allowed to pass through because of the black ink on the original drawing.

The Ozalid and diazo processes have now replaced blueprints. The Ozalid and diazo are more legible, and show black lines or dark lines on a light background. They are cheaper than blueprints, and they change dimensions less than a blueprint during developing.

2. Loosely applied to any method of same-size photocopying from translucent originals. *See also* blueline.

blurb. **1.** A short piece of descriptive material on a book jacket for sales purposes. **2.** A headline intended to persuade a reader to read a magazine story. Also called precede and deck.

boards. Rigid material such as pasteboard used to make covers of a book. *See also* binder's board and pasted oak.

board stock. *See* paperboard.

body. **1.** The metal block of a piece of letterpress type that carries the printing surface of the letter plus extra space below the letter called the shoulder. In letterpress, this block of type determines the point size measured from the top of the ascender to the bottom of the shoulder. The body of type is larger than the actual size of most characters. These measurements are the same even when typesetting is done photographically. *See also* shoulder and type. **2.** The consistency, viscosity, and flow of an ink.

body copy. The text of a story as opposed to the display headings.

body size. The height of the printed letter from the top of the ascender to the bottom of the shoulder, measured in points. So called because of the metal block on which the character was cast for letterpress. The character could also be cast on a larger body than that of the size of the type font in order to obtain the effect of leading between the lines. For example, 10 on 12 means 10-pt. characters on a body with 12 points from base-to-base of each line. This measurement is still used with phototype today.

body type. The type used for the main part of the story, or the text, as opposed to display type used for headings and advertisements.

boldface. A heavyweight version of a regular typeface. Abbreviated bf. A wavy line under the words indicates to the typesetter that the type should be set in boldface. **It looks like this.**

bond paper. A grade of writing and printing paper treated so as to take ink well and have good erasure qualities, strength, and durability. It is also suitable for offset printing. Cheaper grades are made from all-wood fiber, the better grades have rag content. Four 8½ X 11 sheets can be cut from a 17 X 22 sheet, which is the standard size for this grade. Basic weights are 13, 16, 20, and 24 lbs. Bond papers also come in colors. *See also* basis weight or basic weight.

bone knife. Originally a hand tool known as "ever-in-hand paper-folder." In hand binding it is used to crease each edge as a fold is made.

book. 1. A unified, individual work of some length by an author or editor. 2. Slang term for magazine.

bookblock. One or more sets of the book pages which have been gathered and trimmed and are ready to be fed into subsequent bindery operations. A bookblock does not depend on a certain number of sections, but rather on what will fit into subsequent machinery, e.g., the machine for gilding the edges of pages.

book cloth. *See* book covering materials.

book covering materials. Book coverings are either cloth, called *woven,* or paper, called *nonwoven.*

For a *woven* material to be made for a cloth-covered book, unbleached material called greige goods, is brought from the mill to the manufacturing process. The greige goods still has impurities in it, as it has not been through any refining process. Rolls of greige goods are sewn together and run through a huge web for processing. The material is first singed by a flame in order to burn out impurities. It then passes on to the bleaching stage so that it becomes a pure white, a good basis for the dye which is later applied. The bleached material is then stretched and sized so that it will not lose its shape in the wet process. The material is starch-filled and then dyed. Next it passes through a long, ovenlike drying machine after which it is coated for the finish and dried again.

Cotton cloth which has been sized, glazed, or impregnated with synthetic resins, is available in a large variety of weights, colors, and finishes.

Starch-filled cloth is vulnerable to water spotting and soiling because it cannot be wiped clean. It cannot be printed by offset lithography. Impregnating with synthetic resins does not change the cloth's appearance, but makes it water resistant. Coating conceals the original weave of the cloth, but it may be stamped to carry a pattern or to simulate cloth or leather. Impregnated and coated cloths can be printed with offset lithography.

Pyroxylin, which is another name for cellulose nitrate or celloid, is the most common impregnation or coating, but vinyl and other plastic coatings are sometimes used.

The bookbinder usually buys the cloth for a binding job after the client has specified what is wanted.

Nonwoven covering materials are merely coated paper. Coating is applied from a large vat on a coating machine and the roll of paper passes once or more through a drying machine. After it has been dried, it can be embossed with a design or calendered for a shiny smooth coating. The paper covering is also tested with various paper tests for strength, durability, scuff resistance, etc. Manufacturers of book-covering materials can supply charts of the grades they make and the prices for each.

book jacket. *See* jacket.

booklet. A pamphlet, usually bound in paper covers and used for promotional or informative purposes. *See also* pamphlet.

book manufacturing. Printing and binding of books. The cost of manufacturing should be 1/4 to 1/8 the list price of the book. The higher the print run, the lower the unit cost of manufacturing will be.

book number. *See* ISBN.

book paper. A grade of coated or uncoated paper made for the manufacture of books, pamphlets, and magazines as opposed to newsprint, writing, or cover stock. The basic size of book paper is 25″ × 38,″ and it is measured in weights of a ream of this size. It is less expensive than text papers, and is made in smooth or antique finish. *See also* paper basis weight.

borders. Decorative lines or designs used to surround type or illustrations on a page.

bottom line. The lowest line in a financial statement or estimate, showing the net income or loss.

6 POINT

12 POINT

6 POINT SIDE

6 POINT

6 POINT SIDE

6 POINT SIDE

12 POINT WAVED

6 POINT SIDE

6 POINT

6 POINT

6 POINT

6 POINT

6 POINT

6 POINT

6 POINT

6 POINT

6 POINT

6 POINT

6 POINT

12 POINT

6 POINT

6 POINT

6 POINT

6 POINT

6 POINT

6 POINT

6 POINT

12 POINT

6 POINT

6 POINT SIDE

6 POINT HYPHEN LEADERS ON SIDE

12 POINT

12 POINT

Borders.

bound proofs. A cheap paper binding of galleys or page proofs used for reviews before the book is published.

Bourges color. Trade name for printer's ink colors or color tints on color-coated overlay sheets keyed to standard printing inks. The colors are used for color separation overlays on art; to modify photo backgrounds; to alter color values on transparencies; to determine the result when one color is printed over another such as in duotones; or to make comps or displays.

The sheets can be photographed with full-color art or separately to save separation costs. Bourges color sheets are either made of a cutaway film with pressure-sensitive backing, or with a color coating, removable with a stylus or liquid color remover. The color guide with transparent swatches can be used to choose the exact color.

box. A ruled border that surrounds copy on all four sides. Boxes emphasize copy or set it off from the rest of the page. Boxed copy must be set narrower than copy in the same column that is not boxed.

boxheading. A heading with a rule around it. A box heading is usually centered. *See also* heading.

Box Heading

Box heading.

box printing. *See* container printing.

brackets. A device for setting off material which is extraneous or incidental to the context. *See also* parentheses and proofreader's marks.

break for color. To separate with masks the parts of a job to be printed in different colors. The camera preparation person will put a piece of white paper under an overlay thus creating a window to show where the color goes. The negative will pick up the shape of the overlay so that when the printing plate is made, the hole will expose onto the plate where the color image will be printed by a different plate. Instructions on the layout or proof say "break for color." The origin of the term is from letterpress. A printer is said to break the form when he removes type from a form in which it is arranged and puts it in the proper form for printing another color.

brightness. **1.** The light reflected by the copy in photography. **2.** The reflectance of the paper, which affects the brilliance, snap, and sparkle of the subject.

Artificial brighteners are not neutral and can add excess blue to a color reproduction.

Brightype. Trade name for a machine used to convert letterpress type or engravings into a photographic image that can be used to make offset or gravure plates. The metal type is sprayed with a black lacquer, which is then rubbed to make the printing surface brightly reflective and the background light-absorbent. The form is then photographed in a special camera as if it were line copy, and a film negative is produced. *See also* Cronapress and Scotchprint.

brilliant. Small type size of 3½ or 4 pt.

bristol. A good grade of thin stiff cardboard or pasteboard of postcard weight or heavier with a smooth surface, ideal for drawing and printing. Bristol comes in a variety of colors and finishes, and is used for displays, posters, or any job where stiffness is required. Index bristols will ink and erase well. *See also* basis weights or basic weight and cardboard.

broadside. **1.** Large printed sheet folded for mailing. Usually used for self-mailing advertising circulars. **2.** A page meant to be read by turning it 90 degrees. Usually the gutter side of a broadside page is at the top when turned. *See also* pamphlet.

brochure. An elaborate pamphlet bound in booklet form, usually containing at least eight pages. *See also* pamphlet.

broken letter. A character in which the type has been damaged so that the letter is not whole. Marked with an X and circled on a proof for correction by the typesetter.

broken package. A quantity of paper less than the standard wrapped quantity, usually a ream. A broken package carries a penalty charge for the buyer.

bromide. A print made from a photographic process using silver and bromine, which is a nonmetallic element of a reddish color.

bronze proof. A proof made on transparent glassine paper. The ink is dusted with bronze powder while still wet in order to make the characters more opaque than black ink alone would make them. The proofs are like positive photographic film. Only processes working from positive film can use this shortcut. Also called glassines.

bronzing. Applying bronze powder over a sizing ink while still wet to obtain a metallic luster of bronze, gold, or silver.

brownline or **brownprint.** *See* blueline.

brush drawing. A drawing made with a brush which pulls ink or water color over the paper. A wash drawing which is produced by a brush dipped in watercolor must be reproduced by the halftone process in order to pick up the shadings. A line drawing can be produced by single line strokes of a brush dipped in india ink.

buckram. A heavy-weave, sized cotton cloth used for binding books.

building-up. The process of squeezing air out of the cased-in book with heat and pressure which also produces the indention in the cover along the spine.

built-up letter. A letter in which the outline is drawn first and then filled in.

bulk. The thickness of paper measured in numbers of pages per inch. Paper of different grades but of the same weight bulk differently. A 60-lb book paper may be ordered to bulk 414 pages to the inch, 624 pages to the inch, etc. More calendering, reduces bulk. Books are sometimes printed on bulked paper to make them appear worth a higher retail price. However, bulked paper is inferior to firmer papers in strength and printing qualities because of the fluff which causes trouble on press. Weight, bulk, and finish are controlled during papermaking. *See also* spine-bulk.

bulking dummy. A dummy of the finished book without the printing or stamping used by designers and printers as a guide for the size of the spine, a check on the appearance and feel of the book, and to measure individual cartons if necessary.

bulk mailing. A large quantity of identical pieces of mail addressed to different names but sorted by zip codes before being brought to the post office. This category of mail is third class.

bulk sales. Large quantities of a publication sold to a buyer at bulk discounts of the list price of the items for redistribution at a price still less than the full list price.

bullet. A solid dot used for emphasis or ornamental device. Bullets are available in all the various type sizes.

bulletin. One of a sequence of reports issued at intervals, or a one-time-only notice printed as a single leaf, folder, or booklet.

bull pen. Slang for that part of a graphic arts department where the mechanical artists sit and do paste ups. These artists are supervised by the art director.

bundle. Signatures from the web or folding department compressed by a metal strap which squeezes the air out.

burnish. 1. To rub down the edges of a piece of film which contains a correction so that the ascenders and descenders of the type contact evenly. The back of a fingernail or an ivory or metal burnisher is applied to the back of the film being contacted. If burnishing is not completely done, the type will appear to be partially cut off. 2. To smooth down self-adhering letters or shading sheets.

burst binding. Similar to notch binding in that the edges of signatures are perforated before glue is applied. However, burst binding is done on the web press, whereas notch binding is done for sheetfed jobs. Burst binding is stronger than adhesive binding and the process is cheaper than sewn binding.

burst test. One of many tests of the strength and quality of paper. The burst test determines how easily an object can burst through paper.

butted. Two or more typographic elements placed side by side to produce a single image.

bw. Black-and-white photograph. *See also* halftone.

by-line. The name of the author to whom the story is credited.

C

cabbages. *See* dingbat.

calender. A set of cast-iron rollers stacked at the end of the papermaking machine. The rollers iron the paper as it passes through them, to increase smoothness and gloss of the surface. Calendered paper has a smooth, glossy, mirror-bright finish. The process is used on paper-based book-covering materials as well. The more calendered a paper is, the better halftones will look on it. *See also* finish, papermaking, and supercalendering.

California job case. Tray with individual cubicles in which handset type is arranged in quantities related to frequency of use. This style of case originated in San Francisco. With the demise of hot metal type, these job cases are being sold for use as knick-knack trays. *See also* case.

caliper. Thickness of paper or film measured with a micrometer and expressed in thousandths of an inch, or mils. Film caliper is critical when images on different films are being stripped together. Paper caliper is critical in letterpress, for if it increases, the type punches, or debosses the sheet. If caliper decreases, no impression is made at all. Caliper is also critical to the full reproduction of the image on sheet-fed and web offset.

calligraphy. The art of very elegant and ornate handwritten lettering, the letters being more or less separate. A broad-nib pen is generally used. Calligraphy is often used on maps and in other places where type would be impossible. Calligraphic typefaces resemble different styles of handwriting.

callout. A label or words placed within an illustration itself, designating part of an illustration. A callout is shot as part of the artwork.

CAM. *See* computer assisted makeup.

camera. Large lightproof box equipped with lens, copy board, and darkroom and used for exposure of copy being photographed for printing plates. The copy board has rails which move the copy board closer to or farther away from the lens for exposure. The camera can enlarge or reduce and can be used for color separation.

Copy for photography is placed upside down on the copyboard of the camera. When the lights are turned on, light rays are reflected from the white areas of the copy. These reflected rays pass through the lens of the camera, and are projected onto the ground glass of the camera back. If we looked from inside the camera at the lens side of the ground glass, the image projected would appear right-side up, but backwards. From the operator's side of the camera, outside the ground glass the image appears correct, i.e., readable.

To make a line negative, the film is placed in the camera back with the emulsion, i.e., the sensitized side, facing the camera lens. During the exposure, the light reflected from the white areas of the copy passes through the lens, striking the film emulsion. This causes a chemical change in the silver particles of the film emulsion and creates a latent image. When this film is developed, a black and transparent film negative is formed. The areas of the film which were struck by reflected light from the white areas of the copy are intensified in the developing process and show as black or opaque areas on the negative. The areas that received no reflected light from the black areas of the copy are washed away during the developing, and appear clear in the negative.

When a negative is then placed over a sensitized piece of paper or a printing plate, and light is turned on, the opaque areas of the negative prevent light from passing through, and the clear areas allow light to pass through, thus creating a positive image on the paper or plate. *See also* color, color separation, gallery camera, halftone, line photography, negative, and process camera.

camera copy. *See* camera-ready copy.

camera lucida. *See* lucy.

camera-ready copy. Artwork or type assembled in place and ready to be photographed for reproduction.

Cameron book production system. A low-cost, web-letterflex printing press and in-line binding unit that produces a complete collated book block ready for adhesive binding. The system makes use of letterflex plates on a continuous belt which prints on a web of paper at a rate of 50 to 200 books per minute, depending on dimensions. The printing method is similar to rotary letterpress from flexible plates, but the plates in this case are mounted on two continuous belt conveyors, one for each printing unit. After the first printing operation on one side of the paper, the web is turned over and conveyed through the second printing unit where the other side of the web is then printed back-to-back and registered by means of an automatic edge guide. The conveyor belts, with plates still mounted in place, can be stored for reprinting.

The web continues through slitting and is perforated for folding. The ribbons are then pulled through folding and cut at individual signatures which are collated, trimmed, and bound. The Cameron book production system is most practical for Bibles, catalogs, dictionaries, telephone directories, manuals, and other light-weight paper products. It does not yet produce quality halftones, or any multicolor work. *See also* belt-press book production system.

cancel. 1. To cut out blank or unprinted pages. For example 12 pages are printed as 16 and 4 pages are canceled. 2. A new leaf or signature replacing a defective one, or material substituting for deleted material.

cap height. The actual height in points or inches of a character used in a display head. The point size of characters is actually larger than the characters measure because space is allowed in the typeface for ascenders, descenders, and shoulder. When a designer knows exactly what size caps he or she wants in an all-cap heading, the designer will sometimes specify the face in cap height, leaving it to the typesetter to determine the point size of the face that is needed.

caps. Capitals, or uppercase letters. ALL CAPS WOULD LOOK LIKE THIS.

caps and lower case. Both upper- and lower-case letters of one typeface. Indicated clc. Looks Like This.

caps and small caps. Two sizes of capital letters of one typeface, the small caps being the same size as the body of the lowercase letters of that typeface. Indicated as c&sc. LOOKS LIKE THIS. Most italic faces have no small caps.

caption. Originally a title or headline placed above or below an illustration, to be distinguished from a legend, which is descriptive material about the illustration. Now loosely used as any description of the subject of an illustration. The caption should be at least 6 pt. away from the illustration, or else in stripping the illustration and type into a negative, different thicknesses of film may form a ridge of a few thousandths of an inch at the cut mark and require double burning of the plate, which is an additional expense.

Captions are usually written to size specified and sometimes include the photo credit or source for artwork. *See also* copy fitting, credit line. Also called cutline.

captive plant. 1. Bindery that is owned by a printer. 2. A printing plant that is owned or controlled by a publisher.

capture the original keystroke. To utilize the original typing of a manuscript by keyboarding on an in-put terminal that produces either a tape, a floppy disk, or some device for running the output unit; or by typing for an optical character recognition scanner that scans the copy and produces a paper tape for running the output unit. Capturing the original keystroke eliminates the double keyboarding step that occurs when a typist or author types a manuscript that is rekeyboarded by the typesetter.

cardboard. Several layers of low-quality paper pasted together to form a stiff, strong sheet. Cardboard is bought by the pound, in different grades, finishes, and prices. The basic sizes, however, are not the same as for paper.

Cover paper is used for pamphlet covers, *bristolboard* for mechanicals, and *crude board* for protecting the contents of packages, mounting posters, etc. Since there is a limit to how thick paper can be made, heavier weights of stock are made by combining two or more webs of paper. Cardboard can be made in the same finishes as paper.

Bristol is 6-pt. thick or more (heavier than cover papers) and takes ink and erasures well. Printing bristol, mill bristol, or wedding bristols have good smooth printing surfaces. *Bogus Bristol* is a cheaper grade. Bristols can be coated one side, colored, or made to take lacquer or lamination.

Tagboards are made of manila rope, jute, or kraft pulp for tags. The word manila does not necessarily mean that rope fibers have been used.

Cardboards are usually built of several plies. Generally a cheap filler is used with a better grade of lining, or outside layers.

Paperboards are cardboards over 0.012-in. thick. *Binder's board,* the strongest grade is .030 to 0.300-in. thick. Other grades include *chipboard, strawboard, boxboard, millboard, pulpboard, newsboard, pressboard,* and *corrugated board.*

The cheapest cardboards are not bleached white. They are made from reprocessed newsprint.

Special cardboards are made for artists' *drawing board,* as well as *mat board* for mounting pictures. Artists' drawing board such as Ross board and scratchboard can be surfaced to take watercolor and ink.

carding. Inserting strips of heavy paper between lines to lengthen a column or page, in letterpress. The printer inserts thin strips of card stock less than 1 pt. thick, between lines of hot metal type to make a column a little deeper, for example, in order to match an adjacent column or advertisement. In phototypesetting the lines of type are adjusted on the mechanical when such a problem as column depth arises.

caret. A sign indicating insertion of a correction or the addition of written material. The caret is written slightly below the line at the point of the insertion and the material to be inserted is written above the line or at the side separated from it by a solidus. *See also* proofreader's marks.

carry-over line. A line of type usually in the top left corner of a page or column which identifies the story in a magazine of which that page or column is a part. *See also* running head.

cartouche. Ornamental box, frame, or border which looks like a partially unrolled scroll or other similar graphic flourish. Often used to carry a title.

case. 1. A type tray in which each character of a font has its own section. Originally, the capitals were kept in the upper rows, and the lower-case letters in the lower rows. Hence, "uppercase" and "lowercase." In the so-called California job case, both uppercase and lowercase are kept side by side. 2. The cover of a hardcover book. *See also* backing, binding, casing-in, and round-backing or rounding.

case-bound. Hardcover books. Case binding is comprised of approximately 18 different operations, hand and machine. *See also* binding and edition binding.

casing-in. The part of the binding process in which the signatures, which have been gathered and sewn, have also been glued to their end sheets and are assembled into the case, which has been manufactured as a separate process. In hand bookbinding, the cover is not assembled as a separate process but is built around the book itself. *See also* binding.

cast coated paper. Coated paper dried under pressure against a heated polished cylinder while the coating is in a highly plastic condition. A high-gloss enamel finish similar to that of a glossy photograph is produced.

casting. **1.** Forcing molten metal into type molds, or matrices, as single letters or as complete lines. **2.** Making duplicate metal printing plates, or stereotypes from matrices for newspaper or book work.

cast-off. The calculation of the length of manuscript copy in order to determine the amount of space it will take in columns or pages when set in type. This is usually done by the typesetter who takes into account the characters per pica his equipment sets. *See also* copyfitting.

catch line. A line or figure set in type temporarily because the typeface wanted is not available, or a line set for position only until art is made.

cathode ray tube. **1.** A video display terminal that displays copy on a television-like screen. Controlled electron beams present stored data in visual form. The screen is the face of the cathode ray tube. *See also* video display terminal.

2. A device for third-generation typesetting which is electronic as opposed to photographic (as is second-generation typesetting). The first CRT typesetting machine was installed in 1967 by Mergenthaler.

A vacuum tube with a gun, or cathode, at one end emits a spray of electrons which are focused into a narrow beam and projected to a phosphor coating on the television-like screen at the opposite end. On the screen, letter images in the form of dots or lines are displayed for exposure onto photographic material. A vacuum frame holds the film or paper during exposure.

The dots, actually called strokes, are about one mil in diameter and when overlapped and positioned properly, can create a character. The beam is turned on and off, positioned, corrected, and deflected to create characters. The stroking is responsible for the sawtooth effect on diagonal or curved lines. Under a glass this stair-step effect can be seen, but the naked eye should not be able to discern it. The image is focused through a lens onto photo-sensitive paper, microfilm, or offset plates. Because there are no moving parts, the resulting exposure produces the desired characters as fast as 1000 characters per second. This can allow the typesetter to provide material faster and cheaper.

Characters to be reproduced are generated from computerized instructions, so

Case-making machine at the bindery. (*Courtesy Kingsport Press*)

Hardcover book cases coming off the case-making machine at the bindery. (*Courtesy Kingsport Press*)

there is no tangible master for a font. The disc pack (not to be confused with floppy disc) containing format information which was coded in at the video display terminal is integrated with the tape holding the copy which has been keyboarded, and all the information is fed into the photo unit where the setting takes place.

There are two basic CRT systems: formation and projection. In computer logic character formation, the characters to be set are stored as digital information in the computer. The character request comes from the magnetic tape, and the computer sends the configuration of the character as electronic signals to the cathode ray tube where the electron beam forms the image on paper or film.

In character projection, the characters to be set are scanned from a master grid and translated, by breaking them down into thousands of fine lines per inch. Some CRTs are designed to be able to break down continuous-tone copy into lines or dots. This is called photocomposing. The first pictures of the moon were transmitted back to earth this way.

CRT systems are very versatile for changing and mixing fonts. Because the characters are electronically generated, i.e., created by an electrical system of on and off states, they can be expanded, condensed, slanted in varying degrees backwards or forwards, or reproduced in any point size including ½-pt. increments. Dingbats or special characters can be custom made. Thus, the designer can control the number of characters per given measure. All that is needed is the formatting, or set of instructions for the computer. Also, characters are not subject to the stresses and damage of metal matrices as are hot metal type molded characters, and so remain cleaner. Alignment on a CRT is more accurate than that done by hand. Some CRT typesetters can create complete pages of text with headlines and illustrations in place. Abbreviated CRT. *See also* digitized typesetting.

cell. The small etched depression, representing one halftone dot, which carries the ink on the surface of a gravure cylinder.

centered. Placed in the center of a line as opposed to flush right or left. Used as an instruction to the typesetter.

centered dot. **1.** A multiplication sign in mathematical composition. **2.** A heavy dot used as an ornament before a paragraph or item in a list. *See also* bullet.

centered head. A headline placed equidistant from both margins of the page or column.

centered type. Lines of type set centered on the line measure. *See also* arranging lines of type.

center spread. Facing pages on a single sheet of paper in the center of a magazine, brochure, or signature of a book. Artwork may be spread across the two pages easily. On other spreads it is difficult to have art run across the gutter because a folding or stripping error may cause a misalignment. *See also* spread.

Cerlox binding. *See* comb binding.

chad. Waste paper produced from punching holes in paper tape or in cards.

chain lines. Watermark lines, usually about an inch apart, caused by chain marks which run with the grain in laid papers. These lines are natural in handmade papers and can be imitated in machine-made papers. *See also* laid papers.

chain-dot halftones. *See* elliptical dot.

chapbook. A small booklet, usually paperback, of poetry, tales or ballads.

chapter. Main division of a book, treatise, or formal paper.

chapter heading. The number and title of each chapter.

chapter opener. Page or spread which introduces a new chapter. It could include text or graphics, or merely the chapter heading.

character. A letter, numeral, symbol, or punctuation mark. Characters usually vary in width, except on an ordinary typewriter on which they are all the same width.

Cathode ray tube phototypesetter. (*Courtesy Mergenthaler Linotype Company*)

character count. The number of characters including letters and spaces a piece of copy contains. Length can be expressed in character count. The computations of the total number of characters in a line, paragraph, or page of copy is done either by copyfitting or by a minicomputer attached to a phototypesetting machine. *See also* cast-off and copyfitting.

character generation. The projection or formation of typographic images on the face of a cathode ray tube, in association with a high-speed computerized photocomposition system. The character is generated each time it appears, it is not stored on a piece of film or in a metal font.

character recognition. Automatic means of identifying graphic, phonic, or other characters. *See also* magnetic inks, optical character recognition, and scanner.

characters-per-pica. Average number of characters that fit within one pica in a certain typeface. Used as a means of determining the length of the copy when set in type. *See also* cast-off, character count, and copyfitting.

charts. An organized presentation of information contained within rules and boxes either hand drawn on a mechanical or typeset.

chase. The rectangular metal frame in which type and engravings are locked for letterpress printing.

checking copy. A copy of a publication sent to the advertiser for verification of ad.

chemical pulping. Pulp of mainly cellulose fiber, made from sulfite or sulfate processes to produce freesheet, i.e., good quality strong paper free of lignin, resins, gums, and other undesirable components found in groundwood pulp. *See also* groundwood, mechanical pulping, paper grades, and papermaking.

chipboard. Low-grade board made from wastepaper. *See also* cardboard.

choke. To make the strokes of a letter thinner, so that there is more space around the letter and between strokes such as in the letter a. This is the opposite of spread. Choking can be done by hand, or by a graphic modifier in increments from 1/128″ to 3/4″, or it can be done by overexposing repro so that more background is reflected, tending to overwhelm the edges of the letter and lose the thin strokes. Not to be confused with reducing, in which the innerspace of open letters would shrink rather than expand.

chroma. The dimension of strength or intensity of color, the purity free from white or gray. Also called saturation. *See also* color tree, hue, and value.

chrome. *See* color transparency.

ABCDEFGHIJKLMNOPQRSTUVWXYZ AB CDEFGHIJKLMNOPQRSTUVWXYZ abcdefghijklm nopqrstuvwxyz 1234567890 -.,';$...—*.,':?/_ A SPECIMEN BOOK is a cold thing—lifeless. In itself it has no beauty. It is merely a tool with which the artist helps bring out the ideas in his creative mind. *Without the artist the specimen book* of type faces is not much good. No matter what beauty

11 POINT, LEADED 2 2.28 CHARACTERS TO 1 PICA

Century Schoolbook

ABCDEFGHIJKLMNOPQRSTUVWXYZ abcdefghijklmnopqrstuvwxyz 1234567890 - .,';$/.,':!() A specimen book is a cold thing—lifeless. In itself it has no beauty. It is merely a tool with which the artist helps bring out the ideas in his creative mind. Without the artist the specimen book of type faces is not much good. No matter what beauty there may be in the shape of a letter, if used in the wrong way it produces only an inelegant disfigurement and an unsightly distortion,

11 POINT LEADED 2 2.38 CHARACTERS TO 1 PICA

Electra Bold

ABCDEFGHIJKLMNOPQRSTUVWXYZ A BCDEFGHIJKLMNOPQRSTUVWXYZ abcdefghijkl mnopqrstuvwxyz 1234567890 -.,';$...—*.,':? /_ A SPECIMEN BOOK is a cold thing—lifeless. In itself it has no beauty. It is merely a tool with which the artist helps bring out the ideas in his creative mind. *Without the artist the specimen book* of type faces is not much good. No matter what beauty

11 POINT, LEADED 2 2.46 CHARACTERS TO 1 PICA

Times Roman

Characters per pica.

Chrome-guide. Method of color proofing from the color separation in an emulsion-to-emulsion exposure. It is inexpensive but not as accurate as press proofs.

circulating matrix. The mold from which Linotype and Intertype line-casting machines cast type. It is called "circulating" because the matrices automatically return to the magazine for reuse.

circulars. Small sheets of paper printed on one or both sides for delivery by mail, by hand, or as inserts with letters. Also called leaflets.

circular screen. A circular-shaped halftone screen which enables the camera operator to obtain all the different screen angles for shooting color halftones without moving the art. *See also* color separation.

clasp envelope. Envelope in which the flap closes with a metal clasp or has glue for sealing. *See also* envelope styles.

c&lc. *See* caps and lower case.

clean copy. Material which is free of errors, cross-outs, wrinkles, smudges, etc. The cleaner the copy, the faster the typesetting will be. The typesetter will charge a penalty for having to spend time sorting out a high percentage of dirty copy.

clear area. Area on the plate where no image is formed and inked so that the paper adjacent to this area on the press shows through as white or whatever color it may be.

clip book. *See* stock cut or stock photos.

clipsheet. News stories, features, interviews, editorials, fillers, illustrations, ads, or quotes, designed like a newspaper page, printed on one side of the paper and distributed to the press for an editor to clip out and reproduce. The editor may not use the copy verbatim, but may use the clipsheet for ideas. *See also* copywriting.

closing date. **1.** The date upon which advertising must be delivered if it is to appear in a publication. **2.** The date upon which the printer closes his form, i.e., plates are made and no further material can be added.

closed shop. A plant, within an industry, which requires union membership for a craftsman to maintain employment, as opposed to an open shop, which does not.

close-up. **1.** To set type with little space between the words. **2.** Instructions to the typesetter to bring words closer together if a wide space has been left between them, or if some copy has been deleted. *See also* wordspacing.

clothbound. Having a rigid cover of cloth or synthetic material wrapped around stiff cardboard. This type of binding is longer lasting than that with paper. *See also* book covering materials.

cloth printing. Cloth book covers are usually stamped with brass dies in which the spaces between the letters and lines are cut away more deeply than for printing on paper. If ink is used, two hits are usually given for good coverage. Metal or colored foil can be used instead of ink. The foils adhere to the cloth by heat and pressure from the die.

Cloth can also be printed by the same methods as paper. Screen printing is often used for novelty printing on materials such as felt since screen printing lays a thick layer of pigment on the soft material.

coateds or **coated paper.** A grade of paper treated with clay or other pigment, or mineral substances which adhere to the surface to improve the quality for printing, especially for the printing of halftones which require sharper definition, greater color fidelity, greater opacity, smoothness, affinity for ink, and better ink holdout than copy printed on uncoated paper. The coated finish can vary from dull to very glossy and also comes in a duplex finish, which is a different color on each side. Papers may be coated one-side for jackets, labels, adhesive, and packaging, or coated two-sides for book and commercial printing. Papers coated on the papermaking machine are called machine coated and are less expensive than those coated on independent coaters, or off-machine coated. When ordering coated paper it is important to specify how the paper will be used.

cockle finish. The pucker of many bond papers, such as rag bond, which adds crispness to the paper.

cold color. A color which is on the bluish side. *See also* cool colors.

cold type. **1.** Strike-on typesetting in which some form of ink or carbon ribbon produces type on paper from already composed fonts such as on a typewriter or word processor. Hot metal is not used. Cold-type machines can have a computer memory system for justification, corrections, and spacing. Actually, phototype, in which no impression is made, is not cold type, although no hot metal is used. Both hot and cold type utilize a direct impression as opposed to phototype which does not. Cold type is usually very economical. Also called strike-on composition and typewriter composition. **2.** Although it is erroneous, it is now common for phototype to be referred to as cold type.

collate. Gathering sheets or signatures of a book into proper sequence for sewing and binding. *See also* binding.

collating mark. A short rule, letters, or figures printed on the outside of the fold of each signature. When the signatures are collated in the proper order, these marks appear in stepwise fashion. Sometimes a small letter or figure is also printed at the bottom of the first page of each signature.

collotype. A printing process that utilizes an unscreened gelatin-coated plate rather than a halftone screen to print continuous tone copy. In this process, a film of gelatin is chemically treated and exposed to a high-quality film negative so that, where strong light falls on it, it becomes less receptive to moisture than where shielded from light. Thus, the drier areas that received more light accept more greasy ink. It is similar to lithography in that a greasy ink adheres to the image-bearing areas, although it is directly printed from plate to paper. It produces extremely true pictures, but is suitable only for very short runs. It is often used to reproduce paintings, facsimiles of old documents, large photographic illustrations, etc. Also called photogelatin.

colophon. Originally, the statement placed at the end of a book, giving information about the publisher now found on the title page. Today a colophon includes production information or the trademarks of the typesetter, printer, or publisher, and generally appears on the copyright page.

color. The infinite variety of all the shades of the solar spectrum that we see in nature. Red, yellow, and blue exist in all parts of the spectrum, so that it is possible to obtain those three images of the same picture photographically, and recombine them to form an image with all the tints contained in nature.

Since any color is a combination of white, black, and a color, then when white is added to a pure color, a higher tint of that color is obtained. When black is added, a darker shade is created. When both black and white are added, the color value changes. Opposite colors on the color wheel, when mixed, form a neutral gray.

The warm colors are red, orange, yellow, and brown, and give the effect of thrusting forward. The cool colors are green, blue, and gray, and give the effect of withdrawal. The color of paper on which an image is printed also affects the color scheme being printed on it. When working with color it is helpful to have swatch books, paper samples, and ink charts for the printer to match. Ink manufacturers and paper merchants have these samples available.

Intelligent use of color can get attention or create a feeling. Realistic color has been proved to increase sales.

Whether illustrative or decorative, if color is handled so that it has pleasant associations for the audience it can draw attention to the message. Greatest contrast in both hue and brightness has the highest attention-getting value, but the degree of contrast of type of one color run on a background of another color determines legibility and should be considered. Attractiveness of a color depends on how it is used, and the way two or more colors are arranged on the page determines whether or not they harmonize.

A short course on the theory and control of color in print. "Neutral white light contains all the colors of the spectrum. We can conveniently divide the visible spectrum into three primary colors: red, blue, and green, and when the primaries are combined in proper proportions, the result is white. We also can isolate the colors in "white light." A red tomato is red because it reflects that color while absorbing all the other colors from white light. A piece of blue glass is that color because it passes or transmits blue and absorbs the other colors.

"To reproduce color accurately, proper proportions of the three primary colors must be contained in the light presented to the ink film. The most efficient colors for controlling the primaries are the pigments, cyan (blue/green), magenta (blue/red), and yellow (red/green). When yellow and cyan, for example, are overlapped, we see green because that is the only color that each does not absorb. We have produced green by controlling, or in this case eliminating, red and blue.

"What happens when the three pigment colors are overprinted? First, when the yellow and cyan overlap, the yellow absorbs the blue ray from the white light and the cyan absorbs the red ray, leaving only the green ray to be reflected by the combination. In much the same manner, when these pigments are mixed, they retain their light-subtracting qualities so that in the mixture the yellow absorbs the blue ray, leaving only the green ray to be reflected by the mixture. Note that in color-process printing, the primary pigment colors are generally "transparent." The light passes through the pigment film to the white paper beneath and then it is reflected back through the film to the eye.

"There are a number of ways by which light waves reach our eyes. Indirectly, as when light passes through a transparent object held between our eyes and the source of light (called transmission) or directly, as when we stare into the sun or a light bulb or when light bounces from an object to our eyes (called reflection). In printing, we are basically concerned with transmitted and reflected light waves.

"The surface of a red tomato has the faculty of absorbing all light waves that hit it except those that correspond to red. We might say that an opaque substance appears to be a particular color because it reflects the wave lengths corresponding to that color and absorbs those that do not. When all wave lengths are reflected and one does not dominate another, the substance would be perceived as white. Transparent substances absorb some wave lengths and transmit others.

"Pigments, ink, and almost anything else you can think of are perceived as a certain color because we "see" the wave length they reflect or transmit—we cannot see those that are absorbed. Color that results from adding light energy is called additive color. Color that results when an object subtracts wave lengths is called subtractive color.

Interpretation of color. "In the graphic arts we are concerned with such light absorbing materials as film, pigments, and the surfaces of paper. All materials that are not sources of light energy operate by the subtractive method. Each of the process printing inks, cyan, magenta, and yellow, ideally transmits 2/3 and absorbs 1/3 of the spectrum; that is cyan (blue-green) absorbs red; magenta (blue-red) absorbs green; and yellow (red-green) absorbs blue.

"Our brain interprets color sensations in three dimensions: hue, saturation, and brightness. Hue is that characteristic of color by which we distinguish red from green, yellow, blue, etc. Saturation is often called purity of color or chroma, and is often expressed as the strength or amount of a given hue in a color, or the intensity of that hue. Brightness is that quality by which we express similarity to a series of grays, ranging from black to white, such as the difference between a strong red and a light pink.

"A change in the environment in which a color is inspected will influence the discrimination of color. Color is influenced by light under which it is observed and its relationship or proximity to other colors. It is affected by changes in the darkness or lightness of background materials.

"Colors are observed under different varying light conditions. White light, such as daylight, differs, for example, from the color quality of an incandescent light bulb. Daylight at midday, for example, is energy rich in the blue of the spectrum, while incandescent lighting is predominantly rich in the yellow-red end of the spectrum. Candlelight is also distinctly yellow.

Light affects color. "Because of the variation of light sources, color matching and color comparisons become difficult unless such observations are made with the same lighting conditions. Light source has a dramatic effect on color observation. When we view a blue object under a pure red light, the object will appear black. This is explained by the subtractive color phenomenon.

"The influence of the proximity of some colors to others and their background brightness affect perception of color. The color of a transparent subject, for example, may be distinctly or dramatically influenced by background color. The value and saturation of color decrease as the value of the background decreases. Color may also be influenced by the quality of reflected light, as when we view a transparency against an opaque background, such as a sheet of paper.

"When ink is printed on a rough surface, the surface scatters white light in much the same way as do bits of broken glass. This, in turn, adds white light to the printed area and the color appears to be diluted, washed out, or impure. Conversely, when printing on a smooth glossy surface, the ink appears purer and distinguished in hue.

"Inks may be either opaque or transparent. Opaque pigments reflect light at their outer surface and have the property of covering or hiding the background on which they are printed. Opaque white pigments generally produce a light top-tone, and the bulk ink is likely to appear the same as the color which it will print. Transparent pigments do not reflect light at the surface, but rather "transmit" light, or allow the light to pass through the film of the ink and be reflected from the surface on which it is printed. Transparent ink films change the light passing through them by absorbing the color(s) that "aren't there" and passing the color(s) that "are there"—just as a red tomato absorbs blue and green and transmits the red to our eye.

Reproduction of color. "Transparent pigments lie flat against a sheet of paper which, in turn, becomes the (reflecting) light source for the ink placed on it. Overlapping transparent inks produce intermediate colors as each film layer allows light, though altered, to pass through it. Conversely, overlapping opaque inks reflect light and do not transmit or pass light; therefore, they do not produce intermediate colors when overlapped.

"There are as yet no perfect inks. However, theoretically perfect process ink (subtractive) primary colors, which are able to reproduce most of the colors in the spectrum, are:

Cyan—absorbs all red and transmits blue-green.

Yellow—absorbs all blue and transmits green-red.

Magenta—absorbs all green and transmits blue-red.

"To compensate for ink variation to obtain the most accurate result, it becomes necessary to make additional corrections and adjustments when preparing the inks.

"When we introduce halftone screening, we compress the tonal range or range of values available in a printed reproduction, because the small unprinted areas of the white paper reflect white light and dilute the print. When we add white light, we raise the value of a color and decrease its purity. It becomes apparent therefore, that paper is the reflective light source for transparent inks.

Paper source of illumination. "The color judgment of any subject, be it a tomato or a film, is wholly dependent on the quality and quantity of the light which illuminates it. The sheet of paper becomes the source of illumination for transparent ink film. A truly cyan ink film will absorb (subtract) all the red wave lengths from white, which is one-third of the spectrum, and pass the green and blue wave lengths, which are two-thirds of the spectrum.

"Neutral white paper has the characteristic of reflecting the same kind (quality) of light that it is illuminated by, although a certain amount may be absorbed. When paper reflects all wave lengths equally, meaning its characteristics do not alter the quality of light—it is a neutral white sheet. A tinted sheet absorbs some of the wave lengths. A paper that does not reflect any light is black paper. A neutral gray sheet is one that absorbs a part of the quantity of light that strikes it. You can say that ink colors become duller and less brilliant as the brightness of a sheet decreases. The brightest portion of the over-all printed page is the unprinted area of the sheet of paper. The reason for the printed areas being less bright is because they have absorbed part of the light. A paper with low brightness will correspondingly print low in brightness.

"The most accurate color reproduction is obtained on papers that reflect the light that strikes them without changing its quality; correspondingly, most brilliant color reproduction can be arrived at on papers with high balanced reflectance. Rough surfaces scatter light. When light strikes the multitude of uniform reflecting surfaces and debases the print with white light, it becomes grayed because of the addition of uncontrolled and unwanted white light.

"Smooth paper surfaces minimize troublesome light interference, giving uniform directional reflection of light. An open surface paper tends to absorb both ink vehicle and pigment, which in turn leave dull pigment particles on the surface. Measuring "paper surface efficiency"—with limitations—is today one of the many valuable means to ascertain the color printing possibilities of paper.

"Accurate color results are arrived at by printing on a finish which will retain the vehicle and pigment on the surface. Only enough vehicle permeates the surface to provide good bonding of ink to paper. Glossy inks enhance purity of printing in color."[3]

See also color tree, color separation, flat color, and process color.

color acetates. *See* acetate and color key.

color analyzer. Machinery which electronically separates a color transparency or piece of art into its basic process components and recombines them on a viewing screen. The operator adjusts the separated images as desired to correct the color balance before the physical separations are actually made. The analyzer also compensates for effects of inks, paper, and processing steps, and then provides numerical specifications and settings for use in scanning, separating, and screening the art.

color bars. Small rectangles printed on all four-color process proofs which show the amount of ink used, the trapping, and the relative densities across the press sheets. They are a guide to printers and platemakers for adhering to specifications set up by the Magazine Publishers Association.

color bleeds. *See* choke and spread.

color chart. A chart showing all the different possible combinations of percentages of the four process colored inks on press. Mixtures are shown in color blocks. Charts of this nature are available from process color printers.

color conversion. 1. A black-and-white photograph made from a color slide or transparency.

2. A color photograph converted to a negative and then into a black-and-white continuous tone positive. Color conversions are usually done at a conversion house.

There is no way to go from screened, separated copy backwards to continuous tone copy. When a black-and-white copy is wanted from four-color separations, and if the original transparency is not available, the dominant color printer, or film separation, must be used to print from on the black plate, and can be done in same size only.

color copier. A machine that works on the electrostatic principle as does a Xerox or other photocopying machine. These copiers can produce color copies that give an idea of the color, used mostly for presentations, but not good enough in quality for reproduction. *See also* electrostatic printing.

color correction. 1. Changing the color values in a set of separations by such methods as masking, dot-etching, re-etching, or scanning to compensate for

[3] John Deurwaarder, "A Short Course on the Theory and Control of Color in Print," *Printing Magazine*. Source of information for the article, Graphic Arts Technical Foundation, Pittsburgh.

errors in photography, or color separation. 2. Marking color proofs to indicate what corrections the printer should make.

colored masks. Adhesive transparent or opaque masks which can be used to add color to black-and-white photographs or can be rubbed onto the enlargement with a smooth flat tool. Colored masks are available in art stores in different color tones.

colored paper. Paper manufactured in color so that it gives the effect of printing with another color. On short runs this effect can be less expensive than printing with the extra color. Duplex paper has different colors on each side. *See also* paper grades.

color filter. Transparent filters made of dyed glass, gelatin, plastic, or dyed gelatin cemented between glass plates and placed over the lens of the printer's camera to separate the colors in the original copy into the four process colors for color printing. The filters absorb all the colors except those which are allowed to pass through, one at a time, as the art is photographed four times or more, so that the dots of one primary color at a time are recorded on a negative. *See also* color separation.

color guide. Instructions on art or mechanical for flat color work indicating the position and percentage of color required. It can also include an actual sample of the color.

color image material. Transparent, controlled printing ink on a piece of acetate film with pressure-sensitive backing. It is used by artists to add color to any smooth surface which is to be photographed. It comes in continuous tone percentage tints and has no dot or screen.

color key. A method of prepress color proofing on multiple transparent acetate overlays with one piece of acetate for each color of ink to be used on the press. Light sensitive pigmented colors (cyan, yellow, magenta, and black) are exposed to the negatives from the separation and developed after lamination to the base material. The sheets are then assembled as a complete color proof. The color key should show dot for dot exactly what is in the negative supplied to the separator, but since the proof is not ink on paper, it cannot match press colors well. It is used when it is not economically practical to wait until plates are made in order to see press proofs. The client thus can visualize the artwork before it goes to press. A color key can also show flat color proofing adequately. Color keys are manufactured by 3M, but are not to be confused with the transfer key, which is 3M's version of the Cromalin, a one-sheet color prepress proof. Color keys are available in both positive and negative imaging material.

color-matching system. Method of specifying flat color by numbered color samples from a swatchbook.

color overleaf proof. *See* color key.

color print. Photographic print made in color by methods such as Cibachrome, dye transfer, Kodacolor, etc.

color printer. An overlay used in graphic lettering to split the image of the letter in the same illustration, making half of it negative and half positive, usually with an invisible line dividing the two diagonally, vertically, or horizontally. Not to be confused with "printer" referring to film negatives, one for each process color in four-color printing.

color printing. *See* flat color and process color.

color process. Multicolor printing from the four photographic process-separated negatives and plates as opposed to multicolor printing in flat, or nonprocess colors in which any color is achieved by specially mixed inks according to formulas. *See also* process color.

color proof. Printed color image which enables the printer and client to see what is on the film and to make sure the color is in register. *See also* prepress proofs and press proofs.

color scanner. An electronic device which produces quality color separation enlargements, does color correcting, cropping, undercolor removal, and contrast highlighting. Use of the color scanner eliminates the masking and separation steps.

Reflective copy is wrapped around a cylinder, and the image is sent electronically onto four sheets of unexposed film as the cylinder revolves. If a transparency is used, the light beams from inside the cylinder out. Some scanners use the same cylinder and four scans of light to produce the separation, others have four different cylinders, or drums.

The film is screened, and four halftone negatives are made. The image can be stored in a memory and transferred to different plants via satellite or telephone. Separations may be produced in 15 to 20 minutes. Use of the color scanner enables a plant to send four-color separations to the other side of the country within a couple of hours.

Since no two color scanners are operated the same, operators must be specially trained to use a particular type of equipment. Where the most faithful reproduction is wanted, the original artwork, not a duplicate, should be used so as not to lose fidelity and sharpness. A scanner cannot standardize or balance colors, it reproduces what it sees.

color separation. The process of separating full-color original artwork into the primary printing colors in negative or positive form by use of filters in a process camera or by electronic scanners. Secondary colors are produced by overprinting with transparent inks.

The filters subtract all the colors from the original art except each of the sub-

The Magnescan 550 color scanner. (*Courtesy of New Horizons Color Corporation, reprinted by permission of Printing Views Magazine*)

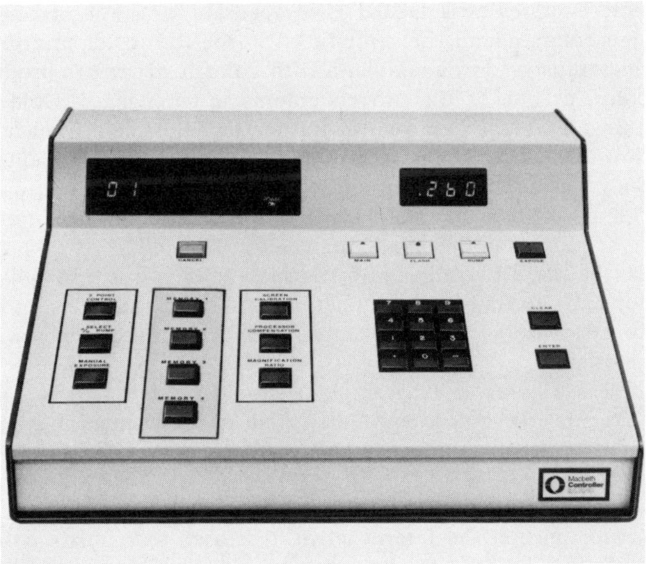

Color separation device designed to simplify color work and to control and calculate exposures for color and black and white screening. (*Courtesy Macbeth, a division of Kollmorgen Corporation*)

tractive primary colors, yellow, cyan, and magenta in turn. In indirect separation, the result is four continuous-tone films which contain the dots of the yellow, cyan, magenta, and black of the original. When projected to the right size and screened, these films are used to make printing plates. Either color transparencies or reflective artwork are used.

In a direct separation, the transparency is put in a camera or enlarger, and a screened halftone negative is made. The angle of the screen and the filter is changed for each color so that the resulting dots will not touch, but will produce an optical illusion of continuous tone colors when printed.

The color separation negative is a single black-and-white negative which carries a record of the proportion and distribution of one of the process colors as found in the original full-color image. A set of separation negatives consists of four black-and-white negatives, one each for the yellow, red, blue, and black. The negatives themselves are black, the color comes from the ink on the plate which has been exposed to the negatives.

On an offset press the sequence of the inks to go down on the paper passing through is yellow, red, blue, and black, the most transparent colors first in order to form the optical illusion of a combination of colors when printed. If black were printed first, it would dirty all the other colors. This is also the order of colors in a Cromalin proof. The number of dots in each of the primary colors combined with the dots of the other primary colors produce the optical illusion of the full spectrum. When examined closely, a small rosette pattern can be seen if the dots do not touch. If the dots do fall on top of each other, an undesirable moiré pattern is produced. There is no such thing as a perfect color separation from filtration. Dot etching is needed to compensate for the shortcomings of the process. Some colors cannot be reproduced in the four-color printing done by the publishing industry. For example, a fifth color is needed to produce a deep chocolate color, or one of the process colors can be changed. Gold cannot be produced from a lemon process yellow. Rather, an adjustment is made in the red and the yellow inks used on press. Many times a compromise is accepted. Reflective copy can be more difficult to match than transparencies, because colors in transparencies are more nearly standardized. Foods and furniture often require a warmer process color than the standard gives.

Money can be saved by ganging up transparencies in position and making all the separations at one time. As many details as possible should be known before the separator estimates a job. For example a duplicate transparency will not separate like the original.

Most people see color as they think it should be, not as it is. Therefore, a proof of the separation can prevent unhappy surprises when a job is printed. *See also* color and subtractive color.

color stat. A photostat of an original piece of art made on paper exposed in a camera/processor without an internegative. It is used to simulate color for layouts or presentations before a final mechanical is made.

color transparency. A full-color photographic positive on transparent film such as Agfa Color, Ektachrome, Kodachrome, etc.

color tree. The spectrum shows only one dimension of color—that of changing hue. Three dimensions are required to identify or specify all possible variations of color—hue, value, and chroma. The value is the lightness or darkness, and the chroma is the saturation or strength of color. These are designated on three-dimensional systems. One is called the Munsell Color System. In this color tree, the hues are arranged in a circle, the value is changed by adding white at the top, graduating through gray to black at the bottom of the center of the tree. Chroma increases from the center out, with the most intense color at the outer edge and the chroma with the most gray at the center. Art suppliers sell sample books with each chip of color numbered.

color photocopy. A color copy made by the electrostatic process. *See also* electrostatic printing.

column inch. A measure commonly used by newspapers based on a space 1-in. deep and a column of type wide. *See also* agate line.

Comb binding, in which plastic combs are inserted into holes punched in the binding edge of pages, is done by hand at the bindery. (*Courtesy Kingsport Press*)

comb binding. A method of mechanical binding using a plastic springlike comb which fits through holes punched in the edge of pages. Pages are inserted onto the comb by hand at the bindery. Also called Cerlox binding.

combination line and halftone. An illustration produced from both a halftone or tint screen and a line negative.

Two shots are made; once to pick up the black-and-white areas and once to screen middle tones. The negatives are superimposed, and the halftone areas show through the line negative.

combination plate. A printing plate or film on which halftone and linework is combined. Abbreviated combo.

command. The portion of the computer instruction that specifies the operation to be performed in phototypesetting. For example, flush right, center, etc.

commercial envelopes. *See* envelope styles.

comp. *See* compositor and comprehensive.

comp copy. Complimentary or free copy usually given to someone who has helped produce a book or magazine.

component. Parts of a book such as jacket, case, signatures, etc., which must be ordered and shipped to the bindery before the book is ready to be bound.

composing room. The area in a typesetting shop or a printing plant in which type is set, or composed.

composing stick. A metal traylike device used to assemble and justify metal type when it is being set by hand.

composition. The setting of type from manuscript copy and the make-up of pages into final film for plate making. Composition can be done by hot-metal casting machines which produce metal type from which a repro galley can be pulled and shot for film. Or, hot-metal type can be locked in a form for letterpress printing. Letterpress will eventually become obsolete because machinery and matrices wear out and are not being replaced. Photocomposition can be run by a computer. This type is set photographically on either acetate film from which the compositor can make up full pages, or on photo repro paper which is then pasted up on mechanicals. In the mid-sixties when photocomposition was rapidly developing for offset lithography, there was no stable base paper on which type could be reliably set, thus, the tendency to have the composition go to final film in the typesetting plant. Now it is more economical and the quality is as good or better if the compositor supplies repro galleys which are pasted up. The mechanicals are then shot by the printer who makes the negatives for printing. Artwork can be shot by either compositor or printer, but shooting quality varies significantly from supplier to supplier. *See also* generations of type and phototypesetting.

compositor. A highly skilled person who sets and arranges type and performs other operations such as constructing tables, charts, etc., whether by hand or machine. Originally, the compositor made up the pages from the slugs of type that came off the hot metal line-casting machine. Abbreviated comp.

comprehensive. An accurate layout showing type and illustrations in position with simulated color, suitable for presentation. It approximates what the job will look like in print. A comp is the most complete type of layout. Abbreviated comp.

computer. A device for performing logical processes, used in typesetting to store information, and make mathematical, grammatical, and typographic spacing and end-of-line decisions, e.g., hyphenation and justification. The output data, often paper or magnetic tape, drives a photounit.

There are four systems by which computers can be programmed to resolve linebreaks: hyphenless, in which no words are hyphenated and lines are justified by increasing or decreasing wordspacing and letterspacing; discretionary, in which the keyboard operator hyphenates every word of three syllables and over, and the computer uses only what is needed; logic, in which the computer is programmed to make decisions; and exception dictionary, in which the computer carries a memory of a number of words that are hyphenated in unusual ways.

The computer is also used in other areas of the graphic arts such as in color separation and in papermaking. In a closed-loop system, the computer is wired directly into the devices that adjust settings such as in a papermaking machine. In an open-loop setting, the computer provides a visible readout of conditions it is monitoring, then an operator makes the adjustments and fine-tune settings.

computer assisted makeup. Composition display units that allow input as to typeface, size, line length, leading and typographic format, and display the result on a screen. The output is a recorded medium such as a tape which runs a typesetting machine. The device allows the typesetter or the designer to see the type on a video screen before it is set and eliminates re-running a job until it is acceptable. Esthetic adjustments for the page makeup are made up front. The cathode ray tube allows full page makeup to be done electronically. Also called aerial composition and pagination. *See also* photocomposing.

computerized composition. The application of electronics to select the keyboarded character from a disc or film strip and expose it in the proper position on photo-sensitive paper or acetate. In indirect composition, a computer produces a paper tape which is used as input for the phototypesetting equipment. Initially, "front-end" systems had a central computer to which all the other units were wired. Now some systems use devices each of which has a small built-in computer with matching programs so that coding used in one unit can be interpreted in the others. Larger systems still employ a central computer. In direct input terminals, the keyboarded information goes directly from the keyboarding unit to the photo output unit.

Some systems incorporate the telephone as an instrument over which type signals can go into the computer for setting. This arrangement is far from perfect. Signals can become confused by bad connections, cutoffs, etc., such as occur in a regular phone call. Satellite transmission of text and picture material also permits composition in one location and page makeup at another.

Computerized composition is more flexible than hot-metal composition in terms of design because of the ability of the machines to vary and combine elements of type design.

computerized bindery. A monitoring and control of binding lines as they are running, in which sensors can inform the control computer of misfeeds. In turn, the control unit can inform other units down the line to hold up the operation as the bad component comes by. The computer can also indicate to operators where jam-ups are in order to speed up their clearance.

The computer can also facilitate selective assembly for individualized copies as well as single-operation addressing and sorting for mailing. It can also set up specifications for a new job much faster than the time-consuming manual setting of equipment.

C-1-S. *See* coateds or coated paper.

condensed type. Narrow version of a regular typeface. *See* expanded type for illustration. *See also* typeface styles.

connected dot. Halftone dots of 50% value or more which are joined together in negative or plate.

consistency. *See* body.

consumable textbook. A self-contained book designed to be written in and completely consumed by one student for one term and then thrown away. The consumable textbook does not depend on any other textbook or material.

contact. A photographic image made from a negative or positive in direct contact with sensitized paper, film, or printing plate in a same-size relationship. Contacting is usually made on a vacuum frame in which light passes through a filter, mask, diffusion sheet, the negative or positive, and onto the film, paper, or plate in order to produce the contacted image. *See also* vacuum frame.

contact screen. A film-base material having a vignetted dot pattern through which light is exposed in order to contact a paper or film original. The result is the dot configuration of the continuous tone original being contacted. The dots will carry the ink on press. *See also* halftone.

container printing. The printing of cartons, cans, tubes, boxes, etc. Offset lithography and silkscreen are often used because they print well on uneven surfaces.

continued line. Line of type at the bottom of the page that tells on which page the story is continued.

continuous tone. A photographic image which has not been screened and has a complete range of tones without the use of dots as in a halftone.

contour line. A line on the outside of graphic lettering which follows the curves of the letter but is separated from the letter by an inline inside the edge of the letter. This process is done on film with a color printer that splits the image, or by hand-lettering and using overlays. A contour outline is any thickness of contour line.

contour shaded. A display font which is shaded so that it appears three-dimensional, with thickness behind the letters. It is a graphic effect with limitless possibilities for dressing up a font.

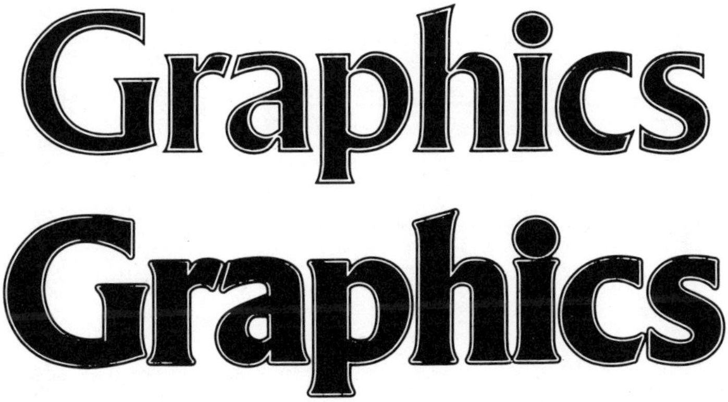

Contour line lettering. (*Courtesy Graphics Modifier, Byers Corporation*)

Contour shaded lettering. (*Courtesy Graphics Modifier, Byers Corporation*)

contrast. The range of tonal gradation between highlights and shadows for either black-and-white or color photographs. The farther apart the tones are, the higher the contrast.

conversion. *See* color conversion.

conversion house. A place that makes black-and-white art from color art.

conversion systems. Systems by which metal type or plates are converted into film images for offset or gravure printing. *See also* Brightype, Cronapress, and Scotchprint.

cool colors. Blue, gray, and violet, as opposed to red, yellow, and orange, which are warm.

copper engraving. **1.** A halftone engraving made on copper. **2.** A plate on which an artist has hand-engraved an image. **3.** The print made from a hand-engraved plate.

copy. **1.** Material such as a typewritten manuscript, to be used in the production of printing. **2.** Sometimes refers to the pictures and artwork to be shot as well. *See also* copyfitting, copy preparation, and copywriting.

copyboard. The board designed to hold the copy to be photographed by a gallery camera. The illuminated copyboard moves toward and away from the lens of the camera.

copy-casting. *See* cast-off and copyfitting.

copy chief. The head of a copywriting group in an advertising agency or publishing company.

copy dot. A method of screenless printing in which previously screened halftones are shot as line art, thus utilizing as copy the screen dots that exist within the copy. Each dot reproduces on the film as line and when printed, recreates the optical illusion of halftone gradations. It is only practical when the copy is shot at same-size so dots don't enlarge or close up. It is often done when the only art available has already been screened.

Very good film must be used, and the dots on the art to be shot must not be too large or too small. If they are too small, the camera will not pick up enough detail. If they are too large, the black will run together, and the whole area will become too solid. If copy dot does not work on a particular piece of art, the art must be rescreened or shot as fine line. Also called dot for dot. *See also* fine line, moiré, and rescreening.

copy editing. Editing the manuscript for grammar, punctuation, and conformity to the publisher's style, as opposed to editing for content. Copy editing includes setting policy in a style sheet for the manuscript, querying the author, rearranging words, polishing, and preparing the accepted editorial material for the typesetter. The copy editor queries the author on points that seem unclear or inappropriate. It is the author's responsibility to see that the information is technically accurate. In dealing with authors, the copy editor should follow the publisher's policy. *See also* copy preparation, copywriting, and style sheet.

copyfitting. Estimating the space required to print a given quantity of copy in a specified size and style of type on a certain piece of typesetting equipment. The characters per pica will vary from one typesetter to another because of different types of equipment involved. Therefore, if copyfitting in-house, the client should make sure the supplier used is consulted for the character-per-pica figure used in the copyfitting. The formula is as follows:
(1) Find the number of typewriter characters in 1-in. of the typewritten copy. Pica typewriter type is 10 characters per inch. Elite typewriter type is 12 characters per inch. Punctuation marks and spaces are included. (2) Multiply the average length of the copy lines by the number of typewriter characters per inch. The result is the number of typewriter characters per line of copy. (3) Multiply the number of typewriter characters per line by the number of lines on the page to arrive at the number of typewriter characters on the page. (4) Multiply the number of typewriter characters per page by the number of pages of copy to find the total number of typewriter characters in the job. Make allowances for partial pages. This is the character count. (5) Compare the length of type line required in picas with an actual printed specimen of the type to be used. Count the number of type characters contained in this number of picas. This is the number of type characters required to set one line of type at the required measure. (6) Divide the total number of typewritten characters in the job by the number of type characters required for one line of the desired length. The result is the *total number of lines of type for the required length of line.* Also called casting off.

copyholder. The person who reads the manuscript aloud to the proofreader, who checks the proof.

copying. *See* electrostatic copying, photocopy, and photostat.

copy preparation. **1.** Directions as to size, position, and other details for photographic reproduction. **2.** Checking manuscript copy to ensure a minimum of changes after copy has been set. Good copy preparation can save money in type corrections. Copy preparation can include catching any omissions; rough character count; checking the layout and specifications; retyping; typemarking; making sure pages are numbered consecutively and insertions are numbered and clearly marked; and marking the copy where it ends.

Poor copy preparation results in expensive corrections and may be penalized by the typesetter if the manuscript is exceedingly dirty.

copyprint. A duplicate of the original art.

copyright. Exclusive right to reproduce, publish, and sell the matter and form of a literary or artistic work. There are extensive rights enumerated in the 1978 copyright statute. *See also* manufacturing clause.

copyright page. The page that carries the copyright notice, the ISBN number, and other information such as the publisher's imprint, credits, or the colophon. The copyright page of a book is usually placed on the verso of the title page.

In a magazine, the copyright is usually placed on the contents page. If a smaller publication such as a brochure is copyrighted, the notice is usually put at the foot of the first or second page.

copywriter. One who is skilled at presenting copy in an interesting, logical, attention getting way.

copywriting. 1. The writing of a manuscript as opposed to editing it. 2. Copywriting usually refers to writing for advertising, i.e., to persuade the reader to do something or think along certain lines by appealing to the reader's self-interest.

coquille. A drawing technique making use of drawing paper with a surface of raised dots. *See also* stipple.

corner marks. Marks, usually open lines or squares, put on a page proof by the compositor to show trim, position of running heads, or register for checking the proofs.

corn starch. Fine dust used on offset sheets to dry the ink as the sheets come off the press.

cottage industry. Method of handling work in which employees work on company-provided equipment at home.

cotton fiber papers. *See* rag papers.

counter. Space enclosed by the strokes of a letter, such as the bowl of the b, e, p. etc.

counter card. An easel displaying material at point of purchase.

counting keyboard. An input keyboard which adds up the unit widths of the characters and spaces set and indicates the space used and the space remaining in a line. The keyboard operator makes end-of-line decisions regarding hyphenation and justification based on the amount of space left at the end of the line.

cover. The two hinged parts of a book binding, or the four surfaces making up a magazine cover, carrying the title or advertising. The sides of the cover, beginning with the outside front are designated cover I, cover II, cover III, and end with cover IV, the outside of the back. C II and C III are the front and back insides, respectively.

covering power. An ink's ability to cover the material beneath to produce a uniform, opaque surface. *See also* opacity.

cover papers or **cover stock.** Paper grades, usually heavier than coated and treated papers, with good folding qualities, uniform printing surface, durability, and dimensional stability. *See also* basic weight or basis weight and paper grades.

CPI. Characters per inch. The measurement of the density at which characters can be packed on a magnetic tape, drum, disc, or any linear device on which information is recorded. Not to be confused with characters per pica.

C-print. A copy print of a color transparency or photo. It is a good-quality copy, suitable for reproduction or separations.

CPS. Characters per second. Measurement referring to the output speed of phototypesetting equipment.

crash. 1. The coarse netlike material that is glued to the spine of a book for strength and also to part of the front and back before end papers are attached. The crash helps hold the book in its cover. 2. A paper finish that simulates the look and feel of coarse linen. *See also* binding.

crawling. The expansion or contraction of ink after printing on a surface that it has not completely wet.

crease. *See* hinge and scoring.

credit line. Line under a photograph, on a separate page, or in a footnote which credits the photographer or artist, or states permission to reprint art or a quote from a previously printed piece. Credit lines are easily overlooked in checking page proofs.

creep. Tendency of film or repro paper to move forward thus throwing off the leading in typeset material.

Cromalin. A color-proofing method manufactured by Du Pont. A dry powder of each color separation is applied separately to latent images on a transparent laminated skin in a dusting process. The Cromalin shows dot for dot what is in the film. It is fast and inexpensive, and as close to the printed sheet as one can come for process colors without printing a press proof. It is much better for process colors than a color key proof which is merely colored plastic. Cromalins are so good that they are sometimes better than the printed sheet in comparison with the original art, causing a client to be dissatisfied with the printing process done on press.

Cronapress. Du Pont's system of converting metal type or letterpress printing plates into film for offset or gravure printing. The material to be converted is covered with a special pressure-sensitive film and pressure is applied with vibrating steel balls or pins which coalesce the film to make it clear or transparent at the points at which the raised letterpress dots or type touch it. The material is then dyed to make the noncoalesced areas light-blocking. The result is a film negative. *See also* Brightype and Scotchprint.

cropping. Eliminating portions of the copy, by physical cutting, or by masking, to better fit a space or to concentrate attention on an important area of an illustration. Crop marks are placed with a grease pencil on a photostat or on the original, or with a pen or pencil on an overlay for the cameraman to follow. *See also* proportion scale or proportion wheel, and scale.

cropmarks. Lines drawn on an overlay or in the margins of an illustration or on a photostat to indicate where the art should be trimmed.

crosshairs. Register marks used in accurate positioning or overlaying of images.

crosshead. An old typesetting term for a straddle head which goes above a straddle rule on a table. A straddle rule is a horizontal rule which covers more than one column.

crossline screen. A grid pattern with opaque lines crossing each other at right angles to form transparent squares or "screen apertures," for halftone photography. It is the screen apertures that allow for the dots. *See also* halftone.

crossmarks. Register marks for accurate positioning of images in step-and-repeat, double or multicolor printing, or for superimposing overlays over a base or on each other.

cross perforation. Perforations made at right angles to the direction of web travel to prevent bursting of signatures during folding.

cross-reference. An instruction in an index or glossary to look under another entry for more information, or to look in another part of the book, on another page, etc.

CRT. *See* cathode ray tube, digitized typesetting, and generations of type.

c & sc. *See* caps and small caps.

C-2-S. Coated two-sides. *See* coateds or coated paper.

curling. *See* relative humidity.

cursives. Script typefaces that resemble handwriting, but have disconnected letters. *See also* typeface styles.

cut. 1. Originally referring to a woodcut, now loosely denotes any kind of engraving plate or illustrative matter. Actually only the letterpress process uses cuts, all other printing processes print from one plate containing both type and illustrations. The name came from the idea that nonprinting areas are cut away. Line cuts used to be produced by engravers who copied line art by hand on metal or wood. Now a line drawing is photographed and the negative exposed to a surface that is eaten away with acid in unprotected areas. Halftone cuts are made from screened negatives.

In a true engraving, the design is cut into the printing plate with a graver, and is printed by the intaglio process. In a cut, all areas that are not to be printed are cut away bringing the design into relief, and the image is printed by the relief process.

2. A hair cut, fiber cut, or calender cut which are weak spots in a web. Any sort of defect that allows the web tension to equal less than approximately 4 lbs per lineal inch across the web will have a tendency to break, thus causing the press to stop.

3. To delete material in order to fit a space allotment.

cut-in head. A headline set in different type from the text and placed in a box of white space cut into the side of the type page usually under the first two lines of the paragraph. It makes extra work for the typesetter or pasteup person, and is more expensive than heads set apart from the paragraph.

The following head is called a cut-in head because it cuts into the text. A cut in head is expensive because the typesetter must calculate the line lengths and the height of the heading to accommodate the cut-in head. In

Cut-in Head

photo-type, the cut-in head can be typeset along with the rest of the copy and put in place by calculations on the video display terminal. But in hot metal type, the cut-in head is usually set separately and mortised into the type after it has been set.

Cut in head.

cutline. *See* caption.

cut-off. The distance between cutting knives which chop the web into individual sheets. It corresponds to the circumference of the plate cylinder on the press.

cutoff rule. 1. A hairline that marks the point where a block of type goes from one column to the next, or marks the end of the story in a column of type. 2. In newspapers, the horizontal dividing line between typographic elements.

cut-out. *See* die cutting.

cut-out lettering. Self-adhering transfer type carried on acetate sheets that is cut out and placed on the working surface. For example, Formatt and Letraset. *See also* pressure-sensitive lettering.

cutscore. A sharp-edged knife used in die cutting to cut part way into the paper or board for folding purposes.

cutting. Trimming the paper both before and after printing. Paper cutters can make square or angular cuts. For round-cornering or die cutting into special shapes, special equipment is used. The ink must dry before printed material can be cut in order to avoid set-off onto the back of a subsequent sheet under the pressure of the cutter.

It is wise to check with the printer before ordering paper to size. The paper supplier can cut the paper before delivery, or the printer can cut it for the binder. *See also* die cutting.

cutting copy. *See* copy editing, copyfitting, and copy preparation.

cyan. One of the process colors, and one of the filters used in making color separations. Also called process blue.

cyanide. Used to cut the silver surface of film to reduce the size of the dot in dot etching. Film must be contacted if the dot is to be enlarged. *See also* dot etching.

cylinder press. The first practical version was invented in 1811 in Germany by Frederick König. A revolving cylinder moved the sheet over a flat bed of type. It printed 11,000 sheets an hour, and was used to print the London *Times.* Even then the pressmen were jealous of the new invention that changed their jobs, and the new press was protected by police to prevent violence.

Now, in a letterpress printing press, each sheet of paper is wrapped around a cylinder that rolls across the inked form to impress the paper upon type which lies flat. To the confusion of the layman, *flatbed press* and *cylinder press* are used interchangeably both having a flat bed for the type forms. A *rotary press* has plates curved around a cylinder.

cylinders for offset press. There are three cylinders for the offset press. The offset plate is mounted on the plate cylinder; the rubber blanket covers the blanket cylinder; and the impression cylinder has a smooth metal surface. When the rubber covered blanket cylinder is brought into contact with the plate cylinder, the readable inked image of the plate prints onto the blanket, wrong reading. The paper is passed through the press between the blanket and impression cylinders, and the image on the blanket is printed onto the paper right reading.

D

dandy roll. The wire cylinder on the papermaking machine that impresses the laid and woven patterns and the watermarks on the surface of better grades of writing and book papers.

data bank. The mass storage of information such as programs for typesetting, which may be selectively retrieved from a computer.

data base. An operation in which information is stored in a computer so it can later be retrieved and printed out for users. Some information systems and publishers use data-base storage for information rather than printing material which must be stored or filed. Some typesetters specialize in data-base storage which makes revisions of the stored material very easy.

dead form. Used hot-metal type which is waiting to be distributed or returned to the job case where it is stored.

deadline. The hour or day after which an advertisement or editorial material will not be printed in a particular publication.

dead matter. Type or illustrations no longer needed for printing, as opposed to live matter which is needed.

dead white. A neutral white that has no perceptible tint.

debossing. A finishing process that produces a sunken, or relief image on the surface of the paper. It can be blind, inked, or foiled. Debossing is the opposite of embossing, which produces a raised image.

deck. *See* blurb.

deckle edge. Untrimmed feathery edges on the outside edges of machine-made paper, produced as water pours on the edge of the unformed pulp as it travels on the wire just before becoming paper. The deckling is formed when the paper fibers flow under the rubber dam, or deckle, that determines the width of the

Deckle edge.

paper. The deckle can later be trimmed off. A deckle edge is sometimes produced artificially to give a handmade effect, and handmade paper is deckled on all four sides unless trimmed. Some books retain the deckle on front and foot edges with plain cut or gilt tops. *See also* papermaking.

dedication. A message in the front of a book or other artistic production expressing affection for a friend or group.

deep-etch. The process by which an offset printing plate is produced using two separate etching operations, when type and line work must be etched separately, or to obtain longer-lasting plate life. Additional bite is given line work or coarse-screen halftones so that the greasy areas that carry the ink are slightly recessed below the dampened surface. Deep-etch plates are used for long runs. They hold more ink resulting in more brilliant halftones, and the metal wears longer on press. Since the plate can break, it is only used for one run. To make the plate, a stencil is formed that covers the nonimage areas with resin but leaves the image areas open, which can be etched with special solution. Deep-etch plates are phasing out because they take so long and require more expensive materials to make than albumin surface plates, for example, which are easier to make, and have a longer life.

definition. The degree of sharpness in a print or negative.

delete. To remove or take out. *See also* proofreader's marks.

delivery date. The date on which bound books are delivered to the warehouse. This is several weeks before the publication date, which is the date the book is released for sale in bookstores. Delivery instructions must be very clear to the supplier so that the product ends up in the right place.

delivery end. The part of the printing press at which the finished, printed sheet is delivered.

densitometer. An instrument with a light-sensitive photoelectric eye that measures a material's reflection or absorption of light by transmittance, i.e., the percentage of directed light that the material reflects or passes. The cameraman uses a densitometer to get the correct exposure when shooting art, and the printer uses it to determine whether the ink on the printed sheets is being run at the proper thickness throughout the run. A flying spot densitometer has been developed for reading ink density on the printed sheet while the press is in full operation, though the majority of printers use the densitometer after the sheet comes off the press.

density. **1.** The measurement of opacity of ink or film. The total ink density in a given area of a four-color proof should not exceed 260% which is the maximum amount of ink that can be trapped on paper for web printing. A sheet could not hold 100% of all four colors of ink being used at one time. The range of density is expressed numerically from 0 to 4.0. **2.** The degree of opacity of exposed and developed type characters.

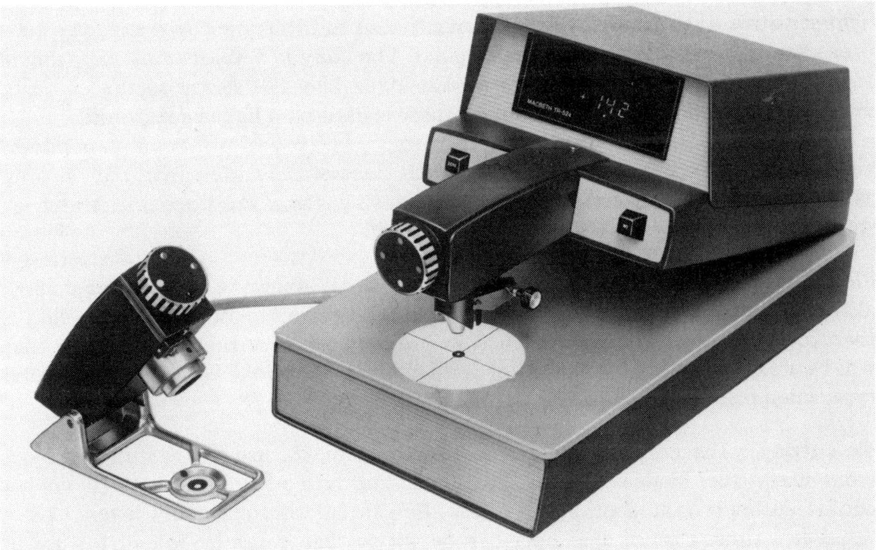

A digital densitometer shows the ink coverage on a color proof or press sheet. (*Courtesy Macbeth Color and Photometry Division*)

department slug. *See* slug.

descender. The lower stroke of a letter that falls below the base line as in p, q, y, and j. *See also* ascender.

design. The conceptualization of a printed piece and the marking of copy so that type and illustrations will be produced and printed according to that concept. Production details such as margins, percentages of color, and any novelties such as gilt edges or rounded corners are considered part of the design. The designer is expected to follow the guidelines of the client as to specification tastes and limitations of the budget. *See also* art, color, layout, margins, and typeface styles.

developer. The chemical agent that renders photographic images visible after the film has been exposed to light.

devil. An obsolete term for a worker in a printing plant with less status than an apprentice.

diamond. Smallest type size in common use, 4½ points. Looks like this.

diaphragm. A disk having a variable opening that restricts the amount of light passing through the lens of a camera.

diazo. A photographic positive same-size proofing process used to produce photoproofs from film positives by contact exposure. In a contact exposure, light-sensitive dyes are destroyed when exposed to ultraviolet light except where protected by the black lines of the original. The copy is developed by exposing it to ammonia vapor that produces an azo dye. The dye serves as the coloring material for the copy. Blue, brown, or black is used on a light background.

The diazo process makes a positive from a positive and prints on plain paper, transparent paper, film, microfilm, or both sides of the same paper, etc., as long as the material is sensitized. Unlike blueprinting, the diazo does not stretch or shrink in the developer. Also called white-print.

die. A stamp of brass, copper, or zinc used in die stamping on covering materials or on cartons. The die can be cut from a negative exposure to a plate that is then routed out, etched, and bathed in order to produce the raised design that will be stamped through a ribbon of foil or inked. Dies hold up better than metal type when printing on an uneven surface.

die cutting. The cutting of paper or cardboard by the use of pressure or a blow from sharp steel blades. The blades are made up into a form that looks like a big cookie cutter mounted on a press. The die can cut through many layers of material at a time. Part of the sheet can be slit so that it can be folded for use in mailing pieces, greeting cards, purchase displays, etc. Die cutting can be done in-line with printing or as an individual operation.

die stamping. Making an impression on book covers, cards, letterheads, etc. by the use of a brass or other hard metal die that stamps the surface with ink or metallic foil and sometimes heat. If there is no color used, it is called blind stamping. The die is cut in the bindery and requires deep and careful routing. An impression of die through foil to the surface is called a hit.

diffusion transfer process. A photomechanical process which uses PMT materials and a camera to produce special lettering effects, reductions, enlargements, screened lettering, to strengthen or weaken copy, clean up copy, drop out backgrounds, etc., without using a film negative. In a diffusion-transfer copier, photographic paper is contacted to the original to be copied on a glass-topped box during a timed exposure. The photo paper is developed to harden the areas that contacted the white areas of the original, leaving the dark areas soft. The photo paper is then contacted to the final copy paper for a permanent image of the original. Defects on an original such as fingerprints, wax, scratches, or dirt can be eliminated by this process.

digitized typesetting. Typesetting comprised of infinitesimal dots or lines that create characters, symbols, lines, art, and photographs. Type fonts can be stored either as digital information in the computer, or on a master grid which is scanned. This information is relayed to the cathode ray tube, which looks like a television screen, where the dots or lines are produced by an electrical system of on and off states. At one end of the cathode ray vacuum tube, a gun, or cathode, emits a spray of electrons which are focused into a narrow beam. They are projected to a phosphor coating on the screen at the other end of the tube. The beam striking the phosphor makes it glow, but only as long as the electrons bombard it. The beam can be directed to any point on the face of the tube. The dots, which are about 1 mil in diameter, are called strokes, and when overlapped and properly positioned, they create a character. The beam is turned on and off, positioned, corrected, and deflected. The stroking quality of the beam is responsible for the sawtooth effect on diagonal or curved lines. Under a glass, the stair-step on almost all CRT characters can be seen, but the naked eye would not be able to discern them. Since there is no tangible master font, there is infinite variation in size and width. Digitized typesetting has created a dramatic change in the possibilities of graphic design for publications which were previously limited to standard hot metal or phototype equipment, or available phototype fonts. *See also* cathode ray tube.

dilitho. *See* direct lithography.

dimension marks. Marks made on mechanicals, tissue overlays, or camera copy outside the area to be reproduced, indicating size of art or type element and often indicating reduction or enlargement.

dimensional stability. Resistance of paper or film to change of size or shape with variance in moisture content or relative humidity.

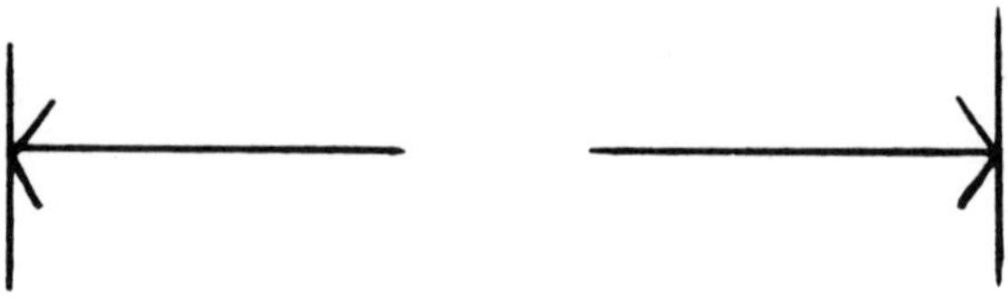

Dimension marks.

dingbat. A small abstract or naturalistic ornament on the printed page used to indicate direction, instructions, or simply used as a motif of the subject matter. Most typehouses carry them. Also called printer's flowers and cabbages.

direct impression. *See* cold type and strike-on composition.

14 Point Special Characters

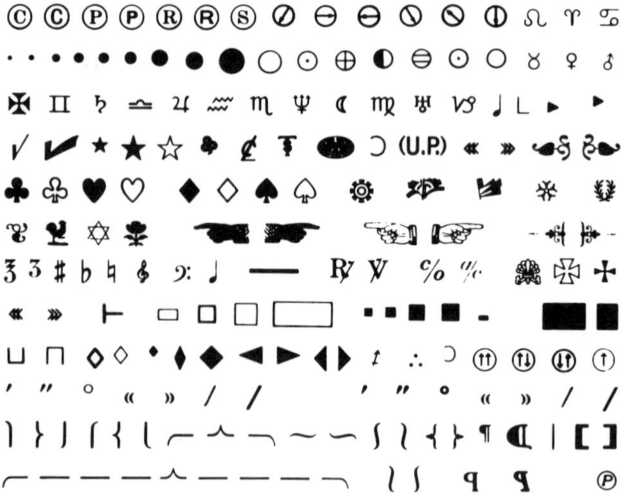

10 Point Special Characters

Dingbats.

direct input composition. An input terminal physically connected to the output unit in phototypesetting so that the system sets type as soon as the keyboarded commands instruct the photounit to set that copy which has been keyboarded. The equipment combines keyboard and photounit. Many advertising agencies, educational institutions, and in-house operations use these machines to free themselves from financial and service dependence on outside suppliers.

direct lithography. Printing with the lithographic process directly from plate onto paper. This is often used as a transitional stage between rotary letterpress and offset lithography because printers can use their previous investment in letterpress rotaries without having to buy an entirely new press. Moreover they can enjoy the lower production costs of lithographic plates. Direct lithography is actually not new. The first planographic printing was done from stones, but was not really successful as offset lithography until there was an improvement in plates beginning around 1970. Direct lithography uses inexpensive wipe-on pre-sensitized aluminum plates and cheap letterpress inks. Quality is almost comparable to offset lithography. Paper waste is higher than in letterpress printing, but not as high as in offset lithography. Web breaks are infrequent. Direct lithography will remain viable in the newspaper industry until the day offset lithography sweeps up the entire newspaper field. Also called dilitho. *See also* printing.

direction of travel. The direction in which the printing stock or web moves through the press.

direct screen halftone. A halftone negative in color separation made by direct exposure on an enlarger or by contact through a halftone screen.

direct separation. A method of color separation in which copy is sized, screened, and separated in one step by the process camera and a halftone negative is made. This is as opposed to the indirect process in which a continuous tone separation negative is made and then projected to the required size and screened.

discount. A fixed rate, given to bookstores or bookclubs, off the retail, or list, price of a book.

disk. 1. A circular image-carrier of negative type styles in some phototypesetting operations. 2. A storage unit for information that is keyboarded on computer typesetting equipment. A disk is similar to a phonograph record, having a flat circular magnetic surface on which data is stored. Data on the disk can be located faster than that on a magnetic tape. A floppy disk can store from 250,000 to 600,000 characters. Rigid disks can store one million to several million characters.

display type. Copy that is set apart from the text and is set 18 pt. or larger to attract attention. Commonly used for headings and advertisements, as opposed to body type. *See also* photodisplay.

distribution. 1. To return the type, leads, rules, slugs, furniture and other hot-type materials to their storage places after use. *See also* California job case. 2. Selling or placing a printed piece into the hands of a reader or prospective customer.

Ditto. Trade name for an office-size duplicator. *See also* spirit duplicator.

ditto. A typographic mark which means repeat what is above. Looks like ″.

doctor blade. A knife-edged flexible metal blade fitted onto rotogravure presses to scrape off excess ink from the nonprinting surface of the engraved printing cylinder. *See also* cells.

do/ht. *See* drop out halftone.

dot. 1. The minute individual elements which carry the ink on a printed surface, formed by a halftone screen. *See also* halftone. 2. Ellipsis points, which indicate an omission in the copy. Looks like . . . 3. *See* leader.

dot etching. Color correction done by hand on film containing screened color separations. Dot etching changes the size of the dots, thereby changing the tone of the separation. Since perfect color separations cannot be produced simply by color filtration, dot etching is needed to compensate for faults of the process.

dot for dot. *See* copy dot.

dot value. Sharpness of the dot on film or progressive proofs. There can be up to 5% gain on the progs due to dot spread on paper. *See also* progressive proofs.

dot spread. A printing defect in which dots print larger than they should, causing a lack of sharpness. It is caused by mechanical mistakes in make-ready or by the press.

double-black duotone. A duotone or a print using two negatives from opposite ends of the gray scale and two impressions on the press in which both plates are printed in black, to achieve greater density and quality like that of gravure printing. The original photograph is shot twice with screens at different angles to obtain the negatives. Also called futuratone. Not to be confused with double-dot halftone or duotone.

double burn. The exposure of two or more films onto a printing plate or a new film, thereby creating a single image. This is necessary when, for instance, type is placed too near an illustration which is stripped into the negative to be exposed to the plate. If the two elements to be stripped together are of different thicknesses, a ridge of a few thousandths of an inch will occur and the type will not completely touch the plate in contact. Thus the plate is required to be burned twice which is, of course, more expensive.

A double burn is also used when two elements such as type and halftones are combined in the same illustration.

double-dot halftone. Two halftone negatives made from the same photograph shot at different screen angles combined into one offset printing plate for one impression of ink on the press. This kind of print has greater tonal range than a conventional halftone because one negative reproduces the highlights and shadows, and the other produces the middletones. Not to be confused with duotone.

double numeration. A numbering system using the chapter number and the individual number of the chart, table, or figures within the chapter. For example, 4–13, 16–1, 8–11b.

double-page spread. *See* spread para no. 3.

double-thick cover. Two thicknesses of regular-weight cover paper pasted together.

double-tone halftone. Imitation of a duotone in which the color plate is purposely printed out of register to produce a duotone effect.

double truck. A page spread made of one unit that jumps the gutter of the facing pages.

doubling. Two impressions of each dot, causing the printed image to appear heavier than usual. Doubling occurs in wet multicolor printing when the first color printed is picked up on the blanket of the second cylinder which in turn prints it back on the next sheet. If it is slightly off register, this will be seen as a light ghost dot next to the original dot, causing variations in color tone and value.

downtime. The time interval during which machinery such as typesetting equipment or a printing press is not operating, or the work is held up waiting for instructions, etc.

down back. Slang for the press room in a printing plate.

drag. *See* slurring.

draw-down. A method of determining color shade of ink. A small glob of ink is placed on paper and drawn down with the edge of a putty knife to get a film of ink. The ink can then be evaluated for color and density.

drawing paper. Papers used for pen or pencil drawing, as opposed to printing. Fiber composition ranges from rag stock to groundwood.

drawing pencils. Pencils ranging from fine to thick points with a soft point for drawing or shading, available from art supply stores.

drilling. Perforating sheets to be bound in spiral-type bindings.

driography. Waterless lithography. Driography simplifies platemaking by using silicone and metal; it eliminates the need for ink and water balance; and it minimizes waste. The problems of the dampening moisture on offset presses and its effect on paper are not of concern in the maintenance of print quality. Not to be confused with *direct lithography, flexography,* or *indirect letterpress,* which is also called *dry offset,* and *letterset. See also* printing.

drop folio. A page number printed at the foot of the page, usually flush outside with the text and a certain number of lines under the text. *See* margins for illustration.

dropout halftone. A halftone in which the screen dots in the highlight areas, or the highlight dots, have been opaqued on the negative so that no dots print in the area and the white paper shows through more brilliantly. Areas are selectively removed and the entire background may or may not be cut away. Because of this selectiveness, this is an expensive process. Abbreviated do/ht. Not to be confused with silhouette halftone.

drop-outs. Portions of artwork that do not reproduce, especially colored lines or background areas. Drop-outs are done on purpose for effect or as an inevitable result of the photographic process.

dropout type. *See* reverse type.

drop ship. To send a book to one address and the bill for it to another. For example, merchandise is shipped to a retailer but billed to the wholesaler.

dry-mounting. A method of adhering photographs to mounting boards by the use of special wax-backed tissue that bonds the photograph to the board under heat and pressure. Dry mounting affixes the art so that there are no wrinkles or bubbles.

dry offset. *See* letterset.

dry-transfer type. A type of adhesive lettering in which the image to be transferred is placed over the artwork and burnished directly to it. No cutting is necessary.

dummy. 1. A facsimile of a proposed issue of a publication. The dummy is a model of the finished printed product, indicating size, shape, and layout. It contains instructions to the compositor as to the design technicalities and type specifications. The degree of finish of a dummy varies from client to client and may contain sketches and lines, or actual photostats or blues, and galleys of type pasted into place. Galleys pasted up into a dummy can contain the galley number so that corrections made on the galleys can be compensated for on the dummy. *See also* mounted reprint copy. **2.** A hand-bound sample showing the paper, cover, size, and bulk of a planned book. Sometimes the dummy contains one printed signature.

dummy type. Sample type used to show what a block of type will look like when set. *See also* Greeking.

duograph or **duotone.** A two-color halftone made from a one-color photograph. The photograph is screened at different angles and shot twice, so that two negatives and therefore two plates are made for printing two colors on the press. The black plate, the light printer, picks up the highlights and shadows, and the plate for the second color, the dark printer, picks up the middletones. The two plates produce a monochromatic color reproduction with a full range of tones. This is not to be confused with a double-dot halftone. *See also* flat-tint halftone.

duotone ink. A special ink designed to bleed into the paper the way a pen stroke on a blotter has fuzzy edges. The ink remains dark where it is laid on the paper; but as it bleeds away from these areas, it turns much lighter and exhibits an undertone of a different color. Photographs reproduce well in duotone ink. However, duotone ink is not so satisfactory for printing a page combining both photographs and type since the tendency of the ink to bleed or fade off has an undesirable blurring effect on the type.

dupe. Duplicate of anything such as film, page proofs, photographs, etc. used in the graphic arts.

dupe neg. A duplicate of a film negative for offset plate making. The negative has to be contacted to make a positive image and then contacted back to a negative in order to obtain the duplicate negative. *See also* Autonegative film.

duplex paper. Paper having a different color or finish on each side.

duplicate plates. Plates made from the same film for offset or gravure, or those produced for letterpress by electrotyping, stereotyping or other molding processes. Duplicate plates make it possible to print multiple images on the same sheet in letterpress work; to use more than one press at a time; to insure against damage of the plate; or to print in several different publications or locations at once. *See also* electrotype, step and repeat, stereotype, two-up.

duplicate transparency. A duplicate of an existing photograph in transparency form, done when more than one piece of art is needed or when the transparency is to be retouched or ganged up with others on a flat.

duplicate film. Special color film used for making duplicates of color transparencies to size, so that they can be stripped together and film separated as a unit for platemaking with the image ganged up.

duplicator paper. A smooth, hard-surfaced paper made for use on spirit duplicators.

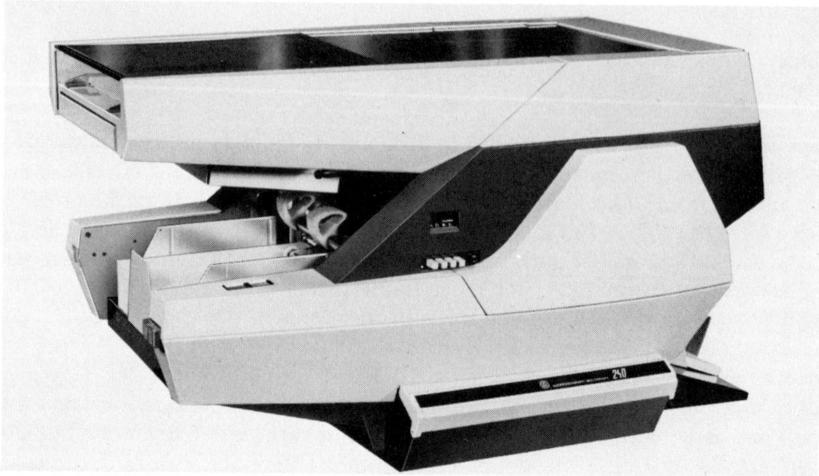

Automated table top offset duplicator, as easy to operate as an office copier and less expensive. (*Courtesy Addressograph Multigraph Corporation, Multigraphics Division*)

dust wrapper. *See* jacket.

dyes. Soluble coloring matter as opposed to pigments, which are insoluble.

dye transfer. A full-color print made from reflective art or transparent copy onto specially coated paper. The art is separated into three colors, and gelatin matrices are made. The matrices selectively absorb the dye and transfer it to the gelatin-coated paper. Often used for retouching or as short-run quantity displays.

Dylux. Trade name for a self-fixing, light-sensitive proofing paper manufactured by Du Pont. Proofs are pulled from either positive or negative film utilizing a dry photo process in which ultra-violet light exposes the paper which is sensitive on both sides. The manufacturer makes the color blue although this has no significance. In some cases the dylux process has replaced the blueline or brownline process.

E

easeling. *See* mounting and finishing.

east, west. From left to right as you read a page of type. North is considered to be the head of the page.

edge gilding. The practice of adding gold leaf to the page edges of finely printed limited editions or bibles.

edge indexing. The use of rules or marks that run right to the edge of the page, corresponding to headings on the table of contents page. To use an edge-indexed publication, the reader must bend it until the pages fan out so the black marks or rules show. *See also* tabbing and thumb cut.

edge staining. Applying a stain by spray onto the edges of pages.

editing. Correcting a manuscript for accuracy, content, consistency, flow, and style, and making sure it meets the standards of the publisher. Actual spelling, grammar, and punctuation are corrected by the copy editor.

editing supervisor. An editor who sets policy and style for the editing of a manuscript. The editing supervisor handles queries with the author and passes the manuscript on to the copy editor for editing.

editing terminal. A visual display unit on which is displayed the results of the keyboarded copy which may have been stored on tape or disk for editing or correcting prior to input into the actual typesetting unit. The operator uses the terminal either for input or for making corrections. With more sophisticated systems, complete page makeup can be viewed and corrected before type is set. (*See* illustration p. 74)

edition. All copies of a book printed from the same type or the same plates including all subsequent copies printed from plates prepared from the original typography. An edition may go through more than one printing or impression. A new edition, as opposed to a new printing, consists of an extensively revised version, a wholly reset version, an old book with extensive new material such as

Editing terminal on which copy is keyboarded and corrections are made. (*Courtesy Addressograph Multigraph, Varityper Division*)

an introduction, or the same book with a different binding and intended for a different audience. In rare book trade, edition and printing are synonymous because the early printer distributed his type after each printing.

edition binding. 1. Specifically refers to case-bound, or hard-cover, books. 2. More generally refers to all commercial bindings including wire-stitched, perfect, mechanical, and case-bound as opposed to custom or hand-made bindings.

editor. One who procures manuscripts for publication, or selects and prepares material for publication. The editor may also set the budget, perform editorial services, or specialize in one professional field so as to pass judgment on manuscripts. *See also* copy editing, copy preparation, copywriting, and proofread.

EF. *See* English finish.

eggshell. Soft, bulky paper with a finish that resembles the shell of an egg. *See also* antique finish.

Egyptian. Square serif typeface style.

electro. *See* electrotype.

electronic scanner. 1. Photoelectric equipment for reading relative densities of full-color copy in order to make separations. The transparency is wrapped around a cylinder, and the image is sent electronically to four sheets of film. The scanner can produce either negative or positive film either screened or unscreened. *See also* color separation. **2.** Device for converting typewritten material to paper or magnetic tape or disk. The device scans copy typed and coded on special paper for typesetting. It recognizes the characters and if the scanner sees anything that is indistinguishable, it stops and asks what it is. *See also* optical character recognition scanner. **3.** An electric eye used in printing to scan the printed sheet as it passes through the press for the purpose of register control, quality control, ink density, and register for cutoff. *See also* scanner.

electrophotography. Image transfer systems used in copiers to produce images using electrostatic forces, for example Electrofax and Xerox. *See also* electrostatic printing.

electrostatic printing. Copying with the use of charges of static electricity, or electrical disturbances to produce inkless printing. The original copy is brightly illuminated and exposed through a lens so as to cast its image on the electrified copy paper or onto a metal surface and then transferred to the copy paper. The paper comes in contact with a selenium surface which varies electrical conductivity with the intensity of its illumination. Thus, it is possible to place an electric

Electrostatic copier makes office copies in sizes from 5½ to 17-inches at a speed of 133 copies per minute. (*Courtesy Van Dyk Research Corporation*)

charge on an unlighted surface, project an image on that surface, and dissipate the charge wherever the light strikes. The copy paper loses its charge where the light strikes and retains it where the light was absorbed by black type or lines of the original. Ink pigment with an opposite electric charge will be attracted to the areas that remain charged and can be heat-fused to the paper for permanence.

The latest types of equipment are controlled by computer tape and can print two pages per second, each one different. Quality is equivalent to that of well-printed offset type and line work. Printing by this method is not as cheap or as fast as conventional printing but it makes it possible to print single copies where special needs may justify higher costs. Some types of electrostatic printing that reduce an image cannot be used when exact size is required.

electrotype. A metal printing plate cast from a wax, lead, or plastic mold of letterpress type and illustrations. Electrotypes may be flat, or curved to fit rotary cylinders and are durable and easy to store. They wear longer than hot metal type. Thus, these duplicates of the original metal type mold are often used for large editions or subsequent printings of a book. *See also* duplicate plates.

elhi. Elementary and high-school textbook publishing.

elite type. The smallest size of typewriter type: 12 characters per inch, as opposed to 10 characters per inch pica type.

ellipses. Three dots that indicate an omission in quoted matter or show a series in shortened form. Looks like . . .

elliptical dot. Halftone dots shaped like footballs. Elliptical dots produce a smoother gradation of tones than conventional dots. Also called chain-dot.

em. A unit of linear measurement equal to the point size of the type being used. So named because the M in early fonts was cast on a square body. One-half an em is called an en; 1/3 of an em is called 3-to-the em; 1/4 of an em is 4-to-the em. Also called mutton quad. *See also* quad.

embossing. A finishing process that produces a raised image on the surface of the paper by means of a die striking from beneath the paper into an intaglio die above the paper. Embossing can make use of printer's ink, metallic foils, be printed on the paper first, or it can be blank. It can be done on book covering materials as well as on paper for printing or writing. *See also* blind embossing.

em-quad. *See* em.

emulsion. The photosensitive coating that reacts to light on film or plate. It is the dull, matte-looking side as opposed to the glossy side of a piece of film. The emulsion contains silver which, when hit with light, turns dark and when contacted will produce the highlight areas.

emulsion to emulsion. Contacting film to film, or film to plates, the emulsion side of the film being contacted to the emulsion side of the duplicating film or bonded to the plate to produce the desired chemical reaction that obtains an image.

en. Half the width of an em but the same height as the em-quad for the particular type size being used. Also called nut. *See also* quad.

enamel. 1. A smooth-coated paper. 2. Coating material used on certain papers.

end matter. Material at the end of a book, including glossaries, appendices, bibliographies, indices, etc. Also called back matter.

end-of-line decisions. Hyphenation and justification decisions made either by the computer or the keyboard operator during typesetting.

end papers or **end sheets.** Sheets at the front and back of a case-bound book that secure the first and last signatures to the cover. End papers are usually of heavier stock than the text pages, and are sometimes printed.

The sheets used for end sheets can also be the outside sheets of the first and last signatures. These would be called self-ends. Self-ends are not used, however, on books that are larger than about 7 × 10, depending on the bulk.

English finish. A grade of book paper with a smoother, more uniform surface than machine finish, but not glossy. English finish is uncoated and gets additional smoothness from supercalendering. Abbreviated EF. *See also* finish and papermaking.

engrave. To cut, etch, or incise a surface.

engraver's proof. A proof of a line or halftone engraving. The proof should, if possible, be pulled on the same paper as that on which the job is to be printed.

engraving. 1. A print made from an intaglio plate prepared by cutting below the surface. The die is inked and wiped, leaving ink below the surface. Paper is laid on the die, and the press forces the paper into the cavities of the die where the ink is transferred to the surface of the paper. Thermography and embossing are cheaper methods of achieving an engraved look. Engraved printing can be glossy or matte, whereas thermography has a matte finish. When the piece is turned over the engraved piece will have a debossed effect where the thermography piece will be flat. 2. A metal printing plate made with acid etching. Here, the term is a misnomer because the etch causes a relief plate rather than an intaglio surface. *See also* cut, halftone engraving, line engraving, photoengraving, and thermography.

engrossing. Decorative hand lettering, especially that done on diplomas and certificates.

enlargement. A photographic print that is larger than the original, made by projecting the image through a lens onto a photographic printing surface. Copy to be enlarged can be illuminated from the front; or if it is transparent, from behind. The process is analagous to a slide projector being projected on a large piece of sensitized paper instead of a screen. Enlargements can be made up to 400% on a gallery camera and up to 1600% with the use of a scanner. For illustrations the size of those in books or magazines, 35mm film can be used for the original artwork. However, enlargements for poster-size illustrations in color will break down when enlarged from 35mm film. Rather, 4 X 5 transparencies should be used.

Photographic paper comes in standard sizes of 4 X 5, 5 X 7, 8 X 10, 11 X 14, and 14 X 20 inches.

Mechanical enlargements can be done by camera lucida, or lucy, and pantograph.

enlarger. A device which makes a print from an optically magnified photographic negative.

enlarger font. Negative film font used to produce type sizes larger than 16 or 18 pt.

envelope stuffer. A small printed promotional piece that can be inserted into an envelope with letters or statements.

envelope styles. *Commercial envelopes* are used for business correspondence, and are made in bond and kraft papers in all standard sizes. (A)

Window envelopes are used for statements and invoices. They save time, and prevent errors by eliminating typing of an extra address. They are made in all sizes, papers, and styles. (B)

Self-sealing envelopes save time in handling because of the latex adhesive on the flaps which seal without moisture. (C)

Bankers flap and wallet flap envelopes are used for bulky correspondence and have reserve strength in excess of regular commercial envelopes. (D)

Baronial envelopes are square envelopes with a deep, pointed flap, used for formal correspondence, invitations, announcements, greeting cards, etc. (E)

Booklet, open-side envelopes are used for direct mail and house organs. They have a concealed seam and lend themselves to overall printing on back and front. (F)

Open-end envelopes are used for mailing catalogs, reports, booklets, and magazines. They have wide seams and heavy gummed flaps for maximum protection. (G)

Clasp and string-and-button envelopes are used for mailing bulky papers. String and button clasps keep contents under tension and better protected, but metal clasps make a smoother back surface. Either type may be opened and closed many times. (H)

Expansion envelopes are used for bulky correspondence, package, and rack sales. (I)

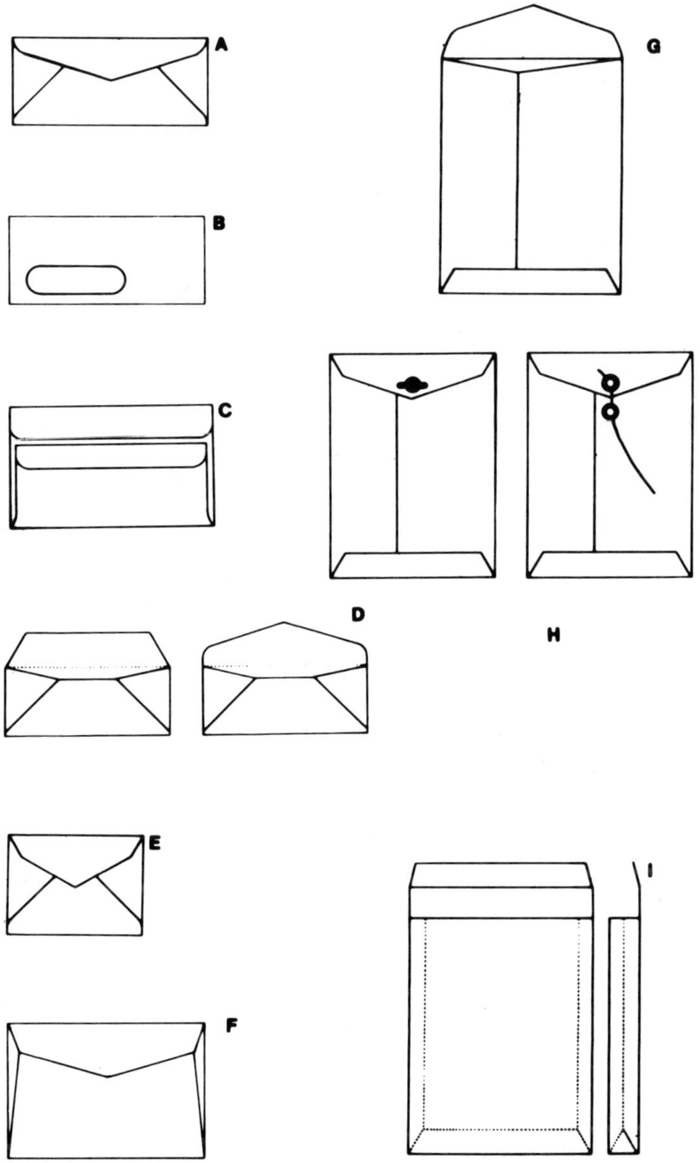

Envelope styles. (*Courtesy Pocket Pal, International Paper Company*)

epigraph. **1.** A motto or quotation at the beginning of a chapter or part-title, used to set the theme. **2.** An engraved inscription.

errata. An error caught after the book has gone to press so that the correction is printed on a slip of paper and tipped in the front or back of the book.

estimate. The costs of producing a book, magazine, or promotion piece, quoted ahead of time. A book is usually priced at four to eight times the total production unit cost of the first printing.

High production costs have a bad domino effect on the rest of an enterprise. If production costs eat up more than 25% of net sales revenue, there is not enough money left to perform the other necessary functions and still leave a profit. Some causes of high production costs which can be controlled are underpricing the book, noncompetitive buying, inexperienced production management, inadequate market, design decisions left up to the supplier, costly design specifications, and unrealistic specifications. The supplier is usually happy to advise alternatives which will save money. *See also* laundry list, manufacturing cost, and plant cost.

etch. **1.** The acid used to eat away the nonprinting area of metal plates in photoengraving. **2.** The fountain solution used to treat nonprinting areas in lithography so that those areas will not accept ink. **3.** To eat with acid as opposed to cutting away nonprinting areas of the metal which is called engraving. In etching, an image is created photographically or photomechanically, and a relief plate is made from the negative by protecting the image wanted with an acid resist, while corroding the rest of the plate below the surface. **4.** To cut the image into the copper printing cylinder in gravure printing. **5.** The fine art intaglio process. *See also* engraving.

etch proof. A repro proof of a letterpress type page including illustrations to be reproduced.

exception dictionary. Words that are exceptions to the rules of logic for hyphenation carried within computer typesetting units. If a word isn't listed in the exception dictionary, and no rule is applicable, the word will not be hyphenated at the end of a line.

excerpt. A passage selected or quoted from another source.

expanded type. A typeface with a width greater than that of the regular typeface. Also called extended type. *See also* typeface styles.

expansion envelopes. *See* envelope styles.

exposure. The time and intensity of illumination acting upon the light-sensitive coating (emulsion) of film or plate.

Spectra

Expanded—20 pt regular

Expanded—20 pt (24 set)

Expanded—24 pt regular

Expanded—24 pt (28 set)

Regular and expanded type.

extended type. *See* expanded type.

extract. A long quotation set off from the text in smaller type or more narrow measure than the body copy. Also called block quotation.

eyeleting. Reinforcing a punched hole with a metal eyelet so the product can be hung. *See also* mounting and finishing.

F

face. **1.** The printing surface of a piece of metal type. **2.** The design of a certain alphabet of type. *See also* typeface styles.

facing pages. The left- and right-hand pages of a spread. Facing pages traditionally have some design balance.

facsimile. Exact reproduction of a letter, document, rare book, or signature, including such things as paper discoloration. Abbreviated facsim or fax.

facsimile transmission. The process of electronically scanning graphic material to convert the image into electric signals that are then transmitted via satellite or telephone lines to produce an exact likeness of the original. A whole page can be transmitted around the world in as little as 6 seconds if the page contains straight text, and in 3 or 4 minutes if there is halftone copy. Darker halftones take longer to transmit than lighter halftones because there is more information to go into the computer.

fade-out. *See* ghosting.

fair use doctrine. A provision of the copyright law which states that short passages from copyrighted material may be used without infringement on the owner's rights. Though there is no set number of words, the rule of thumb is that use of copyrighted material should not impair the market value of the original.

fake color. A method of reproducing artwork in which the designer separates the color areas by the use of overlays, one for each color. The designer can use a color chart to indicate the screen values of each color on overlays that will be used by the printer in making screens in those areas. It is much less expensive than process color but renders only approximate results.

fake duotone. *See* flat-tint halftone.

fake process. *See* fake color.

family of type. All the type sizes, weights, and widths of a particular type design. The members include roman, italic, bold, condensed, and expanded faces for that family. Not all typesetters carry the whole family of any given type.

fast inks. *See* permanent inks.

feet. The part of a piece of metal type upon which it stands. *See also* type.

felt side. The top side of the sheet in paper manufacturing. It does not contact the wire upon which the paper is made, rather, it comes in contact with the felt blanket of the paper machine. The felt side has a closer formation with less grains and better crossing of fibers, and is smoother for printing. In some papers the felt side is impressed, while still wet, with variously structured felts causing a pattern or watermark. Opposite of wire side.

felt-tip pens. Fibrous-tip pens with a self-contained quick-drying ink supply. They can be used for effective coloring of a black-and-white photograph and other types of color illustrations. The luminosity and intensity of these colors create unusual brilliance and expressiveness.

festoon rollers. *See* flying paster.

f & g. Folded and gathered pages. When the printed sheets have been folded and gathered to other signatures in the book, they are often shown to the publisher trimmed or untrimmed before being sewn or glued.

figure. **1.** A diagram or drawing illustrating the text of a book. Originally, a figure was printed with the text of the book, whereas a plate, a glossy illustration, was printed separately. *See also* plate. **2.** A numeral. *See also* lining figures and old-style figures.

The following are examples of Lining figures: 1, 2, 3, 4, 5, 6, 7, 8, 9, 0

The following are examples of Old Style figures: 1, 2, 3, 4, 5, 6 7, 8, 9, 0

Old style and lining figures.

file. A job or set of commands stored in the computer memory of a typesetting system. A file is usually stored on a floppy disk or other magnetic data storage medium. *See also* floppy disk.

filler. **1.** Small advertisement or editorial piece used to fill space in a layout. **2.** Material such as starch, clay, talc, etc., used to improve the printing properties of paper.

fillet. **1.** A decorative line stamped onto a book cover, usually at the top and bottom of the spine. 2. The part of a type character between the serif and the main stroke. Filleting is found in old style and transitional but not modern Roman faces. *See also* Roman and typeface styles.

fill-in. Name, address, and salutation typed into a form letter by a word processor. Other elements can also be filled-in in the body of the text. Also called personalizing.

filling-in or **filling-up.** A condition in which the ink fills the area between halftone dots or plugs up the type.

film. A transparent sheet such as cellulose acetate. Negative photographic film is composed of a protective coating over a layer of silver emulsion adhered to a mylar acetate base with an antihalation backing. Light passes through the coating turning the silver dark where the light hits, thus forming the highlights. The light continues through the substratum base of the mylar carrier and is absorbed by the antihalation backing, thus preventing the light from reflecting back through the layers of the film. For photographic and reprographic purposes stable base film should be used for constant density. Orthochromatic and monochromatic films, used in the graphic arts, are high contrast films so that black and white copy is either picked up entirely or, if the lines are weak, dropped entirely. Therefore, in line photography, black copy must be even, dense, black. Weak, uneven, black or gray will not reproduce without the use of panchromatic films.

When contacting film the emulsion side makes the contact. For making offset plates, right reading, emulsion down film must be used so that the image which is right reading on the plate becomes wrong reading on the blanket, and again right reading on the press sheet. Today's polyester bases are almost as dimensionally stable as glass. Thickness of film is measured in mils or thousandths of an inch.

Typesetting may be done on either stable base film or paper base, or repro. The image is photographically set and the resulting image appears either on film to be contacted to a plate, or on paper to be photographed and the negative contacted to a plate. Composition in film has been popular in the past but with the development of stable paper base, there is no reason not to do a book in repro and have mechanicals pasted up. This is much less expensive than having the compositor do page makeup in film. Pasting up mechanicals involves meticulous work on the part of the paste-up person. Many typesetters perform this service. The camera work, in that case is done by the printer, so a value judgment must be made by the client as to which supplier is best suited to do the shooting and what the comparative costs are. *See also* monochromatic, negative, orthochromatic, and panchromatic.

film advance. The distance in points that film in a typesetting photounit is advanced between the lines to create leading. The measurement is set on the keyboarding unit. A film advance of 12-pt. for 10-pt. type means that the text is set with 2-pt. leading, or 10/12. *See also* creep and leading.

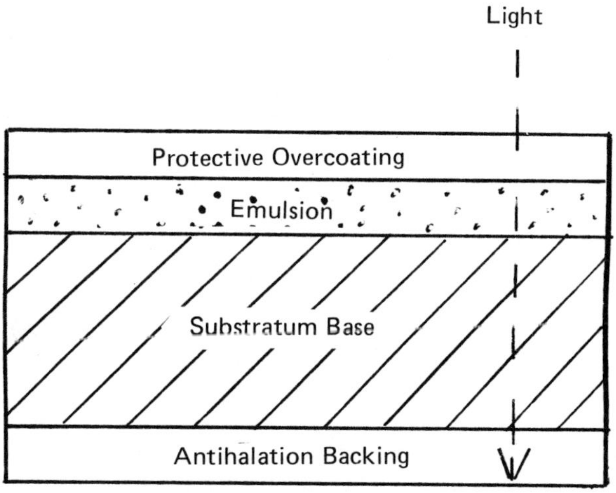

Cross section of stable-base mylar film.

film make-up or **film mechanical.** A sheet of base film onto which all text, half-tone, and display elements are stripped in positive. From this, photo repros or contact films are made for plates. *See also* photomechanical.

film positive. A piece of clear acetate or other film upon which the image appears as it did in the original.

film processor. A machine which develops, fixes, washes, and dries already exposed film or paper.

film split. The split of the ink film off the printing plate or the offset blanket onto the paper or substrate being printed.

filter. A colored piece of gelatin, plastic, or glass placed between the object being photographed and the film in order to eliminate certain colors while allowing the complementary color of the filter to pass through and be recorded on the film which will then be used to make plates. The first exposure is made with a red filter and records cyan; the second exposure is made with a green filter and records magenta; the third, with a blue filter and records yellow; and the fourth exposure either with a yellow-orange filter or three partial exposures with red, green, and blue filters, records black.

final film. Right-reading emulsion down negative film which will be used to make offset plates. The image will be right reading on the plate, wrong reading on the blanket and again right reading on the substrate, or paper.

fine line. A method of shooting already screened art without using a screen and exposing on special film which is more expensive than that used for normal line art or halftone shooting. This is an alternative to shooting halftone copy as line art or to rescreening which can produce the undesirable moiré pattern. Line art may also be shot as fine line in order to pick up more details in the art.

fine papers. The grades of paper used for writing and printing, including bond, ledger, cover, and book papers.

finish. **1.** Pattern characteristic of paper. A laid finish has a pattern of lines or a ribbed effect. A wove finish has no apparent pattern. **2.** Generic term for the surface of a paper. Uncoated book papers are, from least smooth to most smooth: antique, eggshell, vellum, machine finish and English finish. Additional smoothness is obtained if the paper is supercalendered. Paper is a two-sided material. The side directly in contact with the wire on the Fourdrinier papermaking machine is called the wire side. The wire side has less grain and a closer formation. The other side is the top side or felt side. Finish is important in getting the correct reproduction of an image. If the finish changes, a distorted color change or dot will develop on the printed image. *See also* plate finish.

finishing. *See* mounting and finishing.

first color down. The first color printed on the sheet as it passes through the press. It is usually yellow because the lighter colors need to take first in order to form the optical illusion of all the other colors. Black only gives the tone and would dirty the other colors if it went down first, i.e., the other colors wouldn't be seen. *See also* order of colors on press.

first generation typesetting. *See* generations of type.

first proofs. Proofs checked by proofreaders, authors, designers, etc., against the original manuscript.

first revise. The proof pulled after errors have been corrected in the first proof.

fixing. The process by which a photographic image is made permanent by removing unexposed silver halide, thus rendering the film insensitive to further exposure.

flat. **1.** The assembled composite of negative or positive line, halftone, and screens stripped into place in windows cut into the goldenrod, mylar, or other masking material used. The flat is exposed to the plate for platemaking. Flats are more easily stored than plates. **2.** Lack of contrast and detail in photographs.

flatbed press. A press with flat type or plates as opposed to a *rotary press,* which has plates curved around a cylinder. Though it sounds confusing, the term *flatbed press* is synonymous with the term *cylinder press.* Both presses have a

A flat. Page negatives are imposed and stripped in place. (*Courtesy Kingsport Press*)

flat bed for the type forms and a cylinder to carry the paper, not the plates. A rotary press has one cylinder to carry the curved printing plates and one cylinder to press the paper against the plates. *See also* cylinder press.

flat color. Solid colors or tints other than the process colors. Flat colors are not blended to create other colors as in process color. Flat color is any color or percentage of that color the designer asks the printer to match, and it is used for color reproduction of any black-and-white copy, line, or continuous tone. Each color is individually mixed according to a formula. Flat color is less expensive than process color.

flatness. A quality of paper that has freedom from buckles, puckers, wave, and curl. Flatness is important on an offset press.

flat-tint halftone. Printing a black-and-white halftone over a flat tint of a second color. Also called fake duotone.

flexible plates. Photopolymer plates mounted on a belt for in-line production, some of which can produce an entire book on one pass through the press. *See also* belt-press book production system.

flexo or **flexography.** A flexible rotary letterpress process using wrap-around rubber or photopolymer plastic plates with a raised printing surface like a rubber stamp, and special, volatile, fast-drying ink. Originally called aniline printing, a

Mixing flat color ink according to formula. (*Courtesy Lehigh Press, photo by Sid Delmar Leach*)

misnomer since this kind of printing has developed far beyond the original inks made from aniline dyes. Flexo inks are either water or alcohol base. Flexography is often used in the packaging industry or for printing large areas of solid color such as borders or background where sharpness is not required, and on cellophane which letterpress and offset cannot handle well. The flexible rubber-stamp roll covers uneven surfaces, such as corrugated, very efficiently and is practical for short runs. Flexography is beginning to move into book publishing and is starting to turn out color reproductions of a fidelity and quality unattainable a few years ago. Mass-market paperbacks have been produced economically by flexography for years and its printing of newspapers is beginning to meet the objectives of low-cost press unit, high-quality reproduction, minimum paper waste, a low-cost plate, and the use of existing or new inks. Not to be confused with letterflex or letterset. *See also* printing.

flier. Usually a one-page advertisement. *See also* broadside and pamphlet.

flock printing. Special finishes such as velvet, glitter, or frost applied to greeting cards, packages, etc. Sticky glue or varnish is applied to the paper by the silk-screen or letterpress process then sprinkled with fibers, lint, or powders. Also called frost printing and glitter application.

Flat color proofing to compare with sample for matching. (*Courtesy Lehigh Press, photo by Sid Delmar Leach*)

flop. To turn a film image so that the right side appears on the left and vice versa. Not to be confused with reverse.

floppy disk. The flexible mylar magnetic memory device that stores material in a computer typesetting unit. A floppy disk can store 250,000 to 600,000 characters. *See also* file and memory.

fluid duplicator. *See* spirit duplicator.

fluorescent colors. Colors that cause the invisible ultraviolet light to reflect and illuminate.

Fluorescent inks result in extreme brilliance, by reflecting and emitting light, when exposed to external radiation, making use of ultraviolet light waves which other inks cannot utilize. White coated papers produce the best results. The sheet is sometimes given two passes through the press, for a heavier ink film will give better results. When printing with fluorescent inks, one must avoid putting small type in the direct line of solids because of the heavy amount of ink carried on the plate. Fine line screens, and halftones should also be avoided. Letterpress can lay down a heavier layer of ink and will usually print a stronger color of fluorescent ink than will offset, though new finer-grind pigments and greater pigment strength now permit colors to be printed in one impression by lithography and gravure as well. Maximum brilliance can be obtained when fluorescent inks are contrasted with dark surrounding hues. Best use is for semipermanent jobs. Fluorescent colors have a limited life when exposed to sunlight, and a thick film is needed for outdoor exposure.

flush. Even with, or aligned with, the right or left side of the type block area. Also called, in a computer typesetting, quad left or right. Used alone, the word flush means left. *See also* arranging lines of type.

flush-and-hang. Instructions to the typesetter for a flush-left heading or beginning of paragraph followed by a hanging indention. I.e. the rest of the column of type is indented a certain amount of space in from the head or first line. *See also* hanging indention.

flush cover. A cover which has been trimmed to the same size as the text pages such as that of a paperback, as opposed to an overhand cover which protrudes slightly.

flush paragraph. A paragraph with no indention at the beginning.

flying makeready. A method of changing the plates used on a web press which has two units in operation and another two units maderead for printing without shutting down the press. The printer lines up several short-run jobs which require the same size plates and paper and operates the press without down time. Only a few signatures are wasted, and the saving in materials, time, and labor is enormous.

flying paster. An automatic pasting device that splices a new roll of paper onto a roll which is almost depleted, without stopping the press, thus eliminating downtime and minimizing waste when shifting over to new paper rolls. This is most often done by the use of festoon rollers, around which the paper is wound. When it is time for the splice, the rollers can move together so that a slack is created in feeding the press thus allowing the end of the roll time to stop for a few seconds during the splice.

flyleaf. A blank sheet following the end sheet and preceding the bastard title. Flyleaves may be used at the front and back of a book or may be omitted altogether.

foil. Metallic or pigment leaf used for stamping lettering or designs on the covers of books. The long roll of the foil is made from pigment and a releasing agent on a mylar backing. When a heated die is stamped onto the roll of foil, the impression comes off onto the surface beneath. A large selection of colors are available. Foil is often used when many impressions of ink would be required for satisfactory cover of a light color on a dark cloth.

folder. **1.** A printed piece with one or more folds, each portion of which presents a page. **2.** One of the devices on a web press that folds the sheets to create signatures.

folding machine. **1.** A piece of bindery equipment on which sheets of paper that have been printed get folded into signatures. The paper moves up a frame, and hits a stop. A blade hits the sheet in the middle causing the sheet to fold in half, then the paper moves under rollers up a second frame where the folding process is repeated and so on until a signature is made. Special folds may have to be done by hand or go through the machine more than once and so cost more. **2.** A small office machine used to fold letters, bills, fliers, bulletins, etc.

Folding machine at the bindery. (*Courtesy General Bindery Corporation*)

foldout. An oversized page, often containing an illustration or table, folded to the trim size of the book and tipped in.

fold test. A paper test to ensure durability of the paper after a number of double folds without a rupture to the paper. If the fold strength is insufficient, surface cracking will appear at the fold exposing the white of the paper. Breaking or cracking at the fold could break the web in printing or jam the folder in binding.

folio. **1.** The page number. Even-numbered folios are on the left-hand page, odd folios on the right. A folio can either be expressed or blind. A drop folio is placed at the bottom of the page below the last line of text. **2.** A sheet of paper folded once. **3.** A large book about 12 x 15 made from sheets folded once.

font. The carrier for the typeface style. In hot metal, the complete assembly of all the characters, figures, punctuation marks, and ligatures of one typeface, including caps, lowercase, italic, and bold face.

Font carried on a disc for phototypesetting. (*Courtesy Varityper Division, Addressograph Multigraph Corporation*)

In phototype the font is contained on a piece of negative film and includes only one style of that face. For example the italic and roman of the same face would be considered different fonts if they were on different film negatives. Actually, the font is whatever is put into the equipment to do the setting, like a package, thus the different use of the word for different equipment. The number of fonts required for one face depends on the equipment. Pi characters are special characters not included in the alphabet font. Phototypesetting equipment requires mechanical loading of the font, the CRT contains no font as such, rather a computer-driven program which instructs digital signals to create each character separately. *See also* wrong font.

foot. The bottom of a book or page as opposed to the head, which is the top. Also called south, whereas the head is north.

footline. Line of type at the bottom of the page which carries the name of the publication and the issue date. Also called running foot.

footnote. Note at the bottom of the page or the end of a chapter referring to an item mentioned in the text. Footnotes are numbered consecutively or indicated by asterisks, daggers, double daggers, etc., when use of a number would be confusing such as in a table or math text. The order of these signs is

When neither system is suitable, superior letters of the alphabet can be used.

foreword. A short introduction to a book, usually written by someone other than the author, as opposed to the preface which is written by the author.

form. 1. The assembly of pages printed on one side of a sheet of paper and arranged in proper order for folding. A form usually contains multiples of eight pages. 2. The flat or the offset printing plate for pages arranged for proper folding. 3. The actual type and engravings locked up in a chase and ready for letterpress printing.

format. All the elements such as size, style, type page, margins, printing requirements, binding, etc., which make up the individual character of a publication.

formating. The marking-up of typesetting codes for computer-oriented photocomposition. The planning involves such things as command codes, correction necessity, updating, and incorporating into other jobs. The designer's specifications are translated into codes which can be read by the computer.

forwarding. The processes in bookbinding between folding and casing-in, such as rounding and backing, putting on headbands, etc.

foul manuscript. A manuscript which has been set in type. The original marked-up copy is called foul.

foundry. The plant which casts individual characters in metal type for hand setting. Hot metal typesetters buy type from the foundry in complete assortments or fonts.

foundry proof. A proof taken from the letterpress type page after it has been locked up. It shows a black border, created by the bearers in which the type is enclosed in locking up. Foundry proofs indicate that the corrections marked on the final page proofs have been made and no further corrections may be made. *See also* proofs.

foundry type. Hand-set metal type characters cast in special hard metal and kept in separate compartments in a type-case. Certain typefaces are not available in film matrices and can only be bought from a foundry. This type is usually only used for special displays or small jobs. It wears out during printing, and must be redistributed to storage places after use.

fountain. The ink reservoir that holds the ink for use while the press is running and from which the ink is metered to the form by rollers. The fountain roller revolves in the ink or dampening fountain and meters out the correct amount of ink to the distributing rollers. The fountain solution, a solution of water or alcohol, gum arabic, acid, and other chemicals, is used to dampen the printing plate and keep the nonimage areas from accepting ink. The fountain solution is also called etch.

four-by-five. A 4" x 5" transparency used for color artwork. It is especially good for enlargements.

four-color process. Method of reproducing full-color artwork by photographically separating the art into its three subtractive primary colors—magenta, yellow, and cyan—plus black. The resulting negatives are made into four printing plates from which each color is printed in transparent ink over the others. The transparent inks act as filters and produce the full-color effect. Magenta inks filter out green and allow blue and red to show. Cyan inks filter out red and allow blue and green to show. Yellow filters out blue and lets red and green show. When printed one over the other, the dots so filter out color that the resulting colors create the illusion of the full-color range. *See also* color, color separation, process color, and subtractive color.

Fourdrinier. The machine which manufactures most grades of paper. It has basically three units: The wet end, the press section, and the drying section. The pulp mixture travels some 30 feet along an endless wire screen that loops around the machine. When the water is drained or sucked away, the semidry matted fibers proceed on a felt or woolen blanket through press rolls and driers. *See also* papermaking.

Four color sheetfed press. (*Courtesy New Horizons Color Corporation, reprinted by permission of Printing Views Magazine*)

fractions. There are several ways to set numerical fractions in type. The *case* fraction is contained in one line of type where the numerator and denominator are small. Looks like $\frac{1}{2}$, $\frac{1}{4}$. *Special* fractions are also contained on one line of type, but a solidus separates the number. Looks like ½, ¼. In *shilling* fractions, both numbers are full size. Looks like 1/2, 1/4. And in *built-up* fractions the numerator and denominator are very large and the whole fraction takes up two or more lines of type. Looks like $\dfrac{1}{2}$ and $\dfrac{1}{4}$. *See also* piece fraction.

special

$^{1}/_{16}$ $^{3}/_{32}$ $^{5}/_{64}$ $^{10}/_{16}$ $^{20}/_{32}$ $^{30}/_{64}$ $^{15}/_{16}$ $^{31}/_{32}$ $^{45}/_{64}$

case

$\frac{2}{3}$ $\frac{1}{3}$ $\frac{7}{8}$ $\frac{1}{2}$ $\frac{1}{8}$ $\frac{5}{8}$ $\frac{3}{4}$ $\frac{1}{5}$ $\frac{2}{5}$ $\frac{3}{5}$ $\frac{1}{4}$ $\frac{1}{6}$ $\frac{5}{6}$ $\frac{4}{5}$ $\frac{3}{8}$

shilling	**2/3**
built-up	$\frac{3}{8}$ $\frac{1}{9}$ $\frac{6}{7}$ $\frac{13}{23}$

Fractions.

Fraktur type. *See* black letter.

free sheet. Paper with no mechanical wood pulp in it. The wood is boiled, and steamed, and chemicals separate the fibers. The paper is highly bleached and more coating can be applied to it than to groundwood. Therefore, free sheet is more expensive, smoother, and of a better quality than groundwood. *See also* mechanical pulp and groundwood.

French fold. A double fold in which the sheet is printed on one side only. Often used for four-page folders or invitations.

French spacing. *See* spacing.

frisket. **1.** Acetate cut to outline a shape on mechanical art. Usually used to indicate color. **2.** A masking agent used when airbrushing artwork. *See also* mask. **3.** A type character cut out of red or amber acetate to be photographed in the making of a photo matrix for a type font. **4.** Protective paper used to cover any part of the printing plate not meant to print.

front-end system. A computer connected to a video-editing terminal on which the information that is in the computer is compared, hyphenated, justified, etc. A computer cannot store all the information that a terminal can edit so information is stored on a magnetic floppy disk or magnetic rigid disk which can store upwards of 600,000 characters. The front-end system is the totality of all the interconnected devices used prior to output including line printers which produce a typewritten proof. Data management controls the sending of information to the terminal, back to the disk, or to the output end for typesetting. Front-end systems are upgraded by type suppliers as they increase their automation.

frontispiece. An illustration facing the title page of a book.

front matter. Half title, title page, copyright page, and pages such as the contents page, and preface, that explain the text which follows. Front matter does not include the introduction, which is considered part of the text. Front matter is usually paginated in small roman numerals. Also called preliminaries.

frost printing. *See* flock printing.

fugitive inks. Inks that fade or change color when exposed to light, heat, moisture, etc., as opposed to permanent inks which do not fade.

full color. *See* process color.

full measure. Copy set the full width of the line flush with both margins. *See also* measure.

furnish. Pulp and additives that go into the making of paper. *See also* papermaking.

furniture. Rectangular pieces of wood, metal, or plastic used to fill in the blank spaces around hot-metal type and engravings when locking-up the form for printing. Furniture is also used for spacing. It is thicker than leads which are 1-, 2-, or 3-pt. thick, or slugs which are 6- or 12-pt. thick. *See also* leading and measurement.

futuratone. *See* double-black duotone.

fuzz. Fibers which project from the surface of a sheet of paper.

G

gallery camera. A camera with a darkroom behind it. Gallery cameras are used for shooting halftone and line copy, and are equipped with a copy board on sliding rails which move the board with the copy closer or farther away from the lens for exposure. The copy is illuminated by xenon high-intensity lights. Readings are obtained from the copy for highlight, intermediate, and shadow area exposure.

galley. 1. A long, shallow metal tray that holds metal type in the form before printing.

2. A proof, approximately 20 in. long, taken from the standing type. The galley goes to the client for corrections to be marked before printing is done.

In photocomposition, the galley is pulled as a proof from the type set on the photocomposition unit. Galleys show one column of type and have wide margins for marking corrections. The marked set of galleys is returned to the typesetter for corrections to be made before page makeup is done. Extra sets of galleys are made for the author, for the designer to paste up into a dummy, for reviewers, etc. *See also* marked set.

gang printing. Printing several different jobs on the same sheet of paper. The sheet is then cut up into individual jobs and the cost divided accordingly.

gatefold. A leaf that folds toward the gutter. When unfolded, it contains information or photographs that would not fit on a regular page, or it can be used to create a special effect. If inserted before trimming, the sheet must be narrower than the trim edge so as not to get cut by the trimming knife.

gather. To assemble individual sheets or folded signatures into correct sequence for subsequent steps in the bindery process.

gauntlet. The illustration of a gloved hand used as a device to show important lines or the turn of a page. Also called printer's device.

gava. A one-piece four-color prepress proof burned with light powders. It does not contain overlays, and is less expensive than a press proof.

gelatin printing. *See* collotype.

generation. Each succeeding stage in reproduction from the original.

generations of type. The various stages of development of photographic typesetting. The first generation adapted a linecaster from use in hot metal to that of photographic characters. Photographic matrices cast the characters according to a paper tape punched from a keyboard. The first generation started in 1950 with Intertype's Fotosetter which eliminated the step of the repro proof produced by hot-metal type and produced type in negative or positive form for making plates that had photosensitive coatings. Linofilm is an example of first-generation typesetting.

The second generation incorporates a keyboard, computer memory, and a photounit. The characters exist on a photographic negative in a strip, disk, or drum, and light passes through the negative image, through a lens for sizing, and onto photosensitive output film or paper. VIP is one example. This is the leading typesetting method used at this time, but it is fast being outdone by third generation, or CRT typesetting.

Third-generation type is produced by the cathode ray tube which electronically creates characters out of lines or dots at amazing speeds by electronic states of on and off. This is called digitization.

A fourth generation has now come into being with the use of a laser for fast production of photo material right onto a film negative or onto an offset plate. *See also* cathode ray tube and phototypesetting.

ghosting. A condition in printing that often occurs around solid areas that are not well enough separated to give the ink sufficient time to build up on the rollers. Thus, a duplicate image appears light, like a ghost, where not intended. For example, a vertical border will strip more ink off the rollers than a horizontal border. If a solid shape follows the vertical borders, the solid will be starved for ink and print lighter in that area. A designer can control this by keeping solid areas evenly distributed so the ink has time to build up on the rollers.

gigo. Computer programming slang for the idea that bad input results in bad output. It means garbage in, garbage out.

gilding. Gold leaf on the edges of book paper used for decoration. The gold color is stamped or sprayed with heat and adhesive onto the edges of the pages from a foil.

glassine. Clear plastic jackets that go around bound books. They are not printed on paper, as are most book jackets but are made of mylar. *See also* bronze proof.

glitch. A line of type which has dropped half a line during typesetting because of an electronic surge or drop in power within the typesetting unit.

glitter application. *See* flock printing.

gloss. The luster or brightness of a surface. Paper gloss affects the appearance of the ink film. PSE, or paper surface efficiency, is measured by ink absorption and gloss, and determines the purity of ink reproduction.

Gloss inks contain an extra quantity of varnish for use on stocks specially coated for gloss inks. The paper should be very resistant to penetration of the vehicle. Gloss inks are used both for letterpress and offset.

glossary. An alphabetical list of words or terms with their explanations, often included in the back matter of a book.

glossy. A photograph with a shiny finish made on glossy paper as opposed to a matte finish. It is good for reproduction because it has a greater range of tone values. The blacks are blacker, and the whites are whiter than in dull, or matte prints. Glossies resist soil and handling better than photos with a matte finish.

goldenrod. Sheets of coated opaque masking paper of orange or yellow used to prepare negative flats that will then be exposed onto offset printing plates. The yellow-orange paper is opaque to the photographic light used for exposure. Goldenrod tears easily and does not store well, so many printers are now using a paper-base material for stripping, called red.

gold-leaf stamping. Eighteen or 22-carat fine metal rolled very thin and sold in sheets or rolls for decorating covers. *See also* foil.

gothic. **1.** Pointed letterforms known as black-letter type that resemble 15th century script. **2.** Sans serif typeface style. The term is confusing since it refers to two vastly different typestyles.

Government Printing Office. The U. S. Government Printing Office is the only source from which federal government departments may order printing and binding, with the exception of certain requirements that are subcontracted outside Washington. The GPO is the largest printing plant in the world and has several divisions. If a congressman reads material into the *Congressional Record,* it will be printed by the GPO, and reprints will be available. There are over 24,000 different publications, periodicals, and subscription services for sale by the Superintendent of Documents, and 3000 new titles every year. Since it would be impractical to use a single catalog to list all the titles sold, the subject bibliography index lists the subject bibliographies from which one can find publications of interest.

graduated margins. Magazine gutter margins that are graduated in size up to ¼-in. difference to allow for thickness of fold in saddle-wire binding. Because the outside pages have to wrap around a greater thickness in the gutter, the inside pages are laid out with smaller gutter margins. *See also* shingling.

grain. 1. The direction of the fibers in paper corresponding to the direction in which the paper flows on the wire screen of the papermaking machine. Grain should run vertically in a printed piece so that folds will work easily, running with the grain, and coating will not rupture. Paper is stiffer with the grain. When ordering paper, grain direction should be specified. The dimension with the grain direction is underlined, e.g., 45" x 69." Moisture can cause the paper to grow in the direction of the grain. 2. Variations of density in a photograph caused by irregular distribution of the silver crystals.

grain long. The specification of the length of a sheet of paper in the direction of the grain. Book paper should be ordered grain long so that the pages will turn easily along the binding edge.

grain short. The second or short side of the paper. A sheet goes through the press grain short.

graphic design or -graphy. Any type of visual communication. Graphic comes from the Greek word *graphein* meaning to write. Thus, words ending in -graphy mean a type of writing in respect to the form designated. For example, photography means writing with light, lithography means writing with stone, etc.

Graphics Modifier. An image modifying device that photomechanically produces lettered images and variations on lettered images for special effect. *See also* lettering.

Graphics modifier.

gravure. A method of intaglio printing in which the ink is held in the etched areas, called wells, of the plate below the surface, as opposed to printing from a raised surface as in letterpress. It generally refers to all forms of art which are printed from the incision of a groove into some resistant material. For example, dry point, mezzotint, and burin engraving. In commercial gravure positive film is exposed to the plate, and the image areas on the plate are etched by an etching machine which has exact depth-measuring features. The plate is immersed in ink then wiped clean with a knife called a doctor blade, leaving only the depressed image areas filled with ink. The ink then transfers to paper by adhesion. It must have sufficient body to be pulled from the engraved wells. It is a direct process, as opposed to offset which uses a blanket to transfer ink from plate to paper. *Rotogravure* prints from cylinders onto a web of paper. The engraved metal roll presses against a rubber-coated roll around which paper is wound to transfer the image. *Sheet-fed gravure* prints from flat plates curved around cylinders onto individual sheets. Gravure inks dry extremely fast.

Gravure printing gets more coverage of ink on paper than any other printing method. Platemaking for gravure printing is more expensive than for letterpress and offset, because of the high cost of cylinders, copper plating, precise etching, and chrome plating, but new technology has recently enabled gravure to increase its marketability. Gravure's fidelity of reproduction produces superior color illustrations and sharp images even on lightweight papers. But small sizes of type tend to get fuzzy. It is mostly used for long runs of around one million because the printer cannot change the images quickly enough on the cylinders to make it practical for shorter runs.

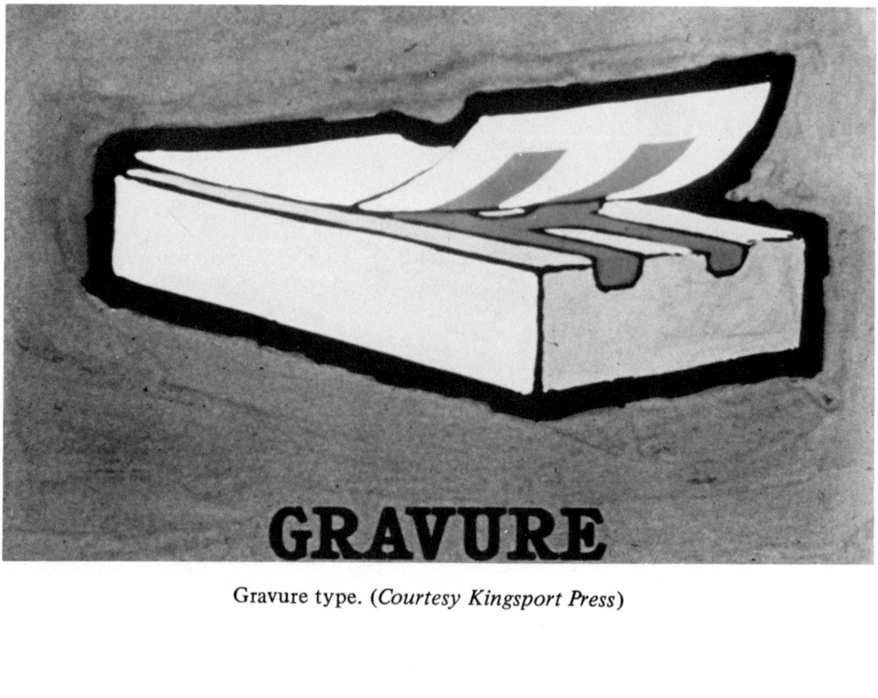

Gravure type. (*Courtesy Kingsport Press*)

Gravure printing needs solutions to the problems of flammability and toxicity of ink solvents, which dry the ink by evaporation, and to the problems of economics and pollution on runs of less than one million. Experiments in this direction are attempting to place gravure in a competitive place with web offset. In runs of one million it may be already competitive. Gravure is expected to experience a growth rate of 15% over the next 5 years. Both electron-beam and laser-engraving devices are now in test stages for use with gravure plates.

gray. The value of a color as to how much black or white the color has, or how clean it looks. *See also* color tree and value.

gray scale. A strip of standard gray values ranging from white to black through logarithmic gradations. It is placed at the side of original copy during photographic processing to measure tonal range and contrast obtained. That which is exposed leaves an image and the chemistry takes all else away. On a printing plate, the gray scale offers a numerical way of determining proper exposure. You can see from the gray scale how well the plate will print. The 3 on the scale should be barely visible and the 6 firm.

Greeking. Nonsense characters used to show what the real copy will look like when pasted into place or to give the illusion of copy in an illustration where real copy is not needed. *See also* dummy type.

> Quto avoi bxyo mnstr laeyo aoiou dxpo. Bzny cmbent dtnsti pxrnxo. Dxpo quto avoi bxyo mnstr laeyo aoiou. Pxrnxo bzny cmbent dtnsti. Aoiou dxpo quto avoi bxyo mnstr laeyo. Dtnsti pxrnxo cmbent. Laeyo aoiou dxpo quto avoi bxyo mnstr. Bzny cmbent dtnsti pxrnxo. Mnstr laeyo aoiou dxpo quto auoi bxyo. Pxrnxo bzny cmbnet dtnsti. Bxyo mnstr laeyo aoiou dxpo quto auoi. Stnsti pxrnxo bzny cmbent. Avoi bxno mnstr laeyo aoio dxpo quto. Dmbent dtnsti pxrnxo bzny. Quto avoi bxyo mnstr laeyo aoiou dxpo. Bzny cmbent dtnsti pxrnxo. Dxpo quto laeyo

Greeking.

greige goods. (Pronounced gray goods) Cloth, usually cotton, used for woven bookbinding material. The greige goods comes from the weaving mill in the natural color and with imperfections still in it. It is not bleached or processed until it goes to the covering material mill to be made into binding material.

grid. 1. The cross-ruled lines on transparent acetate over which all parts of a page layout may be assembled on a light box. **2.** A method of designing layouts in which all elements of the layout make use of rectangles created by cross-ruled outlines into which the page is broken. **3.** The rectangular carrier of a negative type font used in some photocomposition systems.

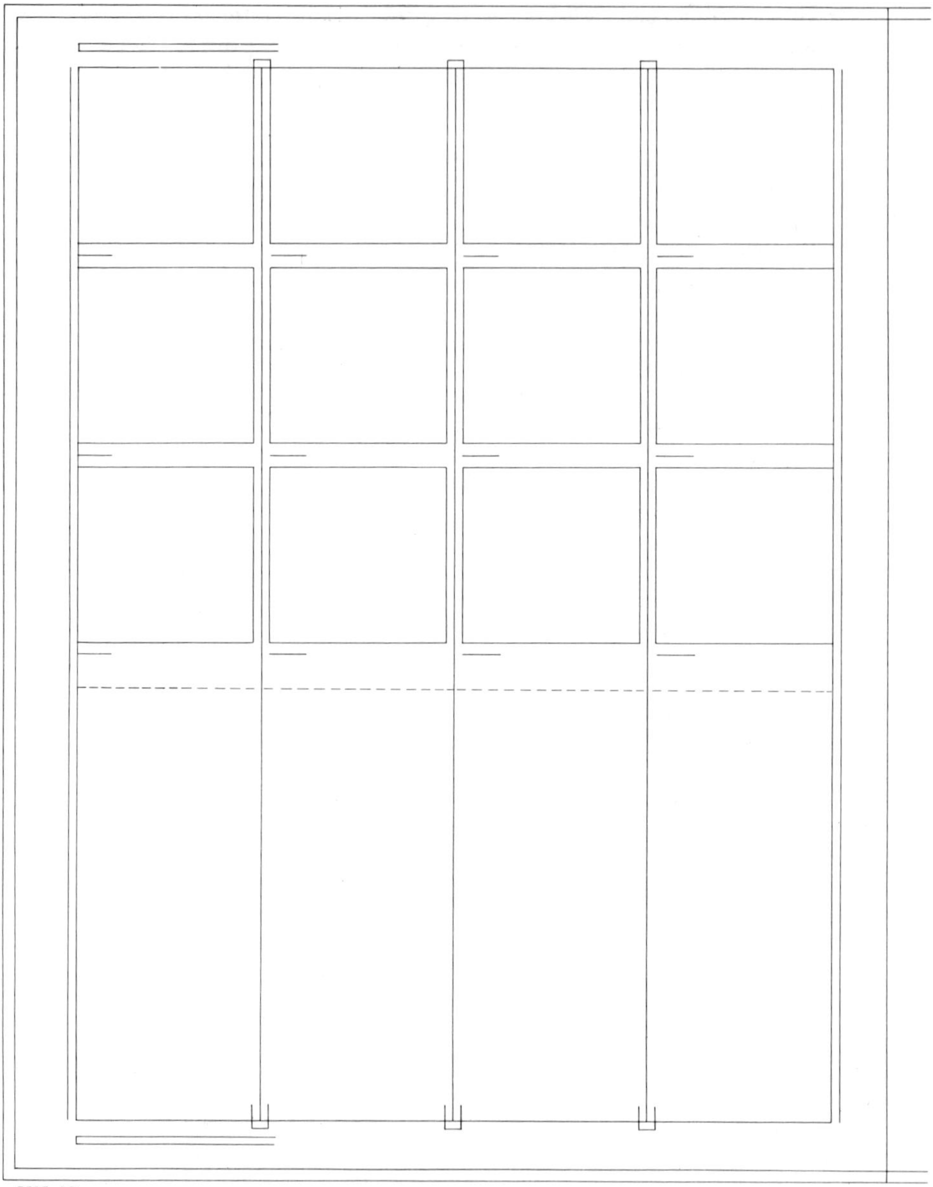

5915-001

Grid.

gripper bite or **gripper edge** or **gripper margin.** The leading edge of a sheet of paper which is clamped by the grippers as it passes through the press. Extra paper must be allowed for the gripper bite of 1/4-in. to 5/8-in., which is the amount of paper that the offset press grippers pick up, depending on the kind of printing press used.

grippers. The metal fingers that draw the paper into the press for the impression. The gripper requirements must be considered when a printing job is laid out, especially if it bleeds.

groove. Valleys or channels on a cased-in book parallel to and at either side of the backbone joints or ridges. *See also* backing and casing-in.

groundwood. Cheap paper made from wood that has been ground up and mechanically separated into fibers. The fibers are not highly processed and the paper will age in sunlight. The fibers are also short and so the paper lacks strength. There are more actual fibers per pound of wood in groundwood than in freesheet, i.e., paper free of groundwood, so groundwood is also more opaque. Groundwood pulp is used in newsprint and cheap publication papers. Also called mechanical pulp.

guideline. 1. A line drawn on artwork or copy to show the limits of the area to be printed. 2. Non-reproducible lines drawn on a mechanical to aid the paste up artist when pasting type on a mechanical.

gummed paper. Paper with an adhesive backing. Gummed paper can be ordered or purchased already gummed.

gutter. Inner margin of a page from the edge of the printing area to the binding edge.

H

Haberule. A yellow plastic ruler for determining how many lines of particular sizes and leadings will fit in a given space. Also used to determine leading of a body of type that has been set. Also called linespacing guide.

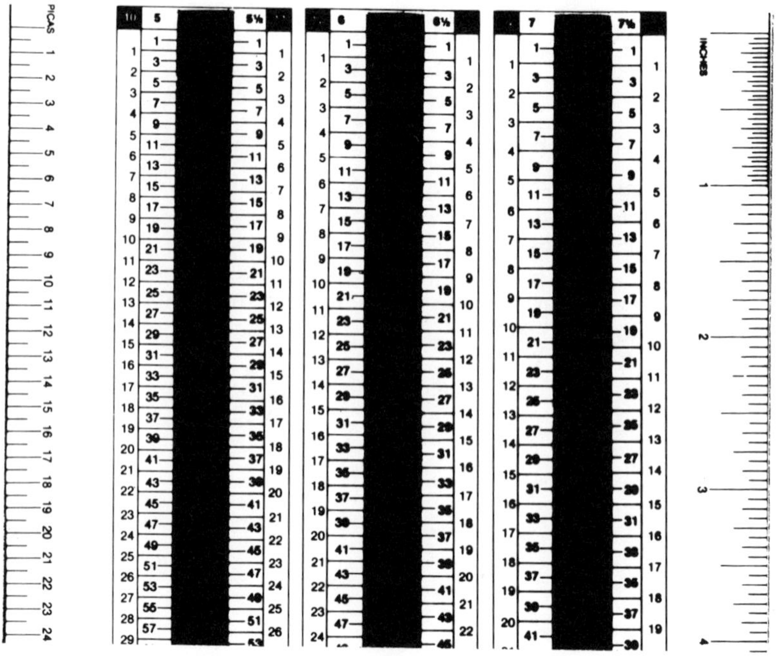

Haberule.

hairline. A fine line in artwork. A hairline is the finest line that printing can produce—½-pt. (1/144-in.) thick or less. It can connect the various strokes of a letter or be used in rules or illustrations. Looks like this:

Hairline rule.

hairspace. ½-pt. thick.

halation. A blurred halo effect found around bright objects or in highlight areas. A halation is caused by light reflected from the back surface of the substrate, i.e., paper or film in the photographic process.

half title page. The title of a book printed on a page immediately preceding the first page of text. Sometimes used interchangeably with bastard title which is the title of the book printed on the right-hand page preceding the title.

halftone. The reproduction of continuous tone artwork such as photographs, wash drawings, and paintings, through a crossline screen which breaks up the image into closely spaced dots. Examination through a magnifying glass shows that the image has been formed not with gradations of tone but with black dots spaced unevenly. The uneven spacing and the variation in the dot size give the illusion of dimension and value.

The first halftone illustration was produced in the *New York Daily Graphic* in 1875. Stephen Henry Horgan conceived of a method of making the gradations of density of a photographic image into lines. He made a negative screen out of a series of parallel fine rulings slightly out of focus. A photographic negative was projected through the negative screen and a print was produced and treated exactly like a line drawing. The single-line coarse ruling was suited to the letterpress equipment and inexpensive paper of the day. At the time, press operators said that only a fool would try to produce crossline halftones without them looking like a "puddle of mud," but the invention greatly expanded the possibilities of the art of illustration in the 1880s.

The term halftone comes from the idea that the screening process eliminates half of the original image, or, the full tone. *See also* double-dot halftone, drop-out, duotone, highlight, silhouette halftone or silo, square halftone, surprint, and vignette halftone.

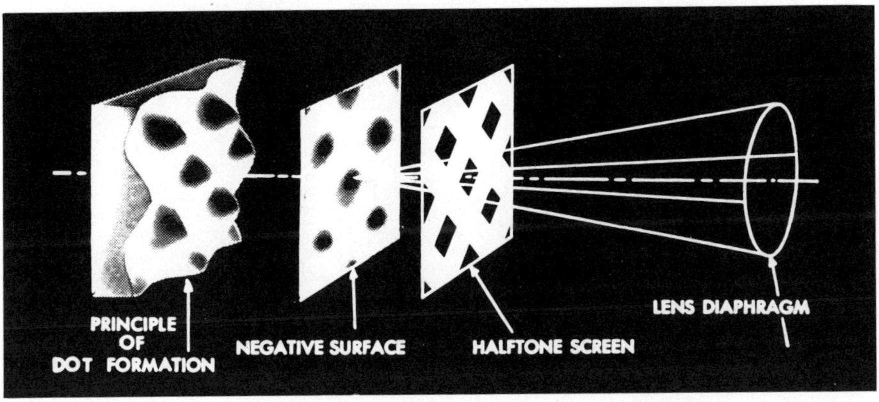

Principle of halftone dot formation. (*Courtesy Kingsport Press*)

halftone dot. The black dot produced by the crossline screen with which the original continuous tone photograph is shot. This is necessary for printing because ink always prints solid ink or it doesn't print at all. The dot carries the ink

Halftone dot. Photo is blown up after having been screened so that dots are visible. (*Courtesy Sid Delmar Leach*)

on the printing press. The gradations of color are an optical illusion of these small dots. It is the size and number of the dots in a given area that create this optical illusion.

When the light hits the original photograph on the copy board of a camera, it bounces off the light areas, goes through the camera lens and exposes the film. Each crossline screen opening acts as a little lens allowing the light to pass through to form a dot on the negative. The light areas of the original appear black on the negative. Since more light will pass through in highlight areas, a larger black dot will be formed on the negative. These are measured in percentages of white. For example gray would create a 50% dot on the negative and no light would pass through at all for solid black areas. When the negative is exposed to the plate, black dots of the various sizes on the negative prevent light from passing through to the plate. Those areas on the negative which remained clear, having reflected small dots from dark areas, now allow the most light through onto the plate, so a bigger dot will be formed for dark areas and the percentages are reversed. Now the dots are measured in percentages of black. The white areas, those that formed black on the negative because of the biggest dots, now prevent the light from going onto the plate. And where there is no dot on the plate, nothing will be printed. The dot on the plate carries the ink. The printing plate prints only one color. It either prints a dot or it does not, there is no in-between. Therefore, where the plate has the largest dots, there will be more ink coverage and the most dark shades will be formed. Where it has fewer dots, little or no ink will go down on the press, and less ink coverage will form the optical illusion of a lighter shading. The eye does not see all the dots, the eye sees the continuous tone which is the illusion created by the size of dots and their density because where the dots are larger, more paper is covered. Where they are smaller, less paper is covered allowing the white paper to show through. There is no printing color of white, only the white paper, or part of it showing through.

Halftone dots are soft or hard. A hard dot has a very crisp edge, whereas a soft dot has a fringe or blurred halo effect around the edge.

halftone engraving. Reproduction of continuous tone copy which is photographed, screened, and the result etched onto a zinc or copper plate which prints an illustration. *See also* etch and engraving.

halftone negative. The negative film produced by shooting continuous-tone copy through a lined screen. The negative is used to make a plate. *See also* halftone.

halftone positive. A positive film image which has been shot through a lined-screen and which contains the dots representing the tonal values of the continuous-tone original to be reproduced. *See also* screened positive.

halftone screen. A fine-line glass or vignetted dot contact screen which breaks the continuous-tone copy into thousands of tiny dots which can then print like line copy. The dots are measured as to how many dots are formed per inch. Screen rulings vary from 65 to 150 lines per inch for normal use, but most common are 55, 65, 85, 100, 120, 133. A 300-lines per inch screen is used for special effects and special paper. The more number of lines per inch, the more dots will be formed. Since the dots carry the ink on the plate, the smaller the line screen, the more detail there will be and the more variation there will be in every gradation. *See also* halftone dot.

halftone shot as line. *See* tone-line.

halo effect. The piling up of ink at the edges of printed letters and halftone dots causing the centers of the dots to appear lighter, or less dense than the edges. Found most commonly in letterpress printing. Not to be confused with halation.

handbill. A single leaf printed for advertising and originally handed out door-to-door by hand. Also called circular.

hand-lettering. *See* lettering.

handset type. Type composed by hand rather than by machine or by computer. Handset type is expensive, but it is often used for display heads or special effects. It can be altered into any sort of line arrangement which computerized photo units cannot handle because computer type is set on strips of a single line at a time. Handset type does not enlarge well, and hot-metal handset type cannot be set tight because of the metal around the letters. Photo handset type can be kerned. *See also* Ludlow and Photo Typositor.

hang for ten. Aligning columns of figures so that ones, tens, and hundreds columns etc., are directly above each other. This applies to contents pages, tables, charts or any list of numbers and is a standard copy-editing style in most publishing houses.

hanging indention. A paragraph in which the first line is set full measure and the following lines are all indented, as opposed to a regular indention in the first line followed by a full-measure paragraph.

This copy is set with a hanging
indention. That means
that the first line of the
paragraph is set full
width and that the rest
of the lines hang down
indented a specified
number of em spaces.

Hanging indent.

hang tape operation. A typesetting plant which only does output. The keyboarding is done elsewhere and a paper or magnetic tape is sent or transmitted to the plant for output. In this way editorial input can be controlled by the client. *See also* in-house and interface.

hard copy. Unjustified typewritten copy produced either on a typewriter or on the keyboard of a phototypesetting unit at the same time the magnetic or paper tape is produced. The hard copy is proofread for errors before the tape runs the photounit. It can also be marked for the photounit operator with pertinent instructions.

hardcover. *See* edition binding.

hard dot. A halftone dot with a very crisp, clean-cut edge as opposed to a soft dot, which has a fringe or blurred halo effect around the edge.

hardware. The actual computer equipment as opposed to software, which is the programming required to run the equipment.

head. 1. The top of the page, as opposed to the foot, or bottom of the page. *See also* north, south. 2. *See* heading.

headband. Decorative tape glued inside the cloth at the top and bottom of the spine of a book. Headbands are not structural, but they give a more finished appearance.

heading. Type set apart from the text as a title, or summarizing what follows. A heading is used to get the reader to read further. *See also* boxheading, centered head, chapter heading, cut-in head, running head, side head, straddle head, and subhead.

headbox. The beginning of the papermaking machine where pulp and additives are mixed to determine the basis weight of the paper. *See also* papermaking.

headline. *See* heading.

head margin. The white space above the first line on a page.

head-to-head come and go. A method of two-up printing in which the folded signatures coming off the press, form two complete books meeting at the heads which must be cut apart to make separate books.

heliotype. *See* collotype.

hickey. A spot or defect in printed matter caused by dust, lint, ink skin, or foreign matter on the printing plate or the blanket. Ink hickies appear as small doughnuts, dark specks with a white ring around them. Paper hickies appear as white specks. *See also* picking.

hi-fi color. Color ads printed like wallpaper so that the paper can be cut at any point without damaging the effect of the ad.

high key. A photograph with most of the tonal values higher, or lighter than a middle gray.

highlight. The whitest part of a photograph, having the smallest dots in the halftone negative and printing plate or no dots at all, as opposed to middletones and shadows. The tonal range of a halftone is designated in percentages of black from 3% to 95%. *See also* dropout halftone.

highlight halftone. *See* dropout halftone.

hinge. The crease where the cover bends from the spine on the binding of a book. Also called joint.

hit. Impression from a stamping die.

holding lines. Lines drawn on the mechanical to show the exact area to be occupied by a halftone, color, tint, or any design element.

holdout. The property of paper that makes it resistant to penetration of the ink vehicle, giving the ink a higher gloss.

hologram. A three-dimensional picture made by the use of a laser beam which strikes the image from all points of view, by bouncing the beam off mirrors. No camera is used, and the image is viewed on a glass plate which is illuminated with a beam of light.

Lasers bouncing off reflective holograms onto glass plates create images to be used in electronic impactless printing onto presensitized webs of paper moving at extremely high speeds through the reproduction devices. The final product of the impactless printing is two-dimensional, however, not three-dimensional as in a hologram (only the plate is three-dimensional). Other new uses of holograms include large 3-D advertising displays and illustrations in books that appear to stand out from the page.

horizontal photo. Of rectangular shape, longer from side to side than from top to bottom.

horizontal publication. A professional magazine written for persons holding the same jobs in various industries. For example, *Today's Secretary,* or *Writer's Digest. See also* vertical publication.

hot foil stamping. Metallic colored, high-gloss adhesive foil in the form of a line motif embossed by pressure and heat onto cardboard, paper, or bookcovering materials. *See also* foil.

hot melt. The adhesive applied to the spine of perfect bound books. It is extremely hot, 350° to 400°F, during the bindery process, and differs from other adhesives because it does not set by cooling, rather by absorption and evaporation of the liquid vehicle.

hot metal type or **hot type.** Metal type cast either by hand or in a linecasting machine. It can be used for letterpress printing, or the resulting repro type can be pasted onto mechanicals which are in turn shot for offset printing. Hot-metal type is more expensive than cold type or phototype. Eventually hot-metal type will become obsolete because machine parts and matrices are no longer being manufactured for the existing machines. *See also* Linotype, Ludlow, and Monotype.

hot spot. A place in copy or art where the wrong angle of light has hit the mounted copy on the copy board of a camera. This shows up in the negative as an extremely dark spot, or in the text copy as uneven density or tone. When the lights are installed on a gallery camera, all of them are aimed at the center, and readings taken at the corners of the board should be the same to avoid hot spots.

house organ. An internal company publication for employees, or external for customers or prospects.

house style. Editorial style decided upon by a publishing house and used for all its manuscripts. Styles vary from house to house.

hundredweight. Hundred pounds of paper. $29 per CWT means that paper is $29 per hundred pounds, or 29¢ per pound. Paper is usually quoted in price per hundred pounds.

hue. The identity of the color such as red, green, blue, orange, etc., that distinguishes it from another color. *See also* color tree.

hydrophobic. Water-hating or water repellent.

hydrophilic. Water-loving, preferring to be wet.

hyphenation. Punctuation between syllables of a word or between the parts of a compound word. In typesetting, the computer hyphenates by logic, or an exception dictionary, or the operator makes the hyphenation decisions.

I

IBM Composer. Strike-on typesetting machine that has a keyboard like a typewriter and changeable type balls which contain various typeface styles. The IBM Composer contains a memory and is coded so that copy may be set, corrected, and played out justified, flush right or left or centered. *See also* word processing.

ideograph. A simple line drawing that symbolizes an idea or concept. Ideographs evolved from pictographs which literally depicted an object. From the ideograph, our alphabet evolved. *See* pictographs for illustration.

idiot tape. Coding for unjustified and unhyphenated copy on paper or magnetic tape produced on a noncounting keyboard. It cannot run a typesetting unit until command codes for end-of-line decisions are added and processed by the computer.

illuminated manuscript. A text, from the incunabula period, that contains ornamental designs, miniatures, or lettering in brilliant colors or precious metals.

illustration. Any form of drawing, halftone, engraving, or color image handled separately from the text and used to enhance or explain the piece. Well-illustrated text will be read more thoroughly than the same material without illustrations. *See also* artwork, design, drawing techniques, halftones, line art, photography, rescreening.

illustrator. An artist skilled in drawing techniques as opposed to a designer who only conceptualizes or sketches a piece of art which will be composed for printing. Not all good layout artists are illustrators.

image area. Area on the plate where ink adheres and thus prints onto a substrate. There is no ink on the clear area.

image master. The disk, film negative, or other image-carrier in a typesetting photounit that holds the type fonts. *See also* matrix.

image transfer. Artwork available in logos, slogans, symbols, titles, call-outs, and phrases for use in color as rub-on art for camera-ready or presentation art. The use of image transfer art eliminates overlays.

imagic. *See* thermography.

impactless printing. Printing methods, such as ink-jet or electrostatic printing, which do not use regular printing presses. Ink-jet printers are directed by digital signals from a computer, and publications or products can be addressed with individual names and numbers as copies pass beneath the printing head, thus producing in-line completion of a product. The physical problem of placing enough ink-jet nozzles together limits the production of commercial presses for full-color halftones or other elements. *See also* ink-jet printing.

Electrostatic printing is used in photocopying such as Xerox. It competes with offset duplicating equipment in small quantities, but will not be used in book manufacture in the foreseeable future. *See also* electrostatic printing.

import. A book imported and distributed by a domestic publisher, usually designated as copublisher with the foreign publisher.

imposing stone. *See* stone.

imposition. The plan for and the arrangement of pages so they will be in correct sequence when the sheet is printed, and folded. By folding a sheet of paper into 4, 8, 16, or 32 sections, numbering them and unfolding the sheet, one can see how this is arrived at. The imposition is determined by the folding machine at the bindery. The binder knows how the pages should be positioned to be handled most efficiently on specific equipment. One quarter inch to 1/8-in. of the paper will be trimmed off the edges when the sheets are squared up.

Formulas for the page numbers on an imposition can also be figured mathematically and are known to printers and binders by name. Imposition of the negative onto a flat for platemaking is done either by the stripper or by computer-driven projection systems which expose plates from 35 mm negatives. Since stripping is such a labor-intensive operation and such a bottleneck in production, automated methods such as step-and-repeat, optical imposition, and micro-stripping are being developed. *See also* Opti-Copy, photographic imposition system, and step-and-repeat.

impregnated. The coating of the cloth for a book cover. Covers can be either pyroxylin-, vinyl-, or starch-impregnated. *See also* book covering materials.

impression. **1.** Each occurrence of plate against paper. The number of impressions per hour is the rate at which a press can deliver. **2.** The pressure of the type, plate, or blanket as it contacts the paper and produces printed copy. The pressman controls the depth of the impression. An impression that is neither too heavy nor too light is called a kiss impression. **3.** All the copies of a book printed

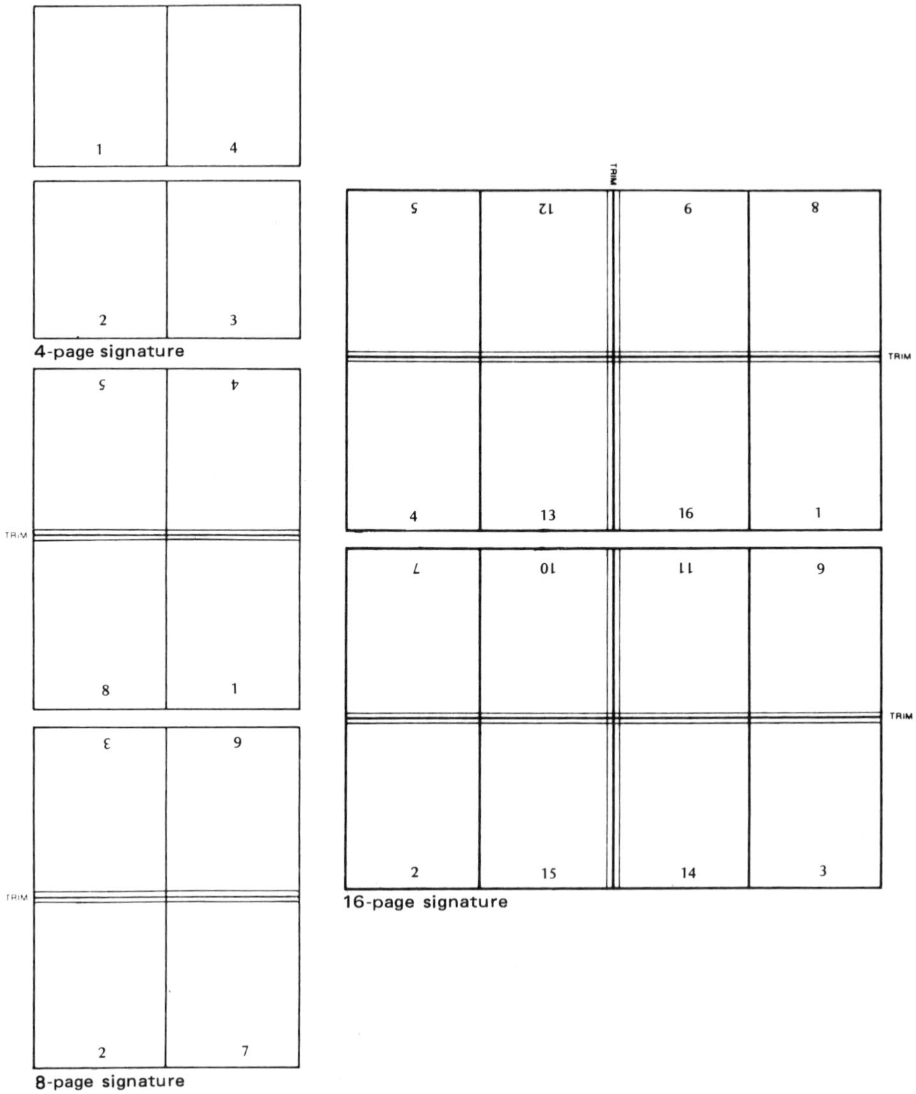

Imposition.

at once, as opposed to an edition, which is all copies, no matter which impression, as long as there is no significant change in the contents.

impression cylinder. The cylinder on the press that holds the paper against the printing plate so that an impression can be made.

imprint. 1. The name of the publisher and the place of publication. *See also* colophon. 2. To print additional copy such as a person's or a firm's name and address on a previously printed piece by running it through a press a second time, or by putting the job on a smaller press, not meant to do high-quality printing but good enough to print in a name and address.

incunabula. The period of early printing in Europe, particularly relating to books printed before 1501.

indent or **indention.** To set a line or lines of type shorter than the other lines on the same page. An indention begins most paragraphs and draws attention to quotes, lists, or special material. The first paragraph of an article or chapter is often not indented. *See* hanging indention and paragraph style indent.

index. 1. An alphabetical list of topics, names, places, or any referenced material a reader may wish to look up in the text. It can be cross-referenced and contain subentries. Any reference or text book should have an index. 2. Binding and die-cutting processes such as the making of the dictionary type thumb indexes, and address book tabs. *See also* binding, edge index, thumb cut. 3. A grade of inexpensive stiff paper either smooth or antique, which is receptive to ink.

indicia. Information printed on cards or envelopes that takes the place of postage or meter impressions. Indicia requires special permission from the post office.

indirect letterpress. *See* letterset.

indirect process. The four-color process in which four continuous-tone or unscreened separations are made. The negatives are then sized and screened. In the direct process separation, sizing, and screening is all done in one step.

inferior figure. A small number printed below the x-line level in a line of type. Also called subscript. *See also* proofreader's marks.

in-house. Work such as editing, keyboarding, typesetting, or design performed within the company as opposed to free-lance which is done outside the company.

initial. A large letter at the beginning of a body of copy which either cuts down into the text or sticks up into the white space above. Some initials are available in a florid version.

THE BASE of the initial letter must align with the base of one of the lines of text. If exact alignment with the first line is not possible, then the initial should project above the top line rather than sink below it. The first word or phrase following an initial is often set in small caps, to give a squared-off start to the block of type. Careful measurement is necessary in specifying sizes for initials.

A stick-up initial is easier for the typesetter and more legible than the set-in.

With the set-in initial, the reader sometimes tries to read the initial letter with other lines as well as with the first line. *See also* stick-up initial.

ink. Fluid or viscous material that passes from the printing plate to a printing surface during an impression. The material includes pigment, vehicle, driers, and other compounds that form the printed impression on the page. Ink is available in a great number of colors and compositions which facilitate sharpness, create scuff resistance, reduce tackiness, and sheet sticking. Printing inks can also be metallic or fluorescent. Pigment and vehicle combinations vary, so that the miscellaneous ingredients are carefully controlled in different inks.

Manufacturers will supply inks to match submitted color samples printed on submitted paper samples. Blade mixers blend together a formulated quantity of each necessary ingredient. After mixing, the ink is passed through an ink mill where steel rollers grind the ingredients to the degree of fineness required. Each finished batch is tested under actual printing conditions. The inks are packed in tubes, cans, drums, or even delivered in tank-truck loads.

Many factors determine the shade of the printed color. Paper coloring will affect inks to some degree. Transparent inks, are greatly affected, as the paper adds another color to the ink by showing through the ink film. Because transparent inks will not print the same color on white paper as they will on a colored stock, a sample swatch of the desired color and a sample of the colored stock should be sent to the ink maker, who can then formulate an ink color that when printed on the colored stock will appear as the desired color.

Paper absorbency is also a factor in printing with transparent inks. If the paper is very absorbent it will require more ink to cover the surface, especially if the paper surface is not smooth. When a heavier ink layer is printed on the paper the transparent ink color will be deeper and more intense.

To check the ink color, tap out a small amount of ink on a paper stock of similar quality or even on the color card itself. In tapping out a color, use a small amount of ink on the fingertip so that the ink goes from heavy to very light and only fingerprints appear. Somewhere in this range of shading should be the color selected. If the desired color is present, then one has to examine the other possibilities that affect color.

Colored inks, when printed, can be affected by the light source used in viewing the printed sheet. Printed color, should be compared with original color swatch under the same light source. One should not judge the color of a printing ink by its appearance in the can, i.e., the mass tone. Transparent inks will appear significantly darker in this form than in the printed state. When a color match appears poor it can be caused by an inadequate color specimen, an incorrect paper sample, or insufficient information regarding the press, job, or form.

ink drying. Ink-drying techniques are either *passive* or *forced. Passive* drying includes absorption, evaporation, or oxidation. *Absorption* means that the ink dries by being absorbed by porous paper, such as newsprint, uncoated text, or cover paper. Also called *penetration.* When ink dries by *evaporation,* volatile solvents in the ink evaporate into the air leaving behind a dry film of ink on the paper. With the *oxidation* process, drying solvents in the ink combine with oxygen in the air in a chemical action that dries the ink through polymerization, which means converting a liquid to a solid. Coated papers and hard-surface uncoated papers require oxidation. Passive drying is frequently accomplished through a combination of all three.

There are two general types of *forced* drying methods—heat responsive and photo-sensitive. The *photo-sensitive* method is more accurately described as curing rather than drying though solvent is involved. With this method, special photo-sensitive inks react when exposed to ultraviolet lights by instantly forming a solid film on the paper. Also called *UV* (*ultraviolet*) drying. UV drying can offer several advantages, such as minimal amount of heat generated eliminating many heat-related problems such as blistering. A UV drying system does not release the pollutants that result from heat-responsive forced-drying systems. Special UV inks cost more and there is less gloss when compared to conventional "heat-set" inks.

There are three methods of *heat transfer: conduction, radiation* and *convection.* In *conduction,* the heated conductor is put in direct contact with the material to which the heat is to be transferred. For example, the printed side of the web of paper is wrapped around a cylinder (drum) that is heated from the inside by steam applied under high pressure. This heat is transferred from the steel drum to the paper, causing the ink to dry. The conduction drying system is suited to press equipment that prints only one side of the paper at a time, such as a common-impression cylinder press.

With *radiation,* the material to which the heat is to be transferred is placed in close proximity to the heat source. The open flame drier is an example of the *radiation* drying principle. Here the printed side of the paper passes in close proximity to the open flame. The resultant radiant heat burns off the solvents in the ink, causing the ink to dry.

Convection drying means that heated air is blown onto the material that is to be heated. A web of paper passes through an oven in which hot air is blown onto the printed web of paper. The hot air extracts solvents from the ink, resulting in a drying process. Another example of the convection drying principle is high velocity drying. Air nozzles placed at close intervals blow hot air onto both sides of a printed web under high pressure. In addition to drying the ink, this procedure helps to support and flatten out the printed web of paper.

Each of these drying principles, when used independently, has certain deficiencies, so many forced drying systems use a combination of these principles.

ink holdout. The characteristic of paper that prevents too much ink from being absorbed. Coated papers have better ink holdout than noncoated papers and therefore can produce finer halftones. Too much absorption causes lack of sharpness and luster.

ink-jet printing. A form of impactless printing in which thousands of tiny droplets of ink are formed as ink comes out of a nozzle. The main body of liquid is vibrated to produce the same number of droplets per second as the rate of vibration of a stimulator. The systems which produce readable characters out of the droplets differ. In one system digital signals from a computer direct the printers and each drop that is to print is given an electrical charge. Unused drops go into a "catcher" and are recycled. Another system electrically charges the droplets not to be used, and the others fall onto the paper as it is moving under the ink jets. The third system produces half a million droplets per second and doesn't use a stimulator. Fifty to one hundred droplets form one dot on paper.

Ink-jet printing is not used for high-quality printing and cannot produce satisfactory halftones but is applicable to batch codes on bottoms of beer and soft-drink cans, printing names and addresses on labels, magazines, or envelopes, production of personalized letters, preprinted mailing pieces, etc. The printing heads can be mounted on a web press so that addresses can be printed in-line with the printing of the document, or the printing heads can be operated off-press.

ink keys. Keys on the inking system of the color press which release a certain amount of color during color printing. At the time of start up, the keys are adjusted until the press sheets meet specified color requirements.

inline. A line around the contours of display lettering just inside the shape of the letters. Inline is done by hand lettering or with an overlay. The inline and the solid portion of the type can be of different colors.

Inline lettering. (*Courtesy Graphics Modifier, Byers Corporation*)

in-line. Continuous processing of books or magazines through lines of machinery linked by conveyors, or integrated mechanically. The most sophisticated in-line processes print, fold, trim, bind, etc. without interruption. The industry is developing various methods of in-line operations to make them competitive with slower methods. *See also* belt-press book production system, Cameron book production system, and on-line.

inline shadow. A style of graphic lettering which contains both an inline and a shadow behind the type to simulate the third dimension which also contains an inline.

input. Computer language for the data to be processed. For example, the copy that is keyboarded on typesetting equipment is the input.

Input terminal editing station increases productivity for typesetting system. (*Courtesy Mergenthaler Linotype Company*)

insert. 1. A separately printed piece or form to be inserted into a publication. It is usually on different paper than the publication and placed between signatures, wrapped around signatures, or tipped within the signature. A tip-in is pasted along the inside edge, whereas a wrap is sewn. Tip-ins are more expensive because of the handwork involved. 2. Copy attached to a page to be set in type and placed where directed within the text.

instant printing. *See* quick printing.

intaglio. From the Italian word for "engrave," or "cut." A method of printing in which the image is cut or etched below the surface of the plate, filled with ink and the plate wiped clean. *See also* engraving and gravure.

interface. To move information in usable form from one device to another. Information is often moved between word processors, phototypesetters, OCRs and editing/makeup terminals to provide economic typesetting. This is usually done by building an electronic device which enables one piece of equipment to communicate with or control another. This can sometimes be done over a telephone line. A good deal of customization in the conversion process is necessary. Command codes must be in the document being sent or, if connected to an editing system, the data will appear on the screen.

Inserts. (*Courtesy Kingsport Press*)

There are certain problems in interfacing word processors and phototypesetters inasmuch as these machines rarely speak the same language, i.e., utilize identical codes. The recording media are not compatible either. Typewriter keyboards are not designed for typesetting input. They lack the additional typographic command keys of typesetting keyboards. This can be overcome by utilizing simple mnemonic codes, e.g., "fr" for flush right, that can be translated in the conversion process. Certain word-processing codes have to be eliminated for typesetting input: underscores, carriage returns, double word spaces after sentence-ending periods, line-ending hyphens, etc. Interfacing is becoming an issue because many firms are finding typeset output superior to typewritten output especially if the specific document is a proposal, catalog, or report intended for wide distribution. *See also* word processing.

Interfont. Trade name for a standard alphabet with added accents, symbols, and diphthongs which enable typesetting in any of 15 languages.

interleave. To insert unprinted sheets or sheets of a different stock between printed sheets. *See also* slip sheeting.

interlinespacing. The photocomposition term for leading, or extra space between the lines. *See also* film advance and linespacing.

International Standard Book Number. Number that identifies a particular book by country, publisher, title, and edition. It originated in England and is now used in English-speaking countries. Also called Standard Book Number. Abbreviated ISBN.

internegative. The negative taken from copying art for blow-up or reduction from which a final-size duplicate transparency or print will be made.

Intertype. Trade name for a hot-metal linecasting machine no longer made. Its matrices are interchangeable with those of the Linotype machine. The Intertype Fotosetter was the first widespread phototypesetter.

introduction. The part of the text that explains what follows and prepares the reader for the book. The introduction is considered part of the text, it is not part of the front matter as are the foreword or preface.

ISBN. *See* International Standard Book Number.

italic. The style of an alphabet which slants to the right for emphasis. Italics are designed to match all roman typefaces and most others. An italic typeface is slightly less legible than roman. Words underlined in manuscript copy will be set in italic. *Looks like this.* Abbreviated ital. *See also* oblique and typeface styles.

J

jacket. The paper covering, usually coated, which wraps around a hard-cover book. The jacket is a selling tool as well as a protective covering, and carries copy about the book on the jacket flaps. Also called dust wrapper.

jobber or **job press.** A platen press used for small jobs such as business cards, envelopes, etc. *See also* platen press.

job shop. A commercial printing plant as opposed to a captive shop belonging to a publisher or publication.

jog. To straighten or align by vibration, the edges of a pile of papers coming off the press so that they are even.

joint. *See* hinge.

journeyman. A craftsman who has completed his apprenticeship.

jump head. A heading which is continued on a subsequent page where the title is followed by the word "continued."

jumping the gutter. Running an element across the gutter from one page onto the facing page. *See also* double truck.

justify. 1. to space out a line of type so that it will fill a predetermined line length. Justified type is flush left and right. Lines of less than 30 characters are difficult to justify. *See also* arranging lines of type, copyfitting, letterspacing, and wordspacing. 2. To insert space between lines in newspaper printing to make top and bottom lines align with adjacent lines of type.

K

keep type standing. An order to the printer to hold the made-up pages for a possible subsequent printing. Abbreviated KTS. *See also* standing type.

Kelvin. Degrees of light by which is measured the effect light has on color. Printers, engravers, and some publishers have these sources available in a viewing box with which to check color proofs. According to the American National Standards Institute 5000° Kelvin is ideal when proofing the original art against the press proof where one is judging dots and ink. 5000° Kelvin is the average color of daylight and appears very white. 7500° Kelvin is ideal for checking proofs against the press run, which is paper against paper. 7500° Kelvin is bluer than 5000° Kelvin. This makes comparison of the yellow printer easier.

The color of the light is the most important factor affecting the appearance of an image. Correlated color temperature can best be described by imagining a large furnace with a small opening in one side. If the furnace is heated uniformly to a high enough temperature, the small opening will first appear red, then yellow, and then progressively whiter, as the temperature rises. The correlated color temperature of a light is the temperature in Kelvins of the furnace when the color of the hole visually matches the color of the light.

The Kelvin scale is an absolute scale of temperature in which the degree intervals are the same as those of the Celsius scale and in which 0° Kelvin equals -273.15° Celsius. *See also* standard viewing conditions.

kerned letters. Characters which are set tight together so that part of their letter shapes extend over each other. To accomplish this in phototypesetting the characters are set with minus letterspacing. In metal type, the body of the type is actually cut for the close fit. Kerning is common in italic, script, and swash forms of type, and is often used for special effect in display type.

kerning. Setting the letterforms closer together.

key. 1. To code copy and artwork to a manuscript or a dummy by means of symbols or letters. Also called key marking. 2. A device used in locking up a letterpress form and a device used in securing electrotypes to a metal base.

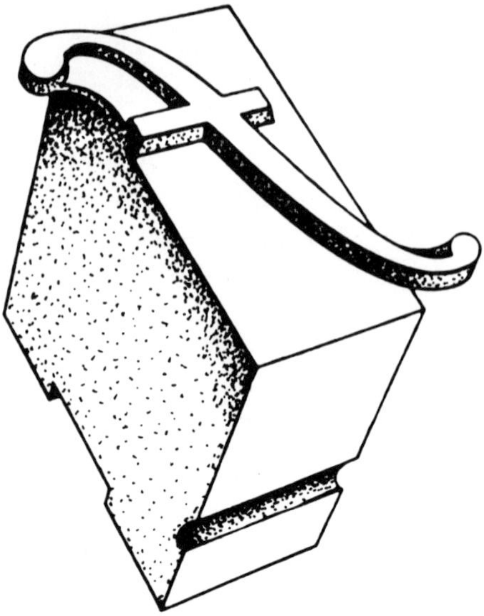

Kerned letter.

−5 Now is the time for all good men
−4 Now is the time for all good men
−3 Now is the time for all good men
−2 Now is the time for all good men
−1 Now is the time for all good men
0 Now is the time for all good men
+1 Now is the time for all good men
+2 Now is the time for all good men
+3 Now is the time for all good men
+4 Now is the time for all good men
+5 Now is the time for all good men
+6 Now is the time for all good men
+7 Now is the time for all good men
+8 Now is the time for all good men
+9 Now is the time for all good men

Kerning.

keyboard. 1. The unit on which copy is typed by a keyboard operator. The keyboarded copy can generate a paper or magnetic tape that runs the photounit, or, in hot metal, the linecasting machine. The keyboard operator sets type directly for strike-on composition and in direct input photo-composition. 2. To type copy on an input terminal for typesetting.

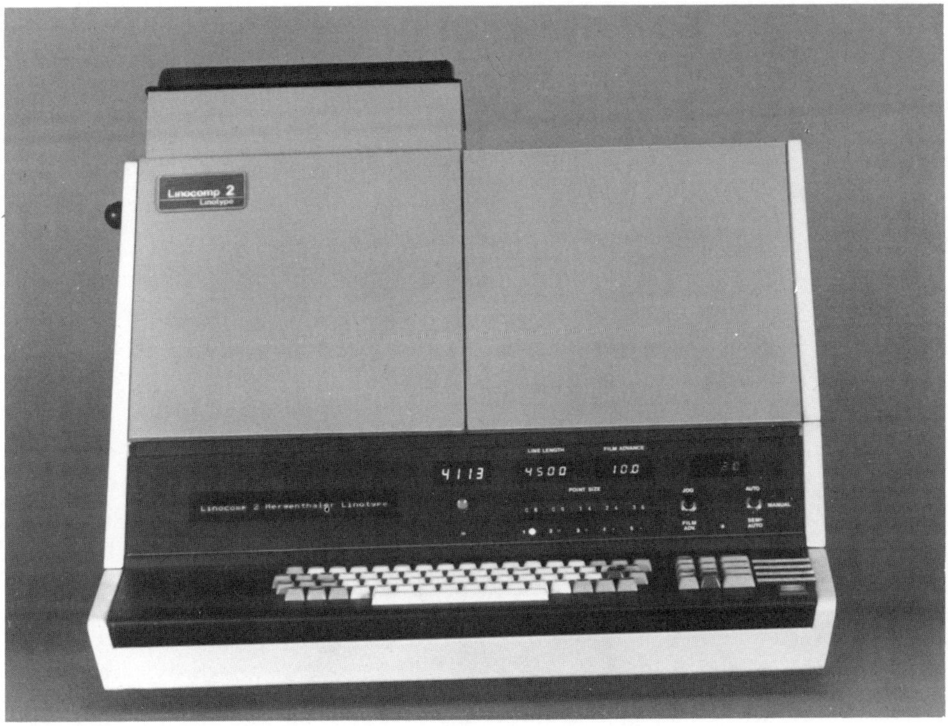

Keyboard. (*Courtesy Mergenthaler Linotype Company*)

keyed advertising. Advertisements with small symbols or letters that identify results when the ad is placed in more than one publication or mailing.

keyline. **1.** The outline on a mechanical indicating insertion of art matter or the shape, cut, perforation, fold, etc., for die cutting. **2.** Sometimes refers to the entire mechanical. **3.** An identification number on business forms, ads, or copyright page including such information as dates, and the name of the company where the piece was printed.

key marking. **1.** Marking on the manuscript what the designer has specified for elements such as headings, extracts, and lists. **2.** Keying artwork by number or letter to a manuscript to indicate where the illustration should fall.

key negative. The film that contains the basic format of a page or illustration. The other separations or tints are registered to the key negative. It serves as a guide for the stripper.

key plate. The plate that carries the most detail of a job and serves as a guide to register the other colors.

kicker. A short line above the headline, printed in smaller type. Also called a teaser.

kid finish. A soft finish used on high-grade or Bristol paper or board.

kill. 1. To delete. 2. To distribute metal type that has already been printed, or to destroy negatives or plates.

kiss impression. The perfect meeting of plate to paper when the ink is properly split from the plate and goes evenly onto the paper. The paper is imprinted but not indented.

Klischograph. An electric eye that scans a picture to be reproduced and controls the movement of a hot vibrating stylus which simultaneously moves from left to right on a metal or plastic surface to produce halftones. The image is transferred from copy to plate by means of electronic impulses which vary according to the intensity of the image of the original. The stylus engraves ink cells of varying depth that act as a screen. Instead of screen angles to separate the colors, cells of different shapes are used for each color. The engraved cells fill with ink giving the effect of a continuous tone.

Kodaline print. A method of proving halftones for position on mechanical.

kraft paper. A strong paper or board made from unbleached woodpulp and commonly used for wrapping. The name comes from the German word for "strong." Kraft paper is attached to headbands that are put onto the spines of quality books. Also called sulfate paper.

Kromecote. A supercalendered paper used for soft covers. Kromecote is uncoated, but the supercalendering makes it so smooth that the ink stays on top of the sheets so there is no need for the varnish that is used on the 10-pt. or 12-pt. Carolina sheets in standard use for cover stock. The Kromecote is brilliant and lustrous but is more expensive than a varnish finish on paper.

Krylon. Trade name for a spray fixative in pressurized cans used for line art and cold-type composition. Used sparingly it prevents lines from rubbing or smudging.

KTS. *See* keep type standing.

L

lacquer. A clear, usually glossy coating applied to a printed sheet such as for a jacket, for protection and appearance. The printer must use inks which are lacquer-resistant so as not to bleed through the lacquer. The lacquer must meet certain gloss requirements, scuff tests, and chemical resistances specified by the client.

ladder. An undesirable condition in typesetting wherein the ends of several lines contain hyphens stacked on top of each other. The eye tends to travel up the page as if climbing a ladder.

**The ladder effect, or sev-
eral stacked hyphens to-
gether, is to be avoid-
ed. As you can see from
this copy they are un-
sightly and make the co-
py difficult to read.**

Ladder effect.

lading. A bill of lading is a bill for cargo or freight used when a publication is shipped from the bindery to the point of distribution.

laid paper. Paper with a series of parallel lines and crosslines simulating the look of the old handmade, ribbed papers. The pattern comes from the screen in the the frames used in hand-made paper. On a paper-making machine, the decorative pattern is added like a watermark. Paper without the laid pattern is said to have a wove finish. There is no difference between laid paper and wove paper with the exception of the appearance.

lamination. A thin plastic film in liquid form or in sheets bonded by pressure and heat to a printed sheet for appearance or protection. The surface has a hard, high gloss and is unsusceptible to stains.

An adhesive is usually applied to the plastic film as it unwinds from a roll. The web is then brought in contact with the printed material. Alternately, the adhesive can be applied to the printed material instead of the plastic if die cutting has been done to permit window lamination. Finishing operations are usually done after the lamination process.

Like lacquer, the printer must use inks that are lacquer-resistant so as not to bleed through the lamination. The lamination maker must know specifications as to gloss requirements, scuff tests, and chemical resistances required by the client. It is difficult to imprint or emboss some laminates.

lampblack. A carbon black pigment prepared by the incomplete combustion of vegetable oils, petroleum, or asphalt materials and used to produce dull, intensely black ink.

lap. The area in color printing where one color overprints, or overlaps, another adjacent color. The lap is specified in points, the thinnest being a hairline.

laser. Acronym for Light Amplification by Stimulated Emission of Radiation. A device that generates and amplifies light waves in a narrow and very intense beam of light that can be optically manipulated. The device makes use of the natural oscillations of molecules or atoms between different energy levels for generating electromagnetic radiation in the ultraviolet, visible, or infrared regions of the spectrum. The laser beam found the first practical applications in the graphic arts around 1973. Lasers are now used in electronic cameras to reproduce text, line, and single color halftone illustrations; to convert images to positive or negative; to correct; and to perform controlled distortion, magnification or reduction.

"The beam is quite different from the normal type of graphic arts light source—such as carbonarc, mercury, or pulsexenon. When you look at a laser beam, you can immediately tell there's something different about the beam because it doesn't spread out in all directions. The advantages of using the laser beam are that the beam is both monochromatic—that is, it's emitted in a single, pure line—and it is also coherent. It is this property of coherency that allows us to focus the laser beam down to extremely small spots. This ability to focus down to diffraction-limited spots (on the order of a thousandth-of-an-inch or less) allows us to place a tremendous amount of energy into a very small area. As a result, we can rapidly scan a variety of photosensitive materials."[4]

laser camera. An electronic camera used to scan line and halftone copy and create high-definition line work and 65- to 133-line screened halftones. A laser camera can be operated by computer for full-page makeup systems, and can greatly reduce the memory space required for storage of digitized half-tone images. *See also* scanner.

[4] Dr. Mark Kaplan of Eastman Kodak's Research Laboratories, *Book Production Industry,* September, 1978, p. 30.

laser platemaking. Direct platemaking based on either the electrostatic or the laser-writing device in which copy is converted directly from computer to printing plate. Use of the laser makes it possible to go directly from keyboard to plate, using a laser to expose the plate material. The laser scans paste-up copy, and electronic signals control a second laser which scans and exposes the light-sensitive plate coating. The laser generates enough light energy to burn away the solid material of the printing plate.

Laser technology has been used in letter-press, offset, and gravure plate-making where systems can produce multiple sets of press plates at fast speeds and moderate costs. In addition, the laser is used to expose three-demensional objects to presensitized glass plates for use in impactless printing. *See also* holography.

laser scanner. A highly sophisticated method of electronic color separation with the use of the laser. The laser scanner brings the entire separation and screening process under computer control. *See also* color scanner and scanner.

last color down. The last color to be printed in four-color process printing. Usually black, so as not to dirty the previous colors. If colors were printed over black, a muddy result would appear. *See also* subtractive color.

Latin alphabet. An alphabet like our own as opposed to such forms as Greek, Cyrillic, or Semitic alphabets. The Latin alphabet is the parent of alphabets used in printing western European languages, including Old English, German Fraktur, and Irish forms of letters.

laundry list. A price quote comprised of a list of all the various classes of typographic matter found in the specifications of a job. The typesetter does a castoff of the manuscript to find how long it is and how many there are of the various typographic elements. He then adds up the varying page rates, art-work, and handwork required in order to compile the laundry list.

laydown sequence. The sequence in which the colors are printed in four-color process printing. Usually, yellow, red, blue, and black. The transparent inks act as filters for each other and create full color range. Ink films are only 90 to 95% effective so black is added for depth and detail. If the dark colors went down first the lighter colors would not show. *See also* process color and sub-tractive color.

layout. The basic elements of a design shown in their proper positions, with specifications of type, spacing, and general style. Headings, captions, illustra-tions, and margins, are drawn to exact size. *See also* comprehensive, design, dummy, paste-up, and rough.

layout sheets. An opaque or translucent paper strong enough to take erasures. Layouts may be drawn on it to size. Sometimes layout paper is printed with blue graph squares to aid the placing of elements on the page.

layout tissue. A thin translucent paper used for tracing or for making layouts.

lc. Lower-case letters of a font.

lc number. *See* Library of Congress catalog card number.

lead. The thin strips of metal in hot type, used to create extra space between the lines. Leads are less than type high, and so do not print. Abbreviated ld. *See also* leading, and slugs.

leader. A row of dots or dashes used in tabular work, programs, tables of contents, etc., to lead the eye across the page. Leaders can also be used instead of a rule for coupons, etc. They are specified as two, three, or four to the em.

.. ..

4 Point Open Dot Leaders—two dots to the em—

-- --

4 Point Hyphen Leaders—two hyphens to the em—

.. . .

5 Point Open Dot Leaders—two dots to the em—

-- -

5 Point Open Hyphen Leaders—two hyphens to the em—

....

5 Point Fine Dot Leaders—four dots to the em—

....

5 Point Fine Hyphen Leaders—four hyphens to the em—

.. . .

6 Point Open Dot Leaders—two dots to the em—

-- -

6 Point Open Hyphen Leaders—two hyphens to the em—

Leaders.

lead-in. The first few words in a block of copy, such as a caption, set in a different, contrasting typeface or style. For example, the lead-in might be boldface, and the rest of the sentence in the regular face.

leading. (Pronounced ledding.) The insertion of metal leads or slugs between lines of hot-metal type or the placement of extra space between lines of type in phototypesetting. In phototypesetting this is also called linespacing or film advance. When no leading is used, the type is set solid, and there is a chance that ascenders and descenders may overlap.

lead time. The time required for preparation before a job goes to press.

leaf. 1. The single sheet of paper comprised of two pages in a publication. 2. A pigmented stamping material used for decoration.

leaflet. *See* circular.

ledger paper. A tough, smooth grade of business papers with a high degree of durability, usually used for record keeping.

legend. Descriptive material placed near an illustration and indicating figure number, as opposed to the caption which is a title that appears above or below the illustration or at the head of the legend. These terms are often interchanged. *See also* caption.

legibility. The qualities of type that affect speed and ease of the perception of it.

length. The property of printing ink which allows it to be stretched into a long, thin thread without breaking. A long ink does not cut off as cleanly, nor does it permit the printing of delicate type and fine illustrations as does short ink, but it is good for most offset printing.

Leroy. A device used to make neat and straight lettering. A Leroy lettering set consists of a pen, a template with selected letters or symbols, and a scriber to hold the pen and trace the letters on the template.

Letraset. Brand name for a dry-transfer or ruboff type.

letterfit. The quality of space between individual characters which have been typeset. In some systems there is no control over the letterfit of body copy once font structure has been programmed into the computer. For display type, the designer is responsible for an esthetic arrangement of letterfit. Not to be confused with letterspacing which is an overall plus or minus a number of units once the letterfit has been standardized for a single font.

Letterflex. Trademark for long-wearing flexible photopolymer shallow relief printing plates. Letterflex plates are the film version of letterpress printing.

Film is stripped to imposition, and the negative is exposed onto a honey-like substance. The light which shines through the negatives hardens the type image and the nonprinting areas wash away, leaving raised letters as in letterpress. Halftones with no more than 100-line screen are used. Letterflex plates are used on the Cameron belt presses which have a continuous belt that prints by flexography on a web of paper. *See also* belt-press book production system, and Cameron book production system.

lettering. Forming an attractive display or label using hand-drawn characters or a process such as the Graphics Modifier which photomechanically produces lettered images and variations on lettered images for special effect. See Graphics Modifier.

letterpress. Printing from a raised surface, or relief printing such as from hot-metal type, photoengravings, wood, or linoleum cuts. Ink is spread on the wrong reading surface by rollers, and paper is pressed against the inked surface during the impression, by either flat-bed cylinder or rotary presses.

Today, letterpress is used mostly for mass-market paperbacks, daily newspapers, long-run publications, packaging, and short-run titles that do not require halftones competitive in quality with lithography. Letterpress is not usually as economical as web-offset, but competes somewhat in belt-press systems which produce a whole book in one pass through the press using either rotary letterpress plates or flexographic plates. Letterpress is slowly giving way to offset and gravure printing as old machinery wears out and is not replaced. However, 20% of all book printing in the U.S. is done by letterpress and flexography.

For long runs chrome-plated sterotypes or electrotypes are sometimes used. These are duplicate plates of the original locked-up type. For illustrations, engravings on zinc or copper are made from the photographic negatives. However, engraved metal plates were made practically obsolete in the early sixties by photopolymer plates.

Letterpress type. (*Courtesy Kingsport Press*)

letterset. A combination of offset printing which uses a blanket with which to transfer the image, and a low-relief plate such as that of letterpress. Etched to approximately .006-in., the impression is made from plate to blanket and then to the paper without water being introduced. Letterset requires no dampening system and allows the printer to use an offset press to do letterpress work. Any ink pigment used for letterpress may be used for letterset. Letterset is ideal for printing on metal or plastic such as for cans, labels, or cartons and has good consistency of printing quality and color. Also called dry offset and indirect letterpress. Not to be confused with direct lithography, driography, or flexography. *See also* printing.

lettershop. A business which services letters, duplicating, stuffing, mailing, etc. Some lettershops produce personalized form letters, on word processors or automatic typerwriters. They will duplicate letters by such methods as multilith, mimeograph, etc., depending on the sophistication of their equipment. They will also fold various sizes of stationery. *See also* duplicating.

letterspacing. Adding space of a point or less between the characters in a word. This is sometimes done optically, when type is in all caps, to provide for more legibility. Minus letterspacing or kerning is also possible in phototypesetting. Not to be confused with letterfit. *See also* kerning, proofreader's marks, and wordspacing.

PLUS 1 UNIT LETTERSPACING	The quick brown fox jumped over the lazy sleeping dog.
NORMAL LETTERSPACING	The quick brown fox jumped over the lazy sleeping dog.
MINUS 1 UNIT LETTERSPACING	The quick brown fox jumped over the lazy sleeping dog.
MINUS 2 UNITS LETTERSPACING	The quick brown fox jumped over the lazy sleeping dog.
MINUS 3 UNITS LETTERSPACING	The quick brown fox jumped over the lazy sleeping dog.

Letterspacing.

lf. *See* light face.

Library of Congress catalog card number. A number assigned by the Library of Congress and printed on the copyright page of a book. The catalog card gives bibliographical data on the publication. This number must be obtained at the beginning of production of every book published in the United States.

ligature. Means "tied together." Two or three characters joined in one unit. Some typefaces have no ligatures by design.

The following are examples of ligatures: fi fl ffi ffl ff

fi fl ffi ffl ff

Ligatures.

lightbox. A surface illuminated from below so that transparencies may be viewed or artwork pasted onto a grid printed on layout sheets.

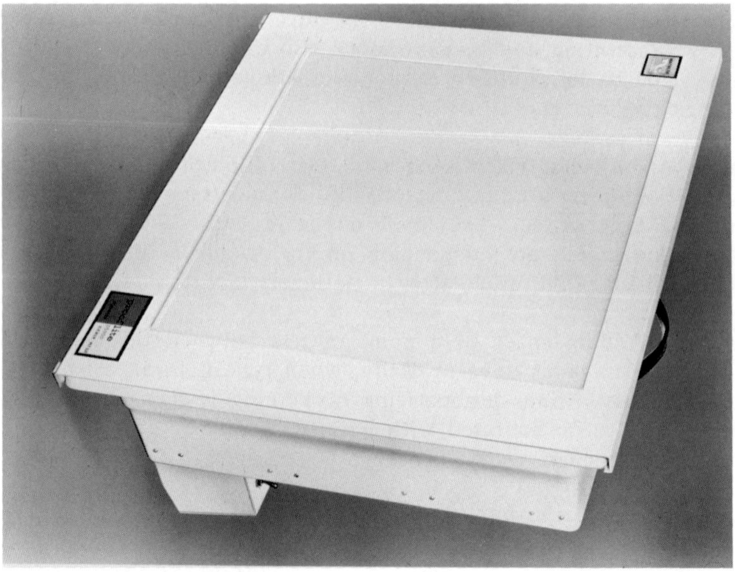

Lightbox for viewing transparencies under optimum lighting conditions. (*Courtesy Macbeth, a division of Kollmorgen Corporation*)

lightface. A lighter version of a regular typeface. Abbriviated lf. *See also* typeface styles.

lightfastness. Resistance to color change when exposed to high-intensity ultraviolet light (either sunlight or artificial light). This is a requirement for inks used on window displays and outdoors.

lighting, standard. Simply stated, color is light. Therefore there are five factors to be considered when viewing the color of a printed piece. First, the light source, which should be color balanced to reproduce natural light; second, the light intensity, which is determined by the distance of the light source from that surface; third, the correct angle and relative positions between the light source and viewing surface; fourth, evenness of illumination; and fifth, the color of the surrounding environment. The graphic arts industry has recommended specifications which have been adopted by the American National Standards Institute. Most printing houses and publishers possess a Macbeth viewing box which meets these standards for color proofing. The effect light has on color is measured in Kelvin. 5000° Kelvin is ideal when proofing original art against press proofs, and 7500° Kelvin, for checking proofs against a press run. *See also* Kelvin and standard viewing conditions.

line art. Any artwork in which there are no middle tones, only pure black and pure white, which require no screen for reproduction. When a continuous tone photograph is shot as line art the middle tones drop out, detail is lost and all that reproduces is the black and white. This is sometimes done for effect. *See also* line photography and tone-line.

Line art. (*Courtesy Van Dyk*)

linecaster. A hot-metal typesetting machine such as the Linotyper that casts entire lines of type in metal, as opposed to machines which cast single characters. Linecasting machines set type at about five characters per second, and are being made obsolete as machinery wears out and is not being replaced, giving way to phototypesetting for offset lithography.

line conversion. The conversion of continuous-tone copy into line copy by the use of specially patterned or conventional halftone or line screens through which the art is photographed. A wide range of effects is available such as mezzontint, circular, random, steel engraving, straight line (vertical and horizontal), and wavy line. To increase the coarseness of a given screen, the continuous-tone copy may be reduced, screened, then enlarged after the screening. To reduce the coarseness of the screen, the reverse process serves. The following article describes some of the various techniques used:

"Line conversions are a graphic art form that changes black and white prints, color prints or transparencies to a line rendering. It's achieved by utilizing screen patterns or masking techniques. No ordinary photo can compare with the impact and reproduction quality of a line conversion. The use of the line conversions relates back to the scratch board method when highly skilled master engravers would spend days etching lines to create their printing plates. As technology advanced in the photo industry, new products came into being. Nowadays process cameras, contact frames, enlargers and textured screens are used to assimilate these artistic effects.

"I will briefly describe three of the basic line conversion methods that are being used by various graphic arts studios. The final quality will be determined by the abilities of the individual doing the conversion and the method he uses.

"First is the camera method. This involves using a process camera. Your original photo is placed in the copy board and set to the proper reproduction size. A textured screen is placed over an unexposed piece of film in the camera back. Various exposures are made to control the density and contrast of the final negative. This film is then processed, dried and prints made. This is known as the in camera direct screening process.

"Second is the contact method. In a process camera, a continuous tone copy negative is shot to reproduction size from your original photo. This negative along with a textured screen and a piece of unexposed film are placed in a vacuum contact frame. Various exposures are made to control the density and contrast. The unexposed film is now impregnated with the screen pattern.

Line conversions. A single line screen over a black and white photograph creates this effect. (*Courtesy Joel A. Levirne/Graphic Images, Ltd.*)

Line conversions. A single line screen over a black and white photograph creates this effect. (*Courtesy Joel A. Levirne/Graphic Images, Ltd.*)

After developing we have a positive screen image. This positive and a new piece of unexposed film are placed into the contact frame and by means of a pinpoint exposure, a negative is made. From this negative final prints are produced.

"The final method to be discussed is the enlarger method. Your negative is placed in the negative carrier. An unexposed piece of film covered by a textured screen is placed in the easel. Various exposures are made through the enlarger's light source to control density and contrast. The unexposed film is then developed, resulting in a positive screen image carrying the texture. From this positive, a contact negative is made which is used to make final prints.

"The different textured screens used in the above mentioned line conversion techniques are readily available. Examples of some of these screens are mezzo tint (mezzo), linear screen, etching screen, linen screen, wood grain and charcoal screens. The mezzo is a stippled, patterned texture that creates a line reproduction from all types of original copy. It has full value range from high contrast down through the middle tones. Linear screens are ruled parallel lines that can be made to run horizontally, vertically or diagonally. It holds most of the original tones. This technique simulates a scratch board feeling with the exactness that can only be achieved photo-mechanically. Variations of this screen are the concentric circle creating a bull's-eye effect and the wavy line screen which gives a contour feeling. The etching screen produces a random scratch line pattern that closely resembles a old time engraving. The linen screen as the name implies is derived from the weave texture of linen material. It is also sometimes called a canvas screen. Wood grain screens are representative of the various types of grains in wood (mahogany, oak, pine, etc.) A charcoal screen is one which closely resembles the embossed texture of an artist's charcoal paper. These are some of the basic screen patterns. There are new textures constantly being sought for use in line conversion work.

"All line conversions are not done by screening processes. There are others made through masking techniques. One of these is the basic line shot. Your original photo is placed in a process camera and a high contrast negative is shot which loses all gray tones and picks up only the detail in the black areas.

"Another is the tone line which is a negative positive masking technique. This process picks up the original grain from your photo and changes that to line. Therefore, the tone line works best from a sharp unretouched photo because retouching destroys the natural grain structure.

"There is also the posterization technique. All continuous tone photos are made up of numerous gray values between the black and white areas. Masks are made to condense these gray tones to two or three values which are then screened for reproduction purposes.

"In recent years, there has been further development of two, three and four color conversions utilizing all the screen and masking processes mentioned. One style is the duotone where one plate is used for the detail and the other for the color. Another is the posterization where the gray values are separated and reproduced as colors. The four color conversion is the newest and most advanced of the color processes. Full color separations are made from color prints or transparencies using special effect screens.

"Here are some of the advantages of using line conversion techniques. It can

Linen screen used for a line conversion creates an interesting effect. (*Courtesy Joel A. Levirne/Graphic Images, Ltd.*)

Linen screen used for a line conversion creates an interesting effect. (*Courtesy Joel A. Levirne/Graphic Images, Ltd.*)

change an ordinary photo into a piece of graphics. Once in line form, butting, overlapping and isolating color and/or images become simplified. Excellent reproduction can be obtained by any printing process, even newspaper if handled correctly.

"As in any photo-mechanical process, it is best to begin with the highest quality photograph available. This is also true with line conversion techniques. However, with the proper skill and technique, even a poor quality photograph can be greatly improved. Most people are under the illusion that a high contrast photograph is necessary to achieve a good conversion. This is not true. It is better to use a full tonal range photo. This way contrast can be increased or decreased with more control. If you use a high contrast original you are limiting the results.

"Some may think line conversions are a new thing. In reality they have been around for many years. Line conversions have advanced to a point where they improve the quality and creativity in the advertising and artistic mediums."[5]

[5] Joel A. Levirne/Graphic Images, Ltd., New York.

Line conversion using a screen to create an effect like old time etching. (*Courtesy Joel A. Levirne/Graphic Images, Ltd.*)

line copy. *See* line art.

line cut. Line art for letterpress printing. A line cut is photomechanically made on a zinc, magnesium, or copper plate by a photo-engraver. Acid etches away the metal surface that is not protected by the image on the negative. The metal plate is mounted either with adhesive, nails, or anchored with solder on a wood block to be type high with the rest of the printing plate. *See also* etch.

line drawing. Any artwork created with solid black tones such as pen and ink. *See also* line art.

line engraving. A plate that prints only black lines. *See also* line art.

line for line. Type set exactly as it appears on the manuscript; ragged right, left, or centered. Commonly used in el-hi publishing.

line gauge. A ruler marked for inches, picas, and centimeters with scales for measuring type lines, usually from agate to 17-pt. sizes. A line guage is used for copyfitting and measuring type. *See also* Haberule.

line mechanical. A paste-up with all line copy in place, ready to be shot by the printer.

linen. A high-quality finish given to book-covering materials or to paper.

line negative. A high-contrast negative made from photographing line art. Areas to be printed are clear, all other areas are opaque so that no light may pass through.

linen finish. *See* pebbling.

line of space. A design specification telling the typesetter to leave the same amount of space blank as if one line of type, the size being used, were set there.

line overlay. Line work put on an overlay used in preparation of line and half-tone art for reproduction.

line photography. Shooting artwork without a screen, for printing. Since light bouncing off the original copy either comes back through the lens to expose the film, or it does not, line art must be a dense even black. There are no little lenses, as in the halftone line screens, to focus on the film; the film either picks up the copy entirely or drops it. There is no in-between, and black or white areas reproduce faithfully. If continuous-tone photographs are shot as line art, the detail is lost in the middletones, all the film picks up is black or white. This is sometimes done as a special effect, and is called tone-line.

A prescreened photograph can be shot as line photography, because each dot is picked up as black line. This is called copy dot and only works if the dot in the prescreened art is the right size and the film used is very good. If the dot is too small the camera won't pick it up and will lose all detail. If the original dot is too big, the whole area goes black or fills in.

Repro type which is photographed for offset printing works on the same principle. Properly shot repro gives a crisp, clear outline. If overexposed, more light is reflected from the background and the letters become smaller. This is called a choke. Ligatures and fine strokes tend to drop out. If underexposed, the letters appear to spread and become fuzzy because less background is reflected. Thus a ragged edge on a letter can come from poor shooting.

line plate. *See* line cut.

line printer. A tape-driven device in phototypesetting capable of printing the line of characters in hard copy rather than in the typeface for correction purposes. This is the output after the keyboarding stage in some systems, though it can be by-passed in order to produce typeset galleys for proofreading rather than hard copy with computer codes.

line printer proof. Copy printed by the line printer and used for checking before type is actually set.

line screen. A screen made of parallel lines closely spaced and running in one direction as opposed to a halftone screen in which the lines are crosshatched. It is used to create an effect when photographing continuous-tone artwork.

line shot. Line art reproduced without using a screen, so the lines are not broken up. Line work can be backed up with a screen in a second step in order to hold detail for a very fine reproduction.

linespacing. The term for leading in phototypesetting. *See also* leading.

linespacing guide. *See* Haberule.

line work. *See* line art.

lining. 1. Reinforcing material such as kraft paper on the spine of a book. The lining is adhered over the crash paper and under the case. The headbands are attached to the lining. 2. The outside ply on a piece of cardboard. The lining is a better grade than the middles. *See also* cardboard.

lining figures. Numerals which align on the baseline with no descenders. Lining figures are the same size as the capitals in any given typeface, as opposed to old-style numerals which fall below the line. Also called modern figures. *See* figure for illustration.

lining-up. That part of the bindery process in which the gathered signatures are fit into the joint of the binding with paste on both end papers.

Linofilm. Trade name for a method of first generation phototypesetting developed in the fifties. Linofilm uses a computer to direct type placement and line justification without manual intervention.

The keyboard operator types the copy on a keyboard which punches a paper tape, and outputs hard copy for proofreading what has been keyboarded before the type is set. The punched tape drives a photo unit which exposes fonts of type from negative images mounted inside the unit. A galley is produced from photosensitive paper or film in the unit. The speed range is about 6 to 12 characters per second, whereas second-generation typesetting machines set from 30 to 100 characters per second.

Linofilm machines are designed for both manual setting and computer setting. Often the keyboardists are so experienced that manual setting is preferred for such things as math tables and charts, until the computers learn enough to set these things with the same facility. Linofilm is also very good for multilevel formulas.

Linofilm is now being outmoded by the more sophisticated cathode ray tube typesetters and in most cases is only being used where equipment already exists.

Linotype. A method of hot-metal typesetting in which one line of type, or a slug, is cast in one piece from molten lead. When a character is keyboarded, brass matrices are dropped with space bands into place. After the line of matrices is assembled, molten metal is forced against the matrices to form the slug or line of type for printing. Linotype sets only one size and face at a time at a speed of about five characters per second. The matrices are automatically returned to the magazine for reuse after the line is cast. Corrections must be made by replacing the entire line. The Linotype was invented by Ottmar Mergenthaler and developed in the 1880s. It is said that when the *New York Tribune's* publisher, Whitelaw Reid, picked up a slug from the machine, he said to Mergenthaler, "Why, Ottmar, you have cast a line-o-type." Originally, the Linotype was used for newspaper typesetting, and some type houses have more faces available in hot metal than in phototype because they've accumulated them over a long period. Linotype is seldom used today as it has been outmoded by computer phototypesetting. The Linotype company is no longer making machinery, parts, or matrices, and so, as they wear out, the Linotype will fall into disuse. Computer type is more flexible for design than Linotype because variations and combinations are more easily made on the computer. *See also* Intertype.

linting. A paper defect in which the fiber is lying loosely on the surface of the sheet. The pulling of fibers on uncoated stock is caused by ink/stock combination, or tacky ink or blanket.

liquid duplicator. *See* spirit duplicator.

list. Copy set apart or indented to show a group or sequence of events.

list price. The price of a publication set by the publisher and listed in the publisher's advertising and suggested as the bookstore or newsstand price for which the item will sell. Distributors of the publication will buy it at a discount in order to make a profit on the sale.

litho or lithography. Means "writing from stone" or "stonewriting." Comes from *lithos,* Greek for "stone" and *graphein,* which means "to write." Lithography was discovered by Alois Senefelder in 1798. Lithography is based on the principle that grease (ink) and water do not mix. Image and nonimage areas are in the same plane on a stone or plate. Artists use the original method of drawing on a limestone surface with a grease pencil then treating the stone with acid to make it water-receptive where there is no image. Ink is applied to the surface and only adheres to the image areas of the grease-pencil drawing.

The commercial form is offset lithography. Zinc or aluminum plates now simulate the surface texture of stones. The offset method keeps plates from wearing out. *See also* offset lithography.

lithographic press. Senefelder invented the first lithographic press between 1798 and 1800. It utilized the limestone slab on a movable flat bed. The image was drawn by hand with a grease crayon material then covered with a water and gum arabic solution. The liquid flowed off the greasy image covering only the nongreasy stone surface. An ink-covered leather cylinder rolled back and forth over the stone. The ink was repelled by the water, but it adhered to the grease image. A dampened sheet was mounted and lowered in a frame to contact the stone, and a wheel was turned to slide the bed under a blade which applied pressure to the paper being inked. Two craftsmen could average 50 acceptable copies per day. Steam power was added to the litho press around 1866, but Senefelder's basic design remained until the offset press was introduced in 1907.

little magazines. Publications of limited circulation, usually on literary or local subject matter.

live matter. The area on the page where type may be placed between margins. To extend artwork beyond this area is to bleed. Not to be confused with dead matter, which is type or illustrations no longer needed for printing.

lockup. To secure a letterpress form in a chase for printing.

logo or **logotype.** The trademark initials or one or more words of a company name. Originally this was cast on one piece of metal, now it is specially designed as artwork for reproduction. Also called adcut.

long ink. Ink that does not break up, but rather flows and forms long filaments on the press. The ink is tested by tapping it with the corner of the ink knife and drawing it out in a long string. A good offset ink is usually long, although short inks are better for very fine artwork, because short inks cut off cleanly and permit printing of delicate type and fine illustrations.

long page. Page on which the lines of type run below the design grid for that page.

long run. A print run of 80,000 copies or more.

long-run platemaking. *See* deep-etch plates and surface plates.

loose blues. Single-page blues as opposed to folded and trimmed book blues. Loose blues are less expensive because they are not accurately folded and trimmed as are book blues.

loose-leaf binding. *See* mechanical bindings.

loupe. Magnifying glass used to examine type and art, especially dot formations, register, and how the dots have printed. Loupe is a jeweler's term.

lower case. The small letters of the alphabet as opposed to the capitals in any given font. In hot-metal days the hand type for small letters was kept in the "lower case" and the type for capitals was kept in the "upper case."

lucy. An optical device used to copy an illustration or an actual object in a size larger or smaller than the original. A simple lucy contains a half-silvered mirror or a prism. A very strong light is put on the original while the copying paper is kept under low illumination. Enlargement or reduction is obtained by adjusting the relative positions of the original copy and the viewing device.

More complex lucies are similar to copying cameras. They throw an enlarged or reduced image of the original onto an inclined or horizontal ground glass where the image is traced.

Ludlow. Trade name for a hot-metal typecasting machine used mainly for display type and newspaper headlines. Matrices are assembled by hand in a composing stick locked into a casting machine and type is cast in line slugs. The slugs are later melted for reuse. Ludlow type is cast new for each use, whereas foundry type is used over and over and wears out with use. Ludlow faces differ from those provided in foundry type. Phototypositor display type is outmoding the Ludlow as hot-metal type gives way to photo offset and foundry type is not being replaced.

luminescent printing. Emission of light produced by chemical actions, friction or electrical action. *Autoluminescence* is visible indefinitely, but it relies on a radioactive element such as radium mixed with a fluorescent salt which will glow under the radiation from the radioactive element. *Phosphorescence* is visible for only a limited period after being exposed to an external light source.

Luminescent printing can be done with tacky varnish over which luminescent powder is dusted; with luminescent paper against which printed lines show; or with a luminescent chemical mixed in ink. Screen printing is often used because it lays down a thick layer of ink. *See also* fluorescent colors.

M

Macbeth. Trade name for a manufacturer of light boxes, which are used for standard color viewing. Color transparencies are viewed with color proofs at 5000° Kelvin. Paper proofs are compared with press sheets at 7500° Kelvin. Macbeth also manufactures transparency viewers and overhead luminaires. Standard lighting for the field of graphic arts refers to a specific set of color viewing conditions recommended and approved by the graphic arts industry and adopted by the American National Standards Institute. For complete accuracy when checking color proofs, this standard lighting must be used. *See also* Kelvin and standard viewing conditions.

Macbeth box. (*Courtesy Macbeth, a division of Kollmorgen Corporation*)

machine coated. An inexpensive grade of paper which is one or two sides coated on the papermaking machine, rather than off-machine coated in a separate process. Not to be confused with machine-finish paper which is not coated. Also called process coated.

machine finish. A smooth calendered uncoated paper. Machine finish is between vellum and English finish in smoothness and is not as glossy as supercalendered paper. *See also* finish and uncoated paper.

machine set. Composition of hot metal type by mechanical means, e.g., Linotype, Monotype, or Intertype as opposed to handset.

magazine. 1. The slotted container for storage of matrices in hot-metal line-casting machines. A magazine holds a font of one size and one face at a time. 2. A periodical publication.

magenta. One of the process colors referred to as process red. In subtractive color which is used in process printing, transparent magenta ink filters out green and allows blue and red to show through. Dots of magenta, cyan, and yellow overlap each other on the paper and allow red, blue, and green to filter through, thus creating combinations of the full range of colors. *See also* additive color, process color and substitute color.

magnetic inks. Inks made with pigments that can be magnetized after printing for use in banks to increase the speed and efficiency of handling checks. The sorting machine first magnetizes the ink then reads it. The magnetized inks can be recognized by electronic sensing or magnetic ink character-reading equipment which passes the information to a computer.

Magnetic inks print in a normal manner, and with a consistent film of ink containing iron oxide. Special type fonts are required, and proper spacing of the encoding numbers is required so as not to confuse the electronic reader.

magnetic tape. A tape or ribbon with magnetic material on which information can be placed in the form of magnetically polarized spots. The tape stores data which can be further processed and set into type by a phototypesetting unit.

makeready. The complete process involved in getting the presses ready to run after plates have been inserted. This includes register, ink control, feeder control, and the proper amount of impression appearing on the printed sheet. The paper and form or plate must come together close enough to transfer the ink, but not so close that the surface will be bruised or the paper punctured. This is called kiss impression. Makeready is charged for by the hour.

makeready on the fly. *See* flying makeready.

make-up. Assembling the photographic and typographic elements to form a page or a group of pages. It is the mechanical and esthetic arrangement of the elements into a legible format for final reproduction. After editorial decisions are made, a designer can do make-up by placing type on mechanicals or merely by pasting up a dummy from which the compositor makes up the page. In composition, this includes shooting and cropping the artwork, contacting to positive film or paper and stripping the elements together into a working flat. Make-up by the compositor is charged for by the hour.

manilla paper. A sturdy, buff-colored paper made from manilla hemp, used for folders, envelopes, and cards. Hemp or jute fibers in the paper give it strength. Loosely used to refer to any yellowish paper or bristol. *See also* paper grades.

manufacturing clause. *See* copyright. The manufacturing clause to the U.S. copyright law is eliminated July 1, 1982. Formerly, the law required that U.S. authored books must have the type set and be printed and bound in the U.S. in order to get U.S. copyright protection. Since 1909, the "Ad Interim" copyright allowed publishers to manufacture 1500 copies of a book overseas, and receive U.S. copyright protection for only 5 years, thus providing U.S. publishers with a way to test the marketability of a title before publishing it here with full copyright protection for a long run.

The new copyright law which went into effect January 1, 1978 raised the 1500-copy limit to 2000 copies, and the 5-year limitation was eliminated giving full copyright protection. The new law also permits U.S. authors whose works are printed in a foreign country to be brought into the U.S. to have copyright protection. Books manufactured in Canada are considered equivalent to those being manufactured in the U.S., so there are no limits on books manufactured there and brought into the U.S. When the manufacturing clause ceases to exist on July 1, 1982, U.S. authored books can be printed and bound anywhere, and become eligible for U.S. copyright protection.

manufacturing cost. Costs for printing, paper, binding, jackets, cartons, freight to the warehouse, and warehousing, which recur every time a book is reprinted. Plant costs, such as design, editing, authors advance, or travel expenses, occur only once but benefit the entire life of the book.

manuscript. 1. Typed copy to be set in type. Abbreviated ms. 2. Handwritten, as opposed to typewritten material.

marbling. Edges of a book or end papers decorated with colors in a pattern resembling veins of marble.

margins. The unprinted space around the printed page. They are called head, outside, foot, and gutter margins. Running heads are counted as part of the type page. Drop folios are counted as part of the margins. Margins must be at least $\frac{1}{4}$-in. to the trim edge and $\frac{1}{2}$-in. to the gutter to allow for folding and trimming, and even $\frac{1}{4}$-in. requires a slow fold at the bindery. Better guidelines are a minimum of $\frac{3}{8}$-in. to the trim edge and $\frac{5}{8}$-in. for gutter margin. It is wise to check with the printer for binding requirements before type is set.

Traditional proportions of margins on a layout are inside margin, two units; top margin, three units; outside margin, four units; bottom margin, five or six units, though many designs incorporate other margins.

marked set. *See* master proof.

markup. The programming language of typography. Usually, the markup person at the publishing house uses standard proofreader's marks, and the compositor uses codes to indicate typeface, size, line length, leading, etc., written in computer language for the keyboard operator to put into the computer. *See also* typographic parameters, and keymarking.

marline. The cost of advertising in newspapers for one agate line per billion dollars of sales in the market area. *See also* agate line.

mask. 1. Lightblocking material to mask portions of an illustration in photographic exposure. An overlay is supplied to create outline shapes for halftones being photographed. Opaque material is also used to protect nonprinting areas of the printing plate during exposure in offset lithography. Masks are used also for multicolor printing or percentages of black. The mask surrounds the area to be printed in color and a piece of white paper is placed beneath the mask creating a window so that when shot, a hole in the negative will expose the printing plate for color in that area. 2. A paper or rubber cement block to allow the printer to take a proof of only certain portions of an inked form. Also called frisket. 3. A photomechanical method in process-color reproduction in which special filters control or modulate color contrast and detail over the total area of each separation negative for color correction.

masking paper. *See* goldenrod.

masking tape. 1. A translucent, light-blocking solid red or black pressure-sensitive tape used to block out unwanted areas of copy on negative or positive film. It can be seen through on the light table for use in stripping art into position. 2. A brown or white pressure-sensitive opaque tape used extensively in preparing artwork and making mechanicals.

massaging. Adding commands to those already programmed in a computer system. A typesetting system can add commands for such functions as kerning and justifying.

mass market paperback. A book bound in paper as opposed to cloth, and sold through newsstands, drugstores, and supermarkets as well as in bookstores. Not to be confused with quality paperbacks, which are sold only in bookstores, direct mail or other normal bookselling channels.

master. Plate for a duplicating machine.

master proof. A galley or page proof containing printer's or typographer's queries and corrections for the client to check, mark, and return to the typographer or printer for further corrections. It is usually stamped MASTER PROOF or MARKED SET. Also called marked set, printer's proof, and reader's proof.

masthead. **1.** Information including title, publisher, address, date, volume, issue number, subscription rates, and the names of the executives and editors on a magazine staff. The masthead is usually printed next to the table of contents of a magazine or on the editorial page of a newspaper. **2.** A design or logotype used to identify a newspaper or publication.

mat. Decorative matboard used to support or frame a picture for esthetic effect. *See also* matrix and matte finish.

mat service. A subscription service supplying advertisers, publications, and printers with ready-made illustrations. *See also* stock cut or stock photos.

match color. *See* flat color and PMS.

matching type. There is a detectable density difference when mixing type from different machines. The design and x-height of a particular typeface will vary from manufacturer to manufacturer. Therefore it is impossible to exactly match typefaces and type sizes from one system to another. The same applies when setting patches. If possible, type for patches should be set on the same equipment as the original text. Also, the typographer should use the same font (the same grid, lens, and type size) for setting enlargements or reductions. For example, if a 10-pt. font is enlarged to 12-pt., the size will be different from that of a 14-pt. font reduced to 12-pt.

matrix. **1.** The glass plate that contains the film font negative for phototypesetting or the mold, usually copper or brass, in which hot-metal letters are cast in linecasting machines. **2.** The paper maché or plastic mold of metal type and engraving forms from which a stereotype is made or a rubber plate for flexography. Also called mat.

matte finish. **1.** A textured, nonshiny, finely grained finish on a photograph or photostat, as opposed to a glossy finish. Matte finishes soil more easily than glossies and do not have as great a range of tonal values. **2.** A paper with an uncalendered, lightly finished surface.

matte print. A photprint with a dull finish.

meaningless words make a line. The editorial idea that the designer sometimes has the editor fill out a line when the page layout requires it.

mean line. *See* x-line.

measure. The width of the typeset line on a page. *See also* full measure and narrow measure.

measurement. The printer's basic unit of measurement is the point, which is approximately $\frac{1}{72}$ of an inch. Twelve points equal 1 pica, which is approximately $\frac{1}{6}$ of an inch.

Letterspaces are measured in ems, which are as wide as the font is high in points. For example, in 10-pt. type, 1 em would be 10 points wide. *See also* em.

measuring type. Type is measured in points; the line length, or measure, is measured in picas. There are 12 pt. in a pica and approximately 6 picas in an inch. To understand how the point size of type is determined a piece of metal type should be examined. It is a rectangular block of metal with a printing surface on top. The block is called the body and the printing surface is called the face. The depth of the body is the dimension of the greatest concern to the designer. It is known as the body size and is larger than the actual point size of the character to allow for ascenders and descenders. It is by this dimension that type size is measured. Type sizes 14 pt. and smaller are called text types and those larger are called display types.

The height of the body is .918-in. This is know as type-high. It is very important to the printer that all hot-metal type be exactly the same height in order to print evenly and consistently.

The type width, which is called set width, is dictated by the width of the individual letter, the letters M and W being the widest and I being the narrowest. *See also* type.

mechanical. Art produced specifically for the printing process in order to simplify reproduction. This is a camera-ready paste-up assembly of all line art, and type from repro galleys, pasted on layout boards in exact position. The mechanicals contain instructions for the printer in the margins or on an overlay. The break for color is indicated.

Mechanical boards are drawn up to show guidelines for the basic grid, columns, margins, placement of running heads, and folios, and boards can be printed in nonreproducible blue from a master to aid the paste-up artist.

mechanical binding. A method of binding in which the pages are held together by mechanical means such as metal rings or plastic coils. Frequently used for calendars, diaries, catalogs, and notebooks, mechanical binding is more expensive than case bindings as pages must be inserted by hand. *See also* comb binding and spiral binding.

mechanical draftsperson. A person who makes mechanicals. This person may or may not also be a designer. He or she can paste up or do a layout once a job has been spec'd. Also called paste-up person.

mechanical pulping. Groundwood pulp produced when logs are cleaned, peeled, and ground against a revolving grindstone or disc mill until they are reduced to fiber. Groundwood pulp is very economical since it uses all the wood, as opposed to chemical pulp in which undesirable components of the wood are removed. It can discolor and tear easily. *See also* groundwood.

mechanical separations. Artwork prepared by the designer with overlays which show each color to be printed, one overlay for each color in register with the base mechanical. Each overlay is shot separately to create a piece of film that will be made into a plate which will print that particular color.

medium run. A print run between 11,000 and 70,000 copies, usually around 40,000. A short run is 10,000 or less, and a long run 80,000 or more.

memory. 1. The electronic circuitry in a machine that actually retains information. 2. The recording medium such as tape or disk used to store information.

"Before the introduction of computers into the composition process, the only form of digital memory storage available was the punched paper tape used to drive typesetting machines. Since then, the media on which coded material can be stored have increased several-fold, all of them involving magnetic recording which can be read by machines at computer speeds. However, while computer tape and disk storage provided ample space to house material for typesetting, it was either relatively expensive or hard to get at quickly and economically in the context needed for editorial processing. One of the major developments that has made in-house editing and composition systems practical for book projects has been the development of inexpensive, portable recording media—specifically, magnetic tape cassettes and floppy disks.

"Tape cassettes have been the primary medium for so-called *word processing* systems, the automatic office typerwriter system that also permit revisions to be made in standing material via electronic sorting prior to final typing of the finished draft. The floppy disk, however, has proved to be far more flexible because it stores data for random retrieval, not linearly. For this reason, it has become the principal portable storage medium for working files in smaller editing and composition systems; and the word processing field currently is moving toward use of floppy disks in place of tapes in its newer equipment. With floppy disks, unlimited magnetic storage capacity is available at almost nominal cost. Many smaller systems use floppy disk storage exclusively, and some larger systems with standard computer disk memory also include the facility to record on floppy disks as well when desired."[6]

merge. 1. A technique for combining items from two or more sequenced tapes into one, using a computer to incorporate new or corrected copy into existing copy to produce a clean tape for the phototypesetting unit. 2. To combine pieces of copy on a video display screen in phototypesetting.

[6] Reprinted from the December 5, 1977, issue of *Publisher's Weekly*, published by R. R. Bowker Company, a Xerox company. Copyright ©1977 by Xerox Corporation.

Mergenthaler. The name of a company which manufactures phototypesetting equipment and type fonts. Ottmar Mergenthaler invented the Linotype in 1886, and this was the first improvement in typesetting speed since the days of Gutenberg in the 1400s.

metallic inks. Special effects obtained by mixing differently colored metal dust such as silver, copper, aluminum, or bronze powder with a varnish base. The bronze powder and vehicle for gold inks are mixed just before printing because gold tends to tarnish rapidly after mixing, thus reducing color brilliance. The varnish binds and holds the powder to the paper surface. Coated papers are used for best results. Cast-coated papers, i.e., glossy, supercalendered paper, must be press proofed to ensure proper binding of the metallic ink to paper. Both aluminum and gold inks can be printed either by offset, letterpress, or gravure.

metric system. A decimal system of measures and weights with the meter and the gram as the bases. Here are some of the more common measures and their equivalents:

kilometer	00.62137 mile
meter	39.37 inches
centimeter	00.3937 inch
millimeter	00.03937 inch
kilogram	02.2046 lbs.
gram	15.432 grs. (av.)
inch	02.54 cms.
foot	00.3048 meter
yard	00.9144 meter
pound	00.4536 kilogram

mezzotint. 1. A form of etching in which the entire surface is burred or made rough. 2. A line conversion of a photograph in which a screen is used to imitate the hand-crafted copperplate engraving effect. *See also* gravure and line conversion.

MF. *See* machine-finish paper.

Microcard. An opaque card with a positive image for insertion into a machine that enlarges the material for reading.

Microfiche. A transparent piece of film with a positive or negative image for use in a special machine that enlarges it for reading.

microfilm. Photographic reproduction of information in a size too small to be read without magnification. It is a photographic method of making low-cost, space-saving copies of text or visual material. A researcher can obtain information located in a distant library by having that library make and send a microfilm copy. A manuscript can be microfilmed as a precaution against loss and a re-

Mezzotints. (*Courtesy Joel A. Levirne/Graphic Images, Ltd.*)

placement copy can be made from the microfilm. Banks use microfilm to make copies of checks. Bulky and seldom-used records can be microfilmed and the originals discarded. The entire Bible has been reproduced on 2 x 2 in. film. Microfilm copies are currently being produced by computer-assisted CRT phototypesetting equipment. Microfilming is usually done on standard size 70mm, 35mm, or 16mm film at about $\frac{1}{10}$th to $\frac{1}{30}$th of its original size. The original negatives can be read, or positive prints can be made from the original negative.

micrographics or **microprinting.** An area of printing utilizing microfilm rather than printing and paper, and taking one quarter of the time. Microfiche can be duplicated at rates of speed up to 650 pages per second. Cost-savings in labor and distribution are enormous. 12,000 pages of paper can be compacted into 1-in. of file space. Industrial catalogs, directories, and business forms are often done by means of micrographics. Color microfilm is just beginning to be explored.

Computer output microfilming, abbreviated COM, is used in such fields as banking, where high volume and meticulous record keeping is a necessity. Digitized information is converted to characters on a cathode ray tube. The tube is photographed on film, all at a speed of 90,000 characters per second.

middle tones. The tonal range between highlights and shadows in a photograph or reproduction, usually the tones between 30 and 75% value of black.

mil. One thousandth of an inch. The thickness of film used for reproduction is measured in mils.

milline. A unit for comparison of newspaper advertising rates in relation to circulation. A milline is the cost of one agate line for one million circulation. *See also* agate line.

mimeograph. Originally the trade name for a direct-stencil duplicating machine, now refers to the process rather than the company, even when another brand of machine is used.

Ink is forced through a stencil made from porous sheets with a coating that is impenetrable by ink. Drawing or typing the stencil with a sharp instrument penetrates the coating and exposes the porous tissue. When the stencil is attached to the printing cylinder it is rotated, and each impression forces the ink from the cylinder through the porous openings of the stencil onto the highly absorbent paper used. The trend is now away from mimeograph and toward photocopying, or electrostatic printing.

mimeograph paper. A paper with a toothy, absorbent surface required for mimeographing.

miniweb. A small web-offset press about one story high. Some miniwebs have four units which print two at a time on both sides of the paper so that at the folding end a full 32-page signature is printed and folded, but not trimmed. A miniweb can also be a smaller one-man operation. Miniweb presses now compete for some of the jobs that were previously done on sheet-fed presses.

minuscules. Small letters, or lower case.

minus letterspacing. *See* letterspacing.

misprint. Typographical error. *See also* printer's error.

mixing typefaces. *See* matching type, and typeface styles.

model release. Permission given by the subject in a photograph for use of the photograph in a publication or for advertising.

modem. A device attached to a telephone connecting computer and telephone lines and converting digital signals to audio tones and vice versa. A modem allows data to be communicated over the phone from word processor to computer for phototypesetting or from one word processor to another. *See also* interface.

modern type. Roman type style developed in the late 18th century. Modern type has pronounced differences between thick and thin strokes and thin, flat serifs. Bodoni is an example. The other Roman type styles are old style and transitional. *See also* roman and typeface styles.

moiré pattern. Undesirable patterns that are caused by optical conflict or meshing between multiple halftone screens shot at less than 30 degrees apart; between the ruling of the halftone screen and the dots or lines contained in the original artwork; or between the halftone screen and a prescreened piece. It can be minimized by finding the matching screen and turning the matching screen to various angles until a minimum oı moiré is found. Moiré can also occur in multicolor halftone reproductions caused by incorrect screen angles or misregister of the color impressions during printing. In four-color process work, the yellow printer is usually screened at a different screen e.g., 133-line, from the other three colors e.g., 120-line, to avoid a moiré pattern. *See also* color separation.

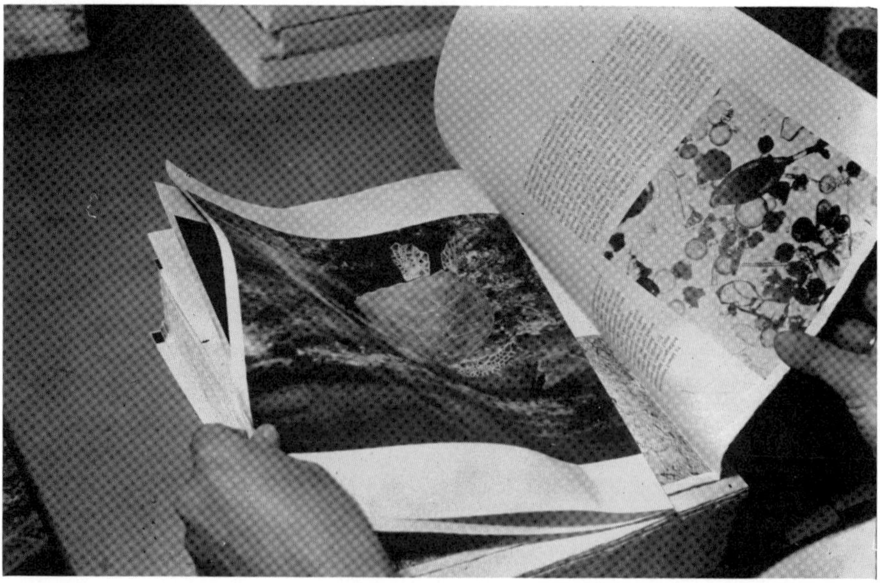

Moiré pattern.

moisture content. The content of moisture in paper. The moisture content should be in balance with that of the pressroom. Humidity in the delivery pile, affects drying time of the ink. An increase in the relative humidity of the pressroom or moisture of the pile can cause wavy edges. If the relative humidity of the pressroom is lower than in the paper, the paper loses moisture, and tight edges are formed. Wavy and tight edges can cause wrinkles and misregister on press resulting in press stoppage.

moisture-set inks. A letterpress ink that is exposed to steam, mist, or water, causing the ink pigment to bind firmly to the paper. Moisture-set inks are ideal for food packaging because they are free from odor.

mold. *See* matrix.

monochromatic. **1.** Artwork made of tints and shades of only one color. **2.** Films coated with color-blind emulsion used for copying black and white originals.

monotone. Artwork produced in one color only. *See also* black-and-white.

Monotype. Trade name for a typecasting machine invented by Tolbert Lanston in 1887. A ribbon of paper, which is perforated on a keyboard activates the typesetting. The font is arranged in a metal tray and a needle pushes through the desired letter, bringing the matrix into contact with molten lead. Letters are cast one at a time and arranged in lines which are justified to the proper length and held together by a string. The operator calculates tabular and formula copy. The speed is about two characters per second in sizes ranging from 6 to 14 pt. As the matrices, machinery, and parts wear out they are not being replaced. Compositors are changing over to computer typesetting, which is hundreds and thousands of times faster per second.

montage. A photograph in which several images are combined photographically at angles, butted, overlapped, cut to various sizes, etc., to tell a story. Ideally each print can be enlarged, cropped, and projected from the original negative onto the final piece of paper in one operation. If prints are overlapped, shadow lines occur. Not to be confused with collage.

morgue. File of reference material and photos used to write a book, story, or any printed piece.

mortise. **1.** A rectangular cavity or hole cut in an engraving block or letterpress printing plate to allow type or other engravings to be inserted. In computer type the term has merely been adapted to use in film. To mortise means to cut the film, strip in a correction and burnish, or rub down the edge so the film matches evenly, leaving no cut mark on the page. **2.** To add or subtract units in certain letter combinations on typesetting systems that allow for it. **3.** To cut an opening for a correction to be pasted into existing type or art work on a mechanical.

mounted reprint copy. Sheets torn from a book or magazine and pasted up, often used as manuscript for revisions. Also called dummy.

mounting and finishing. **1.** Pasting photographic prints or posters onto stiff mounting boards. Mounting is often accompanied by one or more finishing operations, for example die cutting, perforating, creasing, scoring, easeling, varnishing, hinging, stringing, round-cornering, or eyeleting. 2. Backing engravings with blocks of wood to make them type-high.

movable type. Individual characters of type that have been molded and set together for printing. Movable type was used in China as early as A.D. 1050, though the early clay types never gained wide use because of the 40,000 characters in written Chinese. A man named Pi-Sheng cut individual characters in small pieces of clay that were fired to make them hard. They were placed in an iron frame. When cold, the pieces held together and the form was inked and printed. The blocks of type were reheated and the resin mixture that held them together loosened, so the type could be reused.

During the 14th and 15th centuries the Koreans used a version of sand-cast types to produce books. The characters were ideographic, requiring 7,000 to 20,000 characters for a book. In 1403 in Korea, King T'ai Tsung had type cast in bronze and everything he knew of printed in order to preserve a record of Korean civilization. In 1446, King Sejong gave his people a 24-letter phonetic alphabet. The letters were clustered into syllables in order to resemble and harmonize with the existing Chinese characters, and a stick of type was used for every syllable. If the characters had been assembled in lines instead of clusters, Korea would probably have been credited with the invention of movable type.

About the same time in northern Germany, similar events brought Johann Gutenberg the title "father of printing." Actually Gutenberg synthesized existing metals and technology and developed a practical way to create individual sticks of type with the same height, topped with letters of varying widths. A character was filed into the end of a steel bar called a punch. The punch was struck into a bar of copper. The procedure was repeated until a complete set of matrices was made. The matrix was positioned inside a mold into which molten metal was poured to harden into a piece of metal type. Movable type allowed rapid composition of a page with the possibility to edit and correct. Gutenberg's experience with lead in the manufacturing of mirrors finally pointed the way for a combination of lead, tin, and antimony as a suitable metal to cast in the mold. His original formulation (5% tin, 12% antimony, and 83% lead) remains nearly unchanged to this day for hot-metal type. Characters could be perfectly cast with this combination because the alloy expands when cooling to form an exact duplicate of the matrix outline. Two workmen could cast and dress 25 pieces of type an hour. Gutenberg had 292 characters in his font. His Bible of 42 lines to the page contained around 2800 characters to the page. Two pages were printed and two pages were composed at the same time, so at least 11,200 letters were needed even to begin printing. Working a 12-hour work day, it took two craftsmen more than 37 work days to prepare the initial font of working type. At this rate of speed it took over three years to complete just 200 copies.

The use of movable type continued in Korea for 2 centuries and then decayed. In China it was used only occasionally until merchants later brought back the methods of European typographers. Gutenberg's principles of movable type remained in use until the invention of the Linotype machine in the 1880s. His invention of the type mold made possible the widespread dissemination of the printed word necessary for the development of the Renaissance.

ms. Abbreviation for manuscript. *See also* manuscript.

mugshot. Photograph of a person showing the head and shoulders. Mugshot is derived from police jargon for identification photos.

multicolor press. A printing press that has enough units to print more than one color on one run through the press.

multicolor printing. Printing in more than one color with one plate for each color.

Multilith. Trade name for a small offset duplicator press used for small printing jobs such as cards, letterheads, envelopes, and forms.

multiple contours. The effect of more than one type outline or letters within letters created by separate color printers or hand drawing contours around display lettering.

Multiple contours. (*Courtesy Graphics Modifier, Byers Corporation*)

multiple exposures. Photographic effect made by enlargements in varying ratios, by repositioning the subject vertically or horizontally, or by consecutive copying of different images.

multiple inline. More than one line or shaded contour drawn within the shape of display lettering. This can be done with a halftone screen or by hand.

Multiple inline. (*Courtesy Graphics Modifier, Byers Corporation*)

multiple outline. Outlines stacked around each other, around the contours of graphic lettering, and shaded different colors.

Munsell system. A system of numerical gradation used to designate and specify colors. *See also* color tree.

mutt or **mutton quad.** Jargon for an em-quad. *See also* em.

m weight. The weight of 1000 sheets of any given paper, cut to m-weight size for that grade paper. If the m weight of 1000 sheets of 25" x 38" paper is 100 lbs., it would be written 100M. Not to be confused with basis weight which is the weight of a ream (500 sheets) of the standard size for a particular grade of paper. *See also* hundredweight.

mylar. A clear polyester film used in phototypesetting and offset preparation. It is made by Du Pont and is used for stripping positives because of its mechanical strength and dimensional stability. Mylar is also the carrier for the emulsion in negative film. The film is protected by an overcoating and an antihalation backing.

N

narrow measure. A block of copy indented from one or both margins to set it off from surrounding full-measure copy. *See also* measure.

NASTA. National Association of State Textbook Administrators. NASTA provides manufacturing standards and specifications for textbooks, in order that appropriate physical standards of quality and performance for elementary and high school textbook publishing may be maintained. The standards and specs are a guide and in no way preclude a client, whether he has approved the standards or specifications or not, from manufacturing, marketing, purchasing, or using products, processes, or procedures that do not conform to the NASTA standards or specifications.

natural. 1. An off-white, ivory colored paper. 2. A kind of finish given book-covering materials.

negative. A reverse photographic image on film or paper in which the dark areas appear light and vice versa. Intermediate tonal values are also reversed, and the picture is flopped. Film negatives are used to make printing plates.

During the exposure of film, light which is reflected off the copyboard onto the film in the camera produces a latent image on the film. The chemical change in the emulsion of the film cannot be seen until the film is in the developer. The film is placed in four successive tray baths—the *developer,* the *shortstop,* the *fixer,* and *water.*

The *developing bath* causes the latent image to become visible, and the developer solution frees the exposed silver particles in the film emulsion, causing them to form a dense black or opaque background. At the same time, the particles of silver which were not struck by the reflected light form a transparent area on the film. The *shortstop* bath neutralizes the action of the developer. The *fixing* bath removes all unexposed particles of silver and the antihalation backing from the film. Then the *running-water* bath washes away all traces of the chemicals used and prevents later darkening of the clear areas of the film.

When stripping four-color negatives, the stripper follows register marks placed on the film by the compositor or separator. In four-color work, strippers prefer to be supplied with positive film so that they can check for the rosette image which shows if the dots are touching or not. *See also* camera, film, halftone, and line photography.

negative assembly. The assemblage or combination of negatives on a flat in exact position according to layout or impostion so that a plate can be exposed, etched, and printed as one unit.

neon halo effect. Graphic lettering effects done on a halftone so that the letters look as if they glow in the dark.

news ink. Cheap printing inks used on newsprint that dry by absorption. The reason that news inks rub off on the hands so easily is because they do not contain the solvents for drying that are used in more expensive inks.

newspaper fold. One fold such as in a big tabloid.

newsprint. A grade of paper used for printing newspapers and low-cost flyers or broadsides. Newsprint contains about 85% groundwood and 15% unbleached sulfite. The weight is from 30 to 45 lbs and the surface is coarse and absorbent.

nip. A process during the binding of a book in which a machine called the nipper presses the air out of the sewn signatures to reduce swell caused by the thread; to give uniform bulk to all the books; and to make the spine of the signatures very hard before glue is applied.

no good positive. A contact print from the dominant color in the four-color separation, stripped into the page to show the client position but not color on page proofs.

nonconsumable textbook. A textbook intended to be used a number of times, as opposed to a consumable textbook in which the student writes, tears, or which the student uses as a workbook only once.

noncounting keyboard. A keyboard at which the operator types copy to be set without making any end-of-line decisions. A noncounting keyboard produces a paper or magnetic tape called an idiot tape, which is fed into a computer which determines the line length, hyphenation, and justification.

nonrestricted bleeds. Bleeds which fall any place in the publication, or throughout it, as opposed to being restricted to a certain form and number of pages.

nonsilver film. A polymer photographic film without a silver-based emulsion. The nonsilver film has an emulsion made of crystals that take on the electrical charge of an image placed on them. Toner and fixative make the image visible and permanent. The same base material can be used for either positives or negatives, and the film is less expensive and requires less pollution control than that with silver emulsion. Nonsilver film has panchromatic sensitivity, fast-exposure speed, and can be processed onto exposure films, color proofs, or press plates. Nonsilver photosensitive materials make it possible to make color proofs before the printing plate is made. In some instances they have replaced the use of press proofs.

nonwoven. Material that has a paper or reinforced paper base and synthetic coating such as Pyroxalin. Nonwoven material is used in binding. *See also* woven.

north, south. North is the top and south is the bottom of a page as it is viewed when reading.

notch binding. A type of adhesive binding in which notches are cut out of the spines of the signatures so that glue seeps through onto the edges of the pages.

novelty printing. Nonpublication printing such as on T-shirts, balloons, calendars, pencils, and matchbook covers.

novelty typeface styles. *See* occasional typeface styles.

numerals. Numbers written either in Arabic or Roman. Arabic numerals are part of every font both in regular and italic. Roman numerals are made from capital or lowercase letters of the font and are used mostly to number front matter in a book. The series is I, II, III, IV, V, VI, VII, VIII, IX, X, . . . L(50), C(100), D(500), M(1,000). In 15th and 16th century books, IↃ is 500 and CIↃ is 1000 in some cases. *See also* lining figures and old-style figures.

nut. Jargon for en-quad. *See also* en.

O

oblique. Sans serif characters that slant to the right. The same as italic except that italic type has serifs. The term italic is loosely used to refer to oblique.

oblong. A book that is bound on the short end rather than on the long end. In some binderies this incurs more handwork, since the machinery is not designed to handle these sizes on the assembly line.

occasional type. Novelty or decorative typefaces that do not fit into the six standard classes of type. *See also* typeface styles.

OCR. *See* optical character recognition.

octavo. **1.** Term from the incunabula referring to a book made from sheets which have been folded three times, thus forming 16 pages per sheet. **2.** A book measuring about 6 x 9 inches.

off its feet. Type knocked askew on the proof press. Also called pi.

off-line. Equipment not directly controlled by a central processing unit, or operations conducted out of the process, as opposed to in-line, or on-line, which are conducted within one central process.

off-machine coated. Paper that received its coating off the papermaking machine as opposed to receiving the coating in-line with the rest of the papermaking process.

offprint. Reprint of a published article or chapter made from the original type or plates but issued separately. *See also* reprint.

offset. **1.** Jargon for offset lithography. **2.** Formerly the accidental impression from a freshly printed sheet to the back of the next sheet. Now called set-off. **3.** A grade of paper similar to letterpress coated and uncoated book papers except that sizing is added to resist the moisture. Offset papers may be used in letterpress printing, but few letterpress papers are suitable for offset.

offset duplicators. A machine that reproduces what is written, typed, or drawn on a paper master. Offset duplicators are used for small jobs such as letterheads, envelopes, cards, and forms. *See also* offset.

offset lithographic inks. Inks adapted to the chemicals and chemistry used in offset lithography. Lithographic inks contain more water-resistant vehicles than do other inks, and the pigments do not bleed. The inks are strong in color value because less ink is applied than in other processes. They are the strongest of all inks next to collotype inks. The average ink application is about half that of letterpress.

offset lithography. The commercial form of planographic printing in which the image areas and the nonimage areas are on the same plate in the same plane. The images are separated chemically, based on the principle that grease (ink) and water (etch in the fountain solution) do not mix. A negative is usually used to prepare the plate, but for especially fine quality, a positive is used to prepare a deep-etch plate. The ink is transferred from the plate, that is, offset, onto a rubber blanket and from the blanket to the paper.

Offset lithography is especially efficient in work requiring many photographs and/or multiple colors. It is the dominant process for the manufacture of most U.S. books. It may be used for more mass-market paperbacks now being produced by letterpress and flexography, and it is moving into newspaper publishing, although the largest daily papers still use letterpress. The simplicity of makeready in offset lithography is helped by a pre-imposed form on the thin metal plate. Paper waste is still about twice as high on offset lithography as for letterpress and gravure. Also called photo-offset. *See also* litho or lithography, planography, sheet-fed, and web offset.

offset paper. Coated or uncoated paper strong enough to resist the pull of tacky inks used in offset lithography. Sizing is also added to resist the washing away of the coating by the dampening system on the press. Any finish of paper can be printed by offset. Most offset papers may be used to print letterpress, but letterpress papers are not suitable for offset printing.

offset plates. The most common offset plates are *surface plates* on which the image is level with the clear portion of the plate. *Deep etch* plates are plates chemically etched so that the image area is slightly below that of the nonprinting area. *Relief plates* are used in dry offset where the nonprinting areas of the plate are removed to a considerable depth below that of the printing area. Consequently no dampening operation is required on press. *Multimetal plates* are etched so that the image is either slightly raised or slightly lowered to expose an additional metal. The metal on the raised surface will wear better than the usual plate metals. There are many different kinds of all these plates with different types of coatings, and with different methods of transfer for the image exposure.

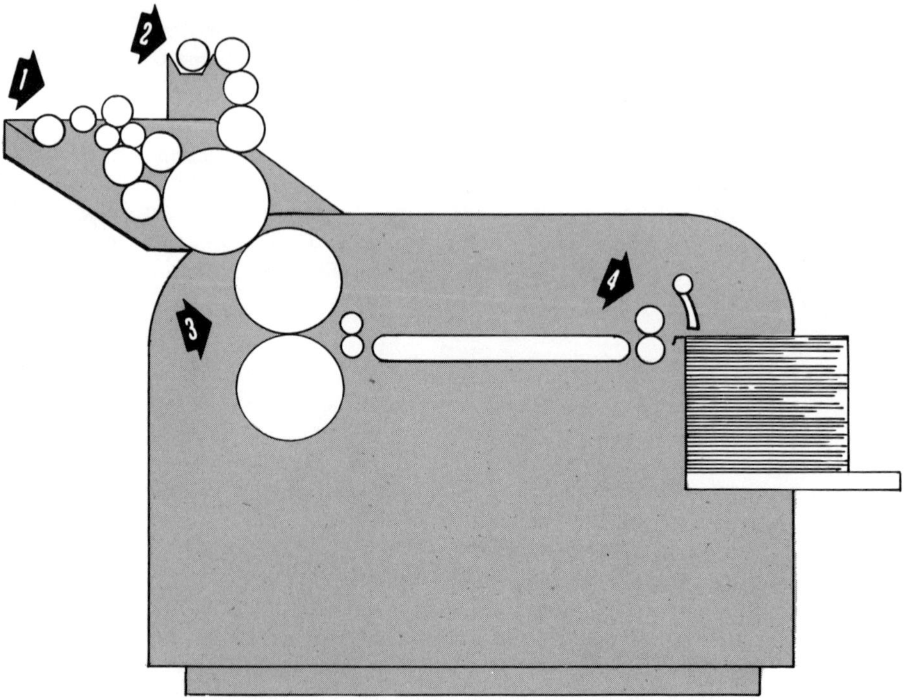

Offset printing. The offset printing process has four interdependent systems: inking, dampening, image transfer, and feeding. The adjustments and operation should achieve good, clean, sharp copies. 1. Inking system, 2. Dampening system, 3. Image transfer system, 4. Feeding system. (*Courtesy New England Printer and Publisher*)

old style. Roman typestyle developed in the early 17th century. It has strong, bold features and strokes of relatively uniform thickness, curves flowing into rounded serifs, and clear contours with no weak hairlines. Caslon is an example. The other Roman typestyles are transitional and modern. *See also* roman and typeface styles.

old-style figures. Numerals with ascenders and descenders, as opposed to lining figures, which align on the baseline. *See* figure for illustration.

one-em dash. A dash the space of an em in the typeface being used.

one-ply. *See* ply.

one-shot. One issue of a magazine rather than a series of issues.

one-up. Making one printing impression at a time, as opposed to ganging up more than one copy of the same image on a plate as in two-up, four-up, etc.

on-line. Refers to equipment directly controlled by a central processing unit, as opposed to off-line, which is not. For example, a phototypesetter on which corrections are made directly into the computer via a video terminal, with no paper or magnetic tape being used as an intermediate recording device. Also called in-line.

OP. *See* out of print.

opacity. **1.** The nontransparent property of paper which prevents type or images printed on the opposite side or on the adjoining sheet to show through. Papers have different amounts of opacity, from 0 to 100%, affected by thickness of the sheet and by clay and fillers added as the paper gets more white. Opacity of 65% means that 35% of the light that falls on the paper goes through. An opacity test, tests for the reflectance power of paper. **2.** The covering power of ink. An opaque ink will show its true color when printed over a previously printed color and conceal all color beneath it, whereas a transparent ink, used in four-color process printing, allows the colors beneath to show through.

opaque. **1.** Nontransparent, or not allowing light to pass through. **2.** To use an opaque solution to paint out areas on a film negative that are not to be reproduced on the plate. **3.** To paint resist on areas not to be etched on metal engravings.

opaque ink. Ink that completely covers what is beneath it. Opaque inks cannot be overprinted to create a range of colors as can transparent inks. *See also* flat color and transparent inks.

open-end envelopes. *See* envelope styles.

open shop. A plant in which employees may belong to a union but do not have to in order to hold their jobs, as opposed to a closed shop in which all employees must belong to a union.

optical alignment. A variation in aligning display type flush left. Characters not having straight vertical strokes are adjusted manually by the operator for handset type, or on the mechanical by the designer, so that stacked lines appear to align.

optical center. A point on the page or layout that appears to be the center. This is about 10% above the mathematical center.

optical character recognition scanner. The recognition of characters by an electronic device. The device optically scans written or printed data and generates their digital equivalents onto a recording medium. The original copy must be typed either with a specially designed alphabet or an alphabet in which each character is accompanied by a series of bar codes. The typewritten copy, including formating codes, is then put through a scanner that scans the copy to convert it to a paper or magnetic tape.

To make a correction, a new line or paragraph is typed, then referenced on the original sheet where it is to go. The OCR scans the insert first and retains it in its memory. When it sees the reference point it inserts it in the text. The variables of paper quality, ribbon quality, typewriter adjustment, scanner accuracy, and cleanliness must be properly balanced to keep errors in line. If the typesetting firm the publisher uses has a scanner, this is the least expensive input method for the publisher, when there are only minor corrections, as it requires only a typewriter and some special procedures. Using OCR, redundant keyboarding is eliminated.

Opti-Copy. Trade name for an optical imposition system, a camera system which combines camera and stripping processes in one operation. A punched paper tape is coded with imposition data and all makeup specifications. The tape controls camera and film movement. Copy mounted on the copyboard does not move.

Camera-ready pages are punched for register pins then placed on the copyboard of the camera. After each exposure the coded tape directs the movements of the camera to the correct position for the exposure of the next camera-ready page and so on until the entire piece of film has been exposed. The end product is composite film. The flat can then be masked and is ready for platemaking.

The Opti-Copy does not shoot halftones, only linework and text, but it is extremely timesaving and economical, by-passing the stripping operation. It also

(a)

Opti-copy. **a)** Copy is punched to register then mounted on copy board for shot. **b)** The copy board doesn't move, rather, the plate behind the camera moves in step and repeat fashion for exposures. **c)** An entire plate is made, thus bypassing the stripping of a flat. (*Courtesy Kingsport Press*)

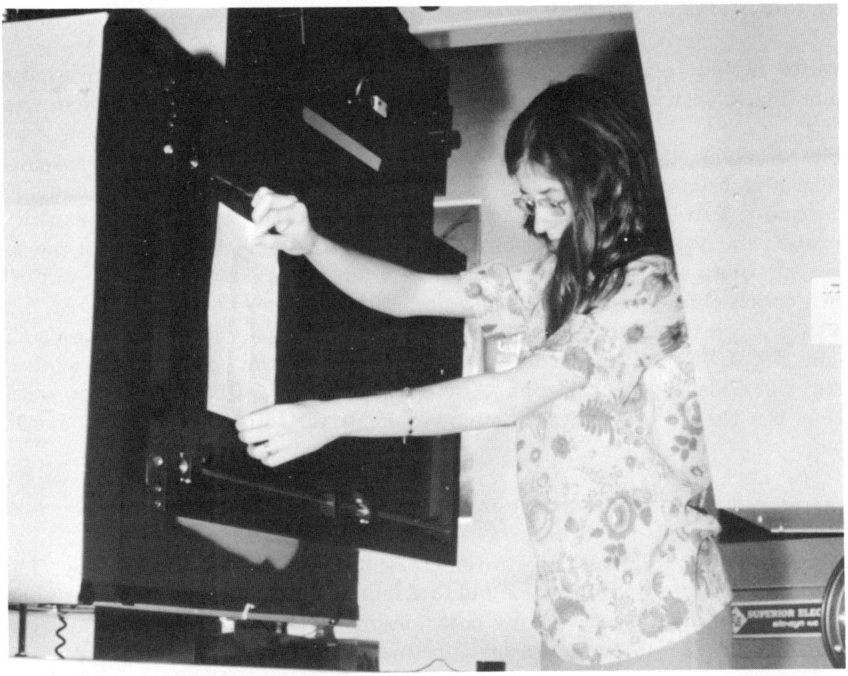

(b)

(c)

Opti-copy.

ensures perfect register for color separations because the film positions itself according to instructions coded into the machine, thus eliminating human error.

order of colors on press. Yellow, magenta, cyan, and black. The transparent subtractive primary colors act as filters. Magenta inks filter out green and allow *blue* and *red* to come through; cyan filters out red and lets *blue* and *green* come through; and yellow filters out blue, leaving *red* and *green.* When two of the subtractive colors are printed, and therefore two colors are filtered out, only the third comes through. By overlapping dots the resulting additive colors, *red, blue,* and *green,* create a full range of colors. This is also the order of colors on a Cromalin proof. If the darker colors were printed first, the lighter colors wouldn't take, since black gives the tone. Any color printed over black is only a mushy black, but the primary colors combine to create the full range of colors. *See also* color.

ornamented. A typeface that is embellished for decorative effect.

orthochromatic. Films that are used for black, white, or orange copy. They will not pick up non-reproducible blue guidelines. These films are used for photostats but cannot be used to copy color originals. The photographic emulsion is insensitive to red light and so is developed with a red safelight.

OS. *See* out of stock.

outline. A typeface that shows only the outline. The solid part of the characters has been chopped out or screened a different color.

Outline. (*Courtesy Graphics Modifier, Byers Corporation*)

outline halftone. Halftone in which all or part of the background has been eliminated to provide a clearer view of emphasized objects. *See also* silhouette halftone or silo.

Outline letter and shadow. (*Courtesy Graphics Modifier, Byers Corporation*)

outline letter and shadow. An outlined letter with a shadow behind to create the illusion of depth.

outline shaded. An outline letter shadowed with a darker color forming the depth dimension.

Outline shaded. (*Courtesy Graphics Modifier, Byers Corporation*)

out of print. The exhaustion of the publisher's present supply of books with no immediate plan to reprint.

out of register. The misalignment of one element superimposed over another such as in an overlay, or in printing several color plates to form a single image with a full range of colors. When color work is out of register, a thin line of a single color is visible to the eye in areas where that color has failed to combine properly with the other colors that have been printed. If all the color negatives have been burned to the same proof, a fuzzy line will show on the proof where the color work is out of register.

out of stock. The temporary exhaustion of the publisher's supply of books.

output. Output refers to a product, whereas input refers to data given to machinery or computer to create the product. For example, the processed tape from a computer which, in phototypesetting, runs the photo unit, or the type that has been set, and which comes out of the photo unit, are output.

overhang. A cover larger than the trim size of the pages it encloses. *See also* flush cover.

overlay. **1.** Shading films, or transparent paper or acetate placed over artwork for protection, containing instructions to the cameraman, platemaker, or printer, and showing the breakdown in mechanical color separations. Stripping films permit the artist to cut out the desired design and peel off unwanted portions, forming a window and giving register for set-ins and color work. Overlays are also available in the form of labels or transfer art to be shot as one piece with the art on the base mechanical. **2.** Transparent or translucent prints which, when placed one on the other, form a composite print.

overprinting. *See* imprint paragraph no. 2.

overrun or **overs.** A publication printed in excess of a specified quantity. There are excess charges when the client requests an overrun of a job already underway at the printer. Printers are allowed to overrun or underrun by a certain percentage, usually 10%, and charge for it. Overruns or underruns occur because it is impossible to predict how much to allow for spoilage during makeready, handling, and binding.

overset. Type or fillers set in excess of space needs in a publication. In page proofs, the editor must decide what to kill in order to make room for overset matter; have the overset matter killed; or save it for another use.

overwrap. A simple die-cut cardboard wrapping used to cover a book for protection in mailing. An overwrap is not as sturdy as an individual carton made for a book.

ozalid. A photocopying process used to produce proofs of phototypeset material. The original positive film or transparency is placed onto photo-sensitized paper. Light is shone through to destroy light-sensitive dyes. The unexposed dye protected by the opaque image is chemically fixed. The simpler equipment develops prints by inserting them into a covered cylinder containing ammonia. An ozalid makes a positive from a positive, and copies retain accurate size in the developing. Prints can be made on various types of sensitized substrates. The background is usually pale and the lines are usually blue or brown. Not to be confused with diazo or dylux.

P

package sale. A journalistic agreement in which the editor buys manuscript and illustrations for one price.

packing. Layers of paper under the printing plate or the blanket used to ensure a perfect impression during printing. *See also* makeready.

padding. **1.** Adding extra space or making illustrations larger in order to fill out the size of a book. **2.** Adding extra time to a production schedule in case deadlines are not met along the way. **3.** Converting paper into pads by trimming, brushing cement across one edge, and applying cloth. Cardboard may be interleaved with the paper for backing and pads cut apart when they are dry.

page. One side of a leaf of a book, either right-hand or left-hand side, as you face the open spread. Page numbers always begin on the right so the right-hand page always has an odd number, and the left even numbers. Pages are made from folded trimmed sheets. *See also* leaf.

page flex. A paper test for the strength of the page which is flexed back and forth a certain number of times after adhesive binding.

page forms. A section of the publication which is printed with one printing plate. A page form is most commonly 16, 32 or 64 pages. *See also* one-up, two-up.

page makeup. *See* makeup and photocomposing.

page makeup devices. *See* computer assisted makeup.

page proof. A proof that shows type and illustrations in place as they will appear in the printed piece. Corrections are marked on the page proofs and made by the compositor before the final plates for printing are made. Corrections are more expensive in page proofs than corrections made in galleys.

page pull. A test for adhesive binding done so that the customer is assured that the pages will not fall out of the book.

pagination. 1. The process of numbering pages of a book, in correct sequence. 2. The total number of pages in the book. 3. *See* photocomposing.

pallet. A portable platform used to move or store materials such as paper, binding material or packages in a warehouse.

pamphlet. A small booklet of a few pages, used for promotion or information.

pamphlet binding. Binding of booklets or pamphlets, usually with saddle-wire or side-wire stitching.

panchromatic. The emulsion of photographic film that is sensitive to all colors visible to the human eye.

pantograph. An instrument for copying originally used in the 19th century to engrave matrices from patterns. A pantograph is comprised of a fixed pivot, a tracing point, and a pencil point, all held in relation to each other. It is used to make enlarged or reduced copies of lettering or drawings, or for making patterns for type matrices from large-scale original drawings. The use of the pantograph revolutionized the production of matrices and so resulted in a proliferation of type designs, many of which were exotic, grotesque, and illegible. Much work formerly done by pantograph is now done by Photostat or a lucy.

Pantone Matching System. Brand name for a color-matching system used by publishers and printers to identify and specify inks for printing. Each shade has a number and a formula as to how exactly to mix the ink to achieve that shade.

paperback. A book bound in paper as opposed to cloth. It can be either a quality paperback (sold by direct mail, in bookstores, and through regular bookselling channels) or a mass-market paperback (sold through newsstands, grocery stores, etc., as well as through regular channels).

paper basis weight. *See also* basis weight or basic weight.

paperboard. A fibrous sheet 12 pt. or more in thickness. It is heavier, thicker, and more rigid than paper.

paperbound. *See* paperback.

paper color. Paper colors vary from cool to warm shades. Type is read most easily against a soft (yellowish) white, while the process colors reproduce best on neutral white paper.

paper cutter. A machine that contains a very fast cutter blade or knife, and is run by a trained operator who cuts stacks of paper to a specific size.

EQUIVALENT WEIGHTS

In reams of 500 sheets, basis weights in bold type

Grade of Paper	BOOK 25 x 38	BOND 17 x 22	COVER 20 x 26	BRISTOL 22½ x 28½	INDEX 25½ x 30½	TAG 24 x 36	GRAMMAGE (gsm)
Book	**30**	12	16	20	25	27	44
	40	16	22	27	33	36	59
	45	18	25	30	37	41	67
	50	20	27	34	41	45	74
	60	24	33	40	49	55	89
	70	28	38	47	57	64	104
	80	31	44	54	65	73	118
	90	35	49	60	74	82	133
	100	39	55	67	82	91	148
	120	47	66	80	98	109	178
Bond	33	**13**	18	22	27	30	49
	41	**16**	22	27	33	37	61
	51	**20**	28	34	42	46	75
	61	**24**	33	41	50	56	90
	71	**28**	39	48	58	64	105
	81	**32**	45	55	67	74	120
	91	**36**	50	62	75	83	135
	102	**40**	56	69	83	93	151
Cover	91	36	**50**	62	75	82	135
	110	43	**60**	74	90	100	163
	119	47	**65**	80	97	108	176
	146	58	**80**	99	120	134	216
	164	65	**90**	111	135	149	243
	183	72	**100**	124	150	166	271
Bristol	100	39	54	**67**	81	91	148
	120	47	65	**80**	98	109	178
	148	58	81	**100**	121	135	219
	176	70	97	**120**	146	162	261
	207	82	114	**140**	170	189	306
	237	93	130	**160**	194	216	351
Index	110	43	60	74	**90**	100	163
	135	53	74	91	**110**	122	203
	170	67	93	115	**140**	156	252
	208	82	114	140	**170**	189	328
Tag	110	43	60	74	90	**100**	163
	137	54	75	93	113	**125**	203
	165	65	90	111	135	**150**	244
	192	76	105	130	158	**175**	284
	220	87	120	148	180	**200**	326
	275	109	151	186	225	**250**	407

Paper basis weights.

paper grades. Paper is categorized in terms of size, weight, and grain, and defined in terms of use; such as offset, book, newsprint, or bond. The following is a summary of the most common classifications, and the size in which a ream is weighed in order to determine the basis weight for that classification:

Book (25" x 38") used for trade and textbooks, available in almost any bulk, made in antique or smooth finishes. Book papers are less expensive than text papers.

Text (25" x 38") used for announcements, booklets, and brochures, and noted for interesting textures and attractive colors.

Coated (25" x 38") used for high-quality printing because of greater surface smoothness and ink receptivity. *See also* cast coated, coateds or coated paper, and machine coated.

Offset (25" x 38") used for offset printing because of its sizing for moisture resistance, and surface treatment to resist picking. Most offset papers can be used for letterpress, but few letterpress papers are suitable for offset.

Newsprint (24" x 36") chiefly groundwood used for newspapers, most commonly used in 30-lb basis weight.

Bond (17" x 22") used for letters and business forms, having surfaces that readily accept ink and can be erased. Four 8½" x 11" sheets can be cut from a 17" x 22" sheet without waste.

Index (22½" x 35" and 25½" x 30½") used when inexpensive stiff paper is required. Index is receptive to ink, available in both smooth and antique finish.

Tag (24" x 36") used for printing, stamping, and writing, has good water resistance, bending and folding qualities, good tearing, bursting, and tensile strength. Tag can be made from groundwood and some waste papers.

Cover (20" x 26") often heavier weights of coated and text papers used for covers on booklets. Some papers are made specifically for covers, having dimensional stability, uniform printing surface, folding qualities, and durability.

Recycled paper is used in newsprint, board, and the more utilitarian grades, but is a problem for printing because of quality and cost. The issue is controversial, and some say it is better and cheaper to use wood fiber. No new book papermaking facilities built in the last 10 years have been designed around recycled paper.

papermaking. Paper is made from cellulose fiber that comes from pulping wood or from waste chips of wood from sawmills. The pulp is either mechanical, chemical, or semichemical.

Mechanical pulping produces groundwood pulp. The first step is to tumble the logs of trees, to strip the logs of their bark, and to grind the peeled logs against a revolving grindstone or disk mill until the logs are reduced to fiber. Groundwood pulp is the most economical because all the wood is used, but its impurities can cause discoloration and weakening. It is mainly used for newsprint, or for parts of magazines where it adds bulk, opacity, and compressibility.

Chemical pulp, made by either the sulfite, soda, or kraft processes, produces freesheet, a more permanent paper. A chipper chews the logs into postage-stamp size wood chips that are stored in massive mountains of chips. A cooking process separates the cellulose fibers from the impurities. At this stage the pulp could be made into unbleached kraft paper for paper wrapping and bags. Pulp converted to paper is bleached white. More water is added, and the fibers are cut, bruised, crushed, and frayed to better mat together on the papermaking machine. This mixture is called furnish. It is the beating, refining, and sizing that largely determines the characteristics such as strength and quality of the paper. Rosin size is added to give water repellency for use in offset printing and for writing with pen and ink. Fillers such as clay are added for smoothness and opacity. Dyes and pigments can be added. The combination of fiber, size, fillers, and alum is known as stock. This is stored in large tanks or chests at the front of the papermaking machine.

The fiber, chemical, and water mixture is jetted out of the head of the papermaking machine called the Fourdrinier machine. The paper-forming section of the modern Fourdrinier paper machine is known as the wet end. The furnish flows across the width of the machine, up to 20-ft. wide, on an endless fine-mesh screen, called the wire. The fibers tend to align themselves with the direction the wire is traveling, but they interweave because of the forward motion of the wire and the added side-to-side motion of the machine from the headbox end. Water is sucked away through the wire and the matted web fibers of the stock tighten. At the point where the sheet is still wet enough to be compressed, the dandy roll helps distribute fibers. If the surface of the dandy roll contains soldered lettering or a design, a watermark is made.

As the paper leaves the wire it still contains 75–85% water. The sheet passes through a number of presses, each consisting of two rolls. At the end of the wire, a huge blotter, called the felt, picks up the mat of newly made paper. The paper passes over, under and around steam-heated rolls enclosed in the machine that dries the paper. Water is squeezed, sucked, and dried out of the paper and recycled. The paper is then pressed between metal rolls if it is to have a smooth and glossy finish ironed on. This is called calendering and is done on a calender stack; vertical cast steel rolls that have polished ground surfaces. Calendered papers are known as machine finish papers.

Supercalendering is a subsequent operation done also in a vertical stack, but the rolls are alternately steel and either cotton or compressed paper. Supercalendering is done for both coated and uncoated papers.

Coated papers are made because of the popularity of reproducing black-and-white and color photographs. Finer halftone screens with stronger definition, improved density and greater color can be reproduced on coated paper which has greater opacity, smoothness, and affinity for ink. Fine papers are coated by rolls, with air knives, or by trailing blades, with white clay powders and adhesives. The paper coated on the papermaking machine is known as machine coated, those coated off the machine are known as off machine coated.

After coating, the paper is calendered again. Papers can be coated on one side only (known as C1S) or two sides (C2S).

Paper is cut from giant logs into smaller rolls by razor-sharp disks in a process called slitting. Rotary cutters convert rolls to sheets if sheets are being provided instead of rolls.

Papers for offset printing require more critical manufacture than paper for letterpress in order to prevent picking on the press and to ensure that they maintain a certain tolerance in moisture content.

Paper must be stored in a dry place, and kept away from water coolers, air conditioners, or other equipment that might cause it to absorb moisture. It

Fourdrinier papermaking machine. (*Courtesy American Paper Institute*)

shouldn't be unwrapped until ready for use. Brand-name paper should be used. So-called "special" buys are often rejects, mill ends, or runs of questionable quality. The better paper mills have standardized papers, and any variance from standardization can cause problems. A paper salesman can apprise his client of manufacturer's studies regarding surface qualities, quality control of alkalinity, moisture content, etc.

Print quality is affected by color of the paper, brightness, opacity, smoothness, gloss, refractiveness. Type is most easily read against a soft yellowish white, while the process colors reproduce best on neutral white paper.

paper master. A paper printing plate for an offset-duplicator on which the image is hand-drawn, typewritten, or imprinted by electrophotography.

paper negative. **1.** Paper used instead of film in the back of a camera. The paper negative can be developed into a positive print. **2.** A photostat made out of negative paper. *See also* negative.

paper surface efficiency. The printability of a sheet of paper, determined by how much ink the paper absorbs, the smoothness of the surface, and the evenness of the caliper.

paper tape. A continuous strip of paper on which information is recorded in the form of punched holes. Some typesetting systems are driven by paper tapes. There are five to eight channels on the tape, on which a unique pattern of holes represents a single character. These channels are similar to those of magnetic recording tape. The codes on the tape signal a combination of electrical ons and offs for the typesetting unit. This works something like a player piano, or morse code.

paper testing. Tests for basis weight, brightness, caliper, gloss, oil absorption, smoothness, opacity, porosity, stiffness, tear, and tensile strength of paper. These tests are necessary for product uniformity, but do not predict the printing characteristics of the paper. The most reliable tests, especially for lithography, are done on the production press. There are not yet any laboratory tests that correlate with performance on an offset press. Letterpress testing for smoothness, ink receptivity, and coverage can be done on a proof press. One example is the Vandercook Universal Test Press. For predictions of picking, ink coverage, receptivity, and even trapping, the IGT Printability Tester can be used. There are also some printability testers for gravure. *See also* burst test, porosity, porosity test, tensile test.

paragraph. A block of copy containing related ideas. *See also* flush paragraph, hanging indention, and paragraph indent.

paragraph indent. The amount of space indented before the first word in a new paragraph. A paragraph indent is measured in ems.

paragraph openers. Signs used in the copy to indicate a paragraph indent. *See* proofreader's marks for illustrations.

parameter. 1. The limits of any given system in the printing industry. *See also* typographic parameters. 2. A special piece of data used as a condition for some kind of computer processing.

parchment. A sheet made from goat, sheep, or other animal skin, treated to obtain a writing surface. Imitation parchment used for diplomas and certificates, is made from paper impregnated with vegetable oils. *See also* vellum.

parentheses. Marks to indicate a thought within a thought. The sequence is

({ [( )] })

({ [( )] })

Order of parentheses.

part title. Heading which begins a division of a book. A part title usually appears alone on a page preceding the text it introduces. Not to be confused with the bastard title or the half title.

pass. A complete cycle of one program from start to finish, from input to output on a machine run. For example, a press sheet usually gets impressions of all four colors on one pass through the press.

pasteboard. Binding board made out of one or more plies of laminated chipboard. *See also* cardboard.

pasted oak. A lightweight board used in hard-cover book bindings. It is not as strong as binders board. Pasted oak is unstable, and humidity can cause problems with glue and board warping. For quality 8½" x 11" hardcover books, binders board should be used rather than pasted oak.

paster. Device on a web press that applies paste to one or both sides of the paper in the direction of travel in order for pasting to replace stitching in finished booklets. Not to be confused with flying paster, which is a device that splices rolls of paper together for the web.

paste-up. **1.** A layout with all elements of type and illustration pasted in place with wax or rubber cement. A paste-up can be used as a guide to the compositor for makeup. Elements can be lifted, moved around, and restuck. Also called dummy. **2.** A mechanical of camera-ready copy in position to be photographed and reproduced as a printed page.

patch film. Strips or pieces of film added to film already prepared for platemaking. Film is often patched into a negative in lieu of having an entire page reset. However, if type is involved, it must match, in size and density, the original type on the film to be patched.

patching. Setting corrections in film or on repro and then stripping them into the one-piece film or mechanical.

p.e. Printer's error. A mistake made by the typesetter or printer. The publisher does not pay for this type of correction. *See also* a.a.

pebbling. A textured or rippled finish made before or after printing by embossing and debossing fine designs. It is difficult to print on rough papers, therefore printing is usually done before pebbling the paper.

penalty copy. Copy which is difficult to typeset because of heavy corrections, lines in foreign language, faintness of typing, or illegibility. The typesetter charges extra to set such copy.

penny-saver envelopes. Envelopes that seal like ordinary envelopes with one unsealed flap to facilitate automatic insertion. They are largely used for third-class matter. Catalog envelopes made like penny-saver envelopes are called booklet envelopes. *See also* envelope styles.

perfect binding. *See* adhesive binding.

perfecting or **perfector press.** A printing press that prints on both sides of the sheet in one pass through the press, with each blanket cylinder acting as the impression cylinder for the other. *See also* cylinders for offset press.

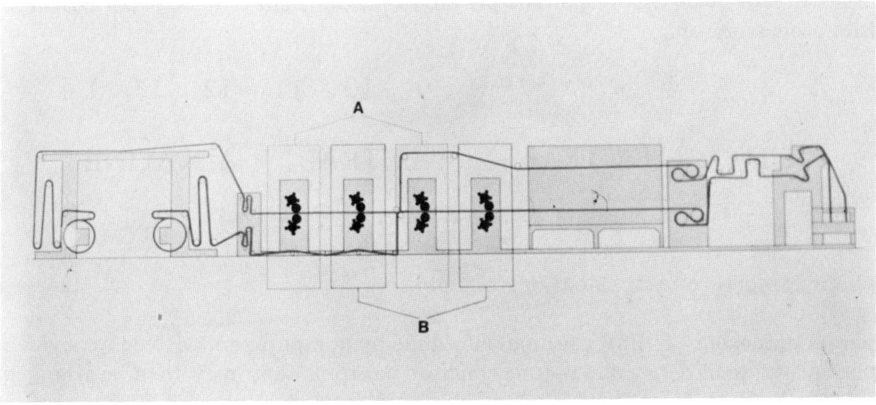

Perfector press. (*Courtesy Kingsport Press*)

perforating. Punching a line of small holes in a sheet so that it may easily be torn off or folded. In letterpress, perforating is done on the press by steel perforating rules. In offset and gravure printing it is done as part of the binding operation. Perforating rules are steel rules, 1- or 2-pt. wide and higher than type high, that are made up in the form of the desired perforation on the press.

perforator. 1. A machine that produces small holes in a sheet to facilitate tearing after the sheet is bound. 2. A unit on a keyboard that punches holes in a paper tape for each character to be typeset according to the computer code.

permanent inks. Inks that do not fade or change color when exposed to artificial light or to the sun, as opposed to fugitive inks, which do. Permanent inks are especially good for signs and posters. Also called fast inks.

permissions. Formal statement in writing that a publisher has permission to reproduce something from another work.

personalize. To type a letter with an automatic typewriter or word processor so that it looks like a personal letter.

pH. A symbol expressing acidity or alkalinity of a solution on a scale having values ranging from 0 to 14 with 7 representing neutrality. The lower numbers represent acidity, and the higher numbers represent alkalinity of a solution. Acids and alkalines have different electrical charges and are attracted to each other. An acid solution is positive, i.e., its molecule can give up a proton to an alkaline molecule, whereas an alkaline solution is negative, i.e., its molecule can give up electrons to an acidic solution's molecule. During the press run the pH factor should not fall too low or it can cause nondrying of ink, short plate life, glazing of rollers, and copy fading. For example, excessive acid fountain solution holds the ink from the image. The pH factor is important in inks, paper coatings, film processors, etc.

1 2 3 4 5 6 7 8 9 10 11 12 13 14

ACID NEUTRAL NEUTRAL ALKALINE

pH factor. A scale of values of acidity and alkalinity in a substance.

photo agencies. *See* stock cut or stock photos.

photocomposing. **1.** Full page makeup done by computer and viewed on a video display terminal. Continuous-tone, line, or halftone copy may then be arranged on paper, film, microfilm, or offset plates for reproduction. *See also* computer assisted makeup. Also called aerial composition. **2.** To expose photosensitive materials onto film or press plates using a photocomposing machine such as in step-and-repeat for jobs that are two-up, four-up, etc. Not to be confused with photocomposition.

photocomposite. The photographic assembly of several color transparencies into one unit. Each part of the transparencies is masked, registered, and exposed with proper color balance and enlargement to produce a single finished composite in the darkroom, and not with the camera.

photocomposition. *See* phototypesetting.

photocopy. **1.** A duplicate photograph, as opposed to the original. A photocopy usually refers to that made on paper rather than on film, although any kind of photographic work that depends on light could be called photocopying. **2.** The correct generic term for the trade name Photostat. **3.** Loosely used to describe copy reproduced on electrostatic copiers such as Xerox or IBM.

photodisplay. Large type for headings or display, set photographically on repro paper or film. It is similar to phototype except in size, and it is set by hand on a Photo Typositor, not by computer. Also called display type.

PROGRESS

Photodisplay type.

photodisplay font. A grid or negative film strip carrying the alphabet of a display font used in a Photo Typositor.

photodisplay unit. *See* Photo Typositor.

photoengraving. A relief printing plate, either an individual unit, or in multiple page forms, produced by photo-chemistry, and used in letterpress printing. Actually engraving is a misnomer because it loosely refers to a cut when it should refer to the intaglio process. Also called engraving, block and cut.

photogelatin. *See* collotype.

photographic imposition system. A system that assembles book pages into finished film flats ready for exposure to printing plates. The use of a page organizer, a page assembler, and an automated camera obviate the need for stripping, and pages are shot on camera in groups, not individually.

Individual pages are sorted into a rack in proper sequence for laying out into press imposition forms. Sorted pages are then glued in position on a carrier sheet. The carrier sheet is accordion folded and fed around a drum and onto a backlighted feed board where punched sprocket holes fit onto pins to provide precise pin registration. A heat sealer bonds the page to the carrier. The movements of the carrier sheet are controlled automatically by computer circuitry to within hundredths of an inch. Carrier-mounted pages are moved to the camera which has automated exposure, film movement, and copy movement controls. The pin register is preserved by punched roll film fed over pin rollers in the camera back. The system is geared for high production volumes. Also called optical imposition system. *See also* Opti-Copy.

Photographic Mechanical Transfer. Photosensitive papers manufactured by Eastman Kodak for making enlarged or reduced copies in a process camera; for making contact proofs of line or halftone negatives in a contact frame; for making positive prints in a diffusion transfer processor; and for making photo-repros. The papers for each use are chemically sensitized differently. PMT prints offer an alternative to halftone stripping because the prints can be pasted right onto the mechanicals for shooting. Abbreviated PMT.

photographic paper. Chemically sensitized paper used for photographic printing. When exposed, an image forms where the light shines through the negative.

photo-graphics. Achieving a special effect by cutting apart the positive and negative of a piece of artwork and mounting them in register in an unusual combination.

photography. *See* additive color, camera, film, negative, subtractive color and process camera.

photogravure. Printing from an intaglio plate that is etched below the surface from a screened photographic image. Commonly called gravure or rotogravure.

photolettering. *See* display type and Photo Typositor.

photolithography. Lithography from photomechanically prepared plates, as opposed to hand-drawn stones or plates. *See also* offset lithography.

photomechanical. 1. Any platemaking process from photographic positives or negatives exposed onto photo-sensitive coated plates, rather than a lithographic stone prepared by hand. 2. Any exposure of a photographic image by the use of the photographic process. 3. In composition, the complete assembly of all the elements on a page in film positive on a transparent film base, from which diazo proofs can be pulled, and from which one-piece film negatives can be made by contacting for the production of offset printing plates.

photomontage. *See* montage.

photo-offset. An offset printing process in which a negative is used to prepare metal plates in a photochemical process. *See also* litho or lithography, offset, and planography.

photopolymer plates. Printing plates made of light-sensitive, polymerizable plastic used in letterpress, letterset, and offset printing.

Plastics with simple atoms are known as monomers. When these link together in chains and solidify or form a new substance, they are called polymers. *Photopolymers* are those in which light, rather than heat or chemistry, causes the linking.

photoprint. 1. A final proof in phototypesetting with all typographic elements in position, ready to be pasted into a mechanical for shooting. A photoprint shows the quality of the shooting. It serves the same purpose as a reproduction proof in hot metal typesetting. Also called photoproof, photorepro, or photocopy. 2. An artwork proof not of shooting quality, and used only for position, such as a photostat.

photorepro. Reproduction-quality proof produced by phototypesetting on photo-sensitive paper or by contact printing phototypeset materials through a film negative. It is used for pasting up, as opposed to a galley proof, which is for reading only and is not reproducible. Abbreviated repro. Also called photoproof.

photosensitive. Chemically wet paper or film that can receive light which will create an image in areas where radiant energy hits the substrate, or surface. It is then processed in a tray or processor in which the image is fixed to keep it from further developing.

It is possible to sensitize almost any surface and print on it photographically—paper, glass, metal, cloth, stone, etc. High contrast substrates make everything either white or black. Low contrast substrates distinguish between subtle shades of gray. Orthochromatic films or papers are sensitive to white and blue light but not to red. Panchromatic film is sensitive to all the colors.

Photostat. Trade name for a photoprint, commonly known as a stat, used to show size and crop on a dummy or mechanical. Original continuous-tone copy is photographed, and a paper negative is made, from which the positive stat is made, having either glossy or matte finish. Some systems by-pass the negative stage and make direct positives.

A Photostat photocopying machine uses photographic paper instead of film and it has a prism so that the paper negatives are right reading instead of being flopped. Photostats are generally not shooting quality. Also called a stat.

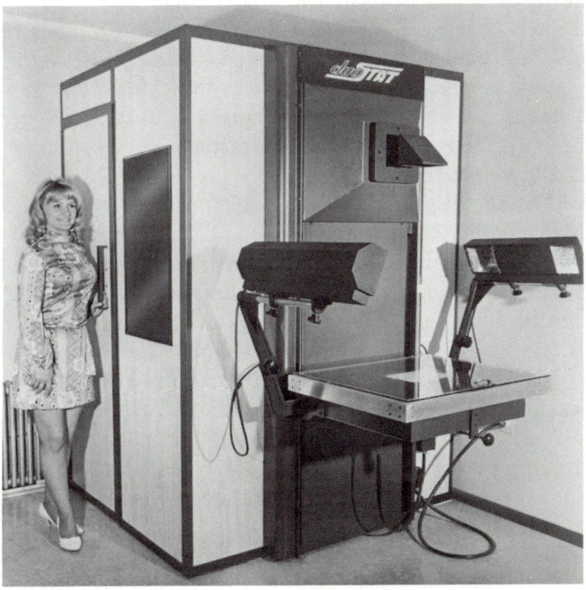

Photostat machine containing copyboard, vacuum film holder, backlight, processor, and solution, requires no darkroom, no plumbing or special wiring. It enlarges and reduces and reproduces positive or negative photostats or films, screen prints or special effects. (*Courtesy Duostat Corporation*)

phototype. Type composed photographically on a phototypesetting machine.

phototypesetting or **phototypography.** The combination of electronic and photographic methods to set type. Images of type characters are projected onto photosensitive film or paper, producing a positive image that is then used for a mechanical or photomechanical, from which the film for offset plates is produced. There are four basic steps to phototypesetting:

1. Input of alphanumeric data, or copy keyboarding. **2.** Input of the typographic parameters, or markup translated into machine language. **3.** Processing and output. **4.** Makeup.

In a phototypesetting system, the manuscript is typed onto a keyboard, and a computer is used to make end-of-line decisions such as those relating to hyphenation and justification. In most systems the output is a paper or magnetic tape which drives the photounit. In direct input the keyboard and video unit are attached to the phototypesetting unit.

The photounit produces the output or typesetting. It makes use of electronics to select the keyboard character from a disc or film negative and expose it in proper position on a photographic medium such as paper or acetate. Phototype is erroneously known as cold type, because in hot and cold type, which use strike-on impression, there is an exchange of ink to paper, whereas in phototype there is no ink, and no impression, only photography.

Photocomposition provides sharper type than hot-metal type because there is no ink squeeze which tends to print the letterforms irregularly. Better letterfit can also be obtained because there is no limitation as in a piece of metal. With the use of prisms, the type can also be extended, condensed, or otherwise altered.

The photographic and electronic industries' and newspaper publishers' concern for more efficient, less expensive prepress and editorial operations have combined to revolutionize the type composition industry that was technologically backwards a few decades ago.

The growth of offset lithography gave rise to the invention of phototypesetting devices which eliminated the steps required to go from metal type through proofs to printing plates. Line-casting machines were prevalent until the invention of the Linofilm machine in the fifties. The first generation of photosetters were modeled on the Linotype and Monotype operating principles.

Phototype is less expensive than hot-metal type. Also, with phototypesetting, it is possible to go directly from film to platemaking without having to make a mechanical, because the type can be set on film and the compositor can make up a flat from which page proofs are pulled and plates made. This saves steps, and the printer is making plates from first-generation material. This is an advantage as far as the type is concerned, but a disadvantage if the illustrations are not well produced at the composition stage.

In the mid sixties the quality of repro was not good and thus justified setting on film, having the compositor do makeup. Repro paper is now of a stable quality, so there is no justification for setting on film, and it is now less expensive for the designer to make up mechanicals than for the compositor to do so.

The second-generation phototypesetters, started in 1954, were electronics oriented, computerized, sophisticated, high-speed devices. But these were too

Phototypesetting processor generates either film or paper for platemaking or paste-ups. (*Courtesy Autologic Incorporated*)

slow to keep up with the capabilities of computers and led to the production of third-generation, cathode ray tube (CRT) typesetters. Digitized characters are formed in these devices by assembling tiny dots or lines on the face of the CRT at tremendous speed.

Digitization allows enormous flexibility in the creation of type images. Type can be produced in an infinite number of sizes, letter widths can be varied, characters can be slanted left or right, and any combinations of these forms can be produced. The dots are created in different densities, depending on the manufacturer, from 975 to 5000 dots per inch.

Some phototypesetting systems now allow the operator to arrange and manipulate, on the screen of the visual display terminal, characters, words, and blocks of copy to fit the desired space. Whole newspaper pages can be made up on the screen. Line art and photographs can be positioned and some machines can even show the work in color.

There are over 300 direct input typesetters, which produce images only as fast as the typist can operate the keyboard. These are relatively low-priced machines with price dependent on capabilities. To take advantage of the ability of the typesetting unit to set type far faster than the keyboard operator, recording media has been added to enable faster production.

Magnetic cassettes are of low capacity, and paper tape may tear, so other recording devices are used such as high-capacity, but expensive rigid disks and different kinds and sizes of floppy disks. An advantage of disks is that they allow for random access in retrieving data at high speed. Bubble memory is being developed that will allow recording the Bible on a disk the size of a quarter. Systems of data management are used so that the location of information is known and it can be quickly recalled.

Photo Typositor. Trade name of a projection-type photographic machine for display typesetting which utilizes a filmstrip font. It will enlarge, condense, expand, slant, interlock, overlap, distort, angle, and letterspace when hand-operated by the typesetter. Also called Typositor.

Typositor

photounit. The unit, in phototypesetting, actually responsible for setting and exposing fonts of type onto photosensitive film or paper for output.

pi. Type that is mixed up accidentally and is unusable until put back in order. Originally, hot metal type that had been spilled. Not to be confused with pi characters.

pica. 1. Printer's unit of measure. 12 pt. = 1 pica, and 6 picas = one inch for practical measurements. Actually, 6 picas = 0.996 inch. In the pica system, the use of fractions is unnecessary. 2. A typewriter that types 10 characters to the inch. So called because its letters are 1 pica high and 6 lines to the inch. Twelve-point type used to be called pica type. An elite typewriter also writes 6 lines to the inch, but differs from a pica typewriter in that there are 12 characters to the horizontal inch.

pi characters. Characters not usually included in the font, such as accented letters, math signs, reference signs, ligatures. Also called sort.

pica grid. A Bristol board printed with a grid comprised of 1-pica squares. It eliminates premeasuring when used for layouts and pasteups.

pica em. A 12-pt. em, i.e., an em in a font that is 12 pts. high. *See also* em.

pica ruler or **pica stick.** A ruler with one edge measuring in picas and points.

pica type. Typewriter type that is 10 characters to the inch, as opposed to elite type, which is 12 characters to the inch. Its name derives from the fact that its letters are 1 pica high, 6 lines to the inch. (What is now called 12-pt. type used to be called "pica.") A typewriter with elite type also writes 6 lines to the inch. It differs from a pica typewriter only in that there are 12 elite characters to the horizontal inch as against 10 pica characters.

picking. Lifting of the coating of the surface of the paper onto blankets or plates. The coating is then transferred to the ink rollers absorbing moisture and creating voids in the final printed image. Picking affects printability and may appear as small white specks in the solid printed area of a paper's surface. It occurs when the pulling force, or tack, of the ink is greater than the strength of the surface of the paper. Highly bulked papers are often fluffy and can cause picking.

pick up. To reuse previously printed material. Abbreviated p.u.

pictograph. Drawings that carry meaning by attempting to duplicate real objects in a one-to-one relationship, as opposed to an ideograph, which symbolizes concepts. As pictographs and ideographs were drawn more quickly, and became less accurate, they evolved into an alphabet.

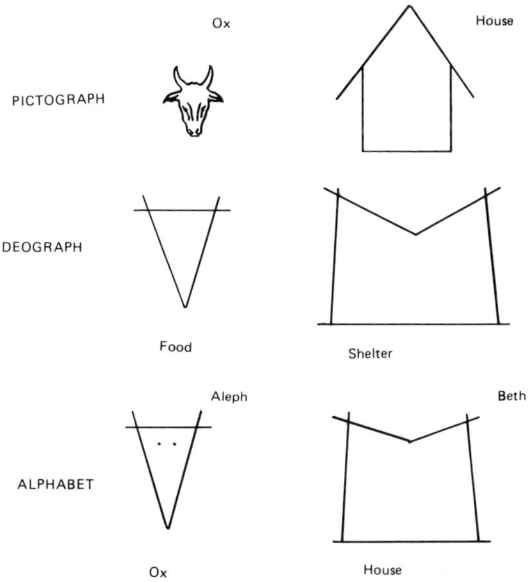

Pictograph.

pictorial statistics. The use of symbols or pictures to represent figures or percentages rather than the usual graph or wedge of pie often used to present percentages.

piece fraction. Combining two matrices to make a fraction when a matrix for the desired fraction is not available. For example 3/4 in which 3 is one piece and 4 is the other piece. In phototype this is often done by using superior and inferior figures combined with a dash. *See also* fractions.

pied. *See* pi.

pigment. The mineral, organic, or dye particles that give ink its color, determine its bleed capacity, and contribute to its opacity and permanence. Pigment particles are fine solid particles which are insoluable. Offset inks are usually made from coal tar, a by-product in the manufacture of coke and fuel gas from coal.

pinhole. A small light-passing hole in the emulsion of a negative. Pinholes must be opaqued before platemaking.

pinholing. Small holes in a printed surface that occur when the printing ink fails to cover a surface completely.

pinks. Pink proofs sometimes sent from the typesetter for use in making a dummy.

pin register. A system of precision registering by the use of accurately punched holes and special graphic arts pins used to secure proper register or fit of colors in platemaking, film, overlay work, and on presses. Copy, film, masks, etc., are punched with a register punch similar to a three-hole binder punch, and the punched holes are carefully placed over precisely positioned register pins, or studs. The pin register is timesaving for printers and compositors when multi-image or corrective work is being done on the negative, and it eliminates the human error inherent in lining up register marks by eye.

piracy. Infringement of the copyright law.

pix. Abbreviation meaning the plural of photograph.

plagiarize. To present material belonging to another source as one's own original ideas.

plain type. Standard typefaces or logos that have not been modified in any way from their original design.

planer. A flat block of wood used in hot metal type to push down the type in the form to a perfectly flat printing surface during lockup.

planography. A printing process in which the image to be printed and the non-image area of the plate are on the same surface, thus in the same plane. In relief printing the image area is raised, and in intaglio printing, the image area is cut below the surface. Lithography is planographic printing, and offset lithography is the commercial form. *See also* lithography and offset lithography.

plant cost. The original costs incurred in order to produce a book including editorial, design, composition, and any cost that will not be repeated in a reprint but will benefit the book over its entire life. Paper, printing, and binding costs are considered manufacturing costs. Plant costs and manufacturing costs are used in estimating the viability of a publication.

plastic binding. *See* comb binding and mechanical binding.

plastic coated stock. *See* acetate, lamination, mylar, and synthetic papers.

plate. 1. The surface from which a print is made, such as a halftone engraving, etching, electrotype, or offset plate, that bears the image to be reproduced. The metal, rubber, synthetic rubber, or plastic surface is treated to carry an image to the printing surface on the printing press. Plates used can be either originals or duplicates. 2. A full-page illustration on smooth or coated paper, printed separately from the text and inserted into the book. *See also* tip-in and wrap.

plate finish. 1. A smooth, hard paper finish achieved by calendering. 2. To mechanically change the formation of dots on photoengravings, for letterpress printing, in order to increase or decrease tonal values. *See also* dot etching.

plateless printing. *See* electrostatic printing, ink-jet printing, and thermography.

platemaking. In all printing plates, the area to be printed and the nonprinting area must stand apart. In letterpress platemaking, the printing area is raised. In gravure printing, the printing area is lowered. And in offset printing, both areas are on the same plane, but treated chemically so that the printing area rejects it. All of these plates can be made from photographing original artwork which produces a film negative. In letterpress, only the engravings, i.e., the illustrations, are produced from photography, the type is set in hot metal and locked into a form. The plates for each printing process differ as to the metal, chemicals, and processors used.

Lasers are now being used to eliminate the film step and go right from the digital codes of a computer-based typesetting system and electronic scanners to the generation of images onto offset plates or gravure cylinders. The laser scans paste-up copy, and electronic signals control a second laser, which scans and exposes the light-sensitive plate coating. The laser generates enough light energy to burn away solid material. *See also* gravure, letterpress, lithography, and surface plates.

platen press. A letterpress in which both the paper and the plate form lie flat and come in direct contact with each other like the opening and closing of a clamshell. The platen refers to the flat surface on which the paper lies. These presses, also called jobbers, are slow, and only suited to short-run jobs. Small hand-presses are usually platen presses, as opposed to cylinder presses or rotary presses.

plate proof. A proof taken from a duplicate plate before printing. Plate proofs are most often taken when halftones and type from different original plates are combined into a single duplicate plate.

ply. The number of thicknesses of paper pasted together to make a stock such as Bristol board. Stock can be 1-ply, 2-ply, 3-ply etc., like plywood.

PMS. *See* Pantone Matching System.

PMT. *See* Photographic Mechanical Transfer.

point. 1. Smallest typographic unit of measure. Points are used to designate type size: 12 pt. = 1 pica, and 6 picas - approximately 1 in., so there are 72 pt. in an inch. Actually, 1 pt. = 0.0138 inch. The leading of any typeface may be determined by dividing 72 by the number of lines per column inch of the type. 2. For measuring the thickness of Bristol board, mounting board, postcards, etc., a point is $\frac{1}{1000}$-inch.

point-of-purchase. Displays or advertising used in or around a retail store.

polymerization. Converting a liquid to a solid. For example, in the making of flexographic plates. *See also* photopolymer plates.

porosity. Quality of paper that allows the passage of air, gas, or liquid. The permeation of air is important for ink penetration.

porosity test. A test for the rate of airflow through paper traveling on a web. The paper needs a certain amount of porosity in order to breathe.

positive. A film or paper reproduction in which the light and dark values correspond exactly to those of the original. The reverse is the negative. Strippers prefer to work in positive when registering more than one image. In the case of color film, the rosette image can be checked to see if the four-color dots do not touch, as in perfect four-color register.

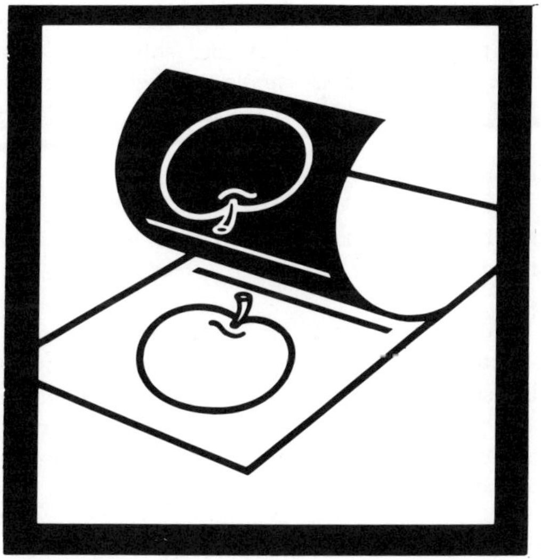

Positive and negative. (*Illustration courtesy Eastman Kodak Company*)

positive paper stat. A photostat with a positive image, sometimes done on repro paper so it can be pasted onto the mechanical and used as camera copy.

posterizations. A high-contrast version of a continuous-tone original. A continuous-tone photograph is broken down into negative films of various densities including solid tone, line or tint variation, and clear paper, or highlight area. These are exposed separately. The first exposure records the extreme highlights, the second, the middle tones, and the third, the solids. The resulting plates, made from the negatives, are used to print a number of colors on the final press sheet. The number of different ink colors counted determines the number of colors used in the posterization regardless of printing on colored paper. Sometimes middle tones and highlight areas are dropped out, so suitable subject matter usually contains little or no important detail in the middle tones.

pot. The receptacle on the typecasting machine in which the metal is melted and stored.

pouch. The service between publisher and typesetter or printer in which material travels, usually overnight by messenger, plane, bus or whatever method is fastest.

p.p.i. Pages per inch. The bulk of a paper, determined by the type of pulp, thickness, and weight of the paper.

precede. *See* blurb.

preface. A preliminary statement at the beginning of a book, written by the author, stating the purpose of the book and sometimes acknowledgments, as opposed to the foreword, which is usually written by someone other than the author. Unlike the introduction, the preface is not considered part of the text.

preliminaries. *See* front matter.

prep or **prepress.** The preparation required to get a job ready for printing, including platemaking, shooting, stripping, proofing, etc., but not makeready.

prepress proof. Proof made directly from the screened separation films and the resulting sheets registered to get the full effect. Prepress proofs provide quality control at an earlier stage than the press proof stage, but they are not as accurate as the final printed sheet in simulating color. Prepress proofs are also less expensive than press proofs which are done on the actual production press prior to the run. *See also* color key and Cromalin.

preprinted. Material which is printed separately from the overall job and later added to, inserted, or used in the production of the final product. Many book covers are preprinted and then shipped to the bindery to be put onto cases.

presensitized plate. A metal or printing plate that has been precoated with a light-sensitive coating by the manufacturer. Some printers prefer to sensitize their own plates.

presses. *See* printing.

pressman. The printer who actually runs the press.

press proof. A proof pulled on the actual printing press with the exact paper and ink to be used on the press run to show how the job will run. Press proofs are expensive, and so are usually done and checked at the plant just before the actual press run.

press run. **1.** The number of copies of a publication to be printed. **2.** The number of sheets to be printed. **3.** The number of impressions made from a printing plate.

press sheet. The sheet of paper that actually takes the image on press.

press type. Derives from trade name Prestype. Now refers to any dry-transfer pressure-sensitive lettering. Type is printed on waxy transparent sheets and will transfer to another surface when rubbed.

pressure-sensitive lettering. Dry-transfer self-adhering type mounted on transparent sheets in various sizes and styles to be cut out, peeled from the backing

Pressmen adjusts the Heidelberg press for a run. (*Courtesy New Horizons Color Corporation, reprinted by permission of Printing Views Magazine*)

sheet, and used on artwork. The characters are usually positioned with tweezers and rubbed down. Letters will not smudge, as they are printed under cellophane. They are aligned with a faint blue guideline. Pressure-sensitive lettering is available in letters, symbols, borders, arrows, music notes, etc., and logos can be made to order. When used on other artwork this can eliminate changes ordinarily made by the stripper. Examples are Artype and Prestype.

pressure-sensitive paper. Paper with an adhesive coating on the back which is protected by a sheet that will peel off when ready for use. Many preprinted labels, address labels, and logos are printed on pressure-sensitive paper for special use.

presswork. The actual printing of a job as opposed to composition, makeup, and binding.

primary colors. The three basic colors from which all other colors can be mixed. The additive primary colors are red light, green light, and blue light.

Pressroom. (*Courtesy Lehigh Press, photo by Sid Delmar Leach*)

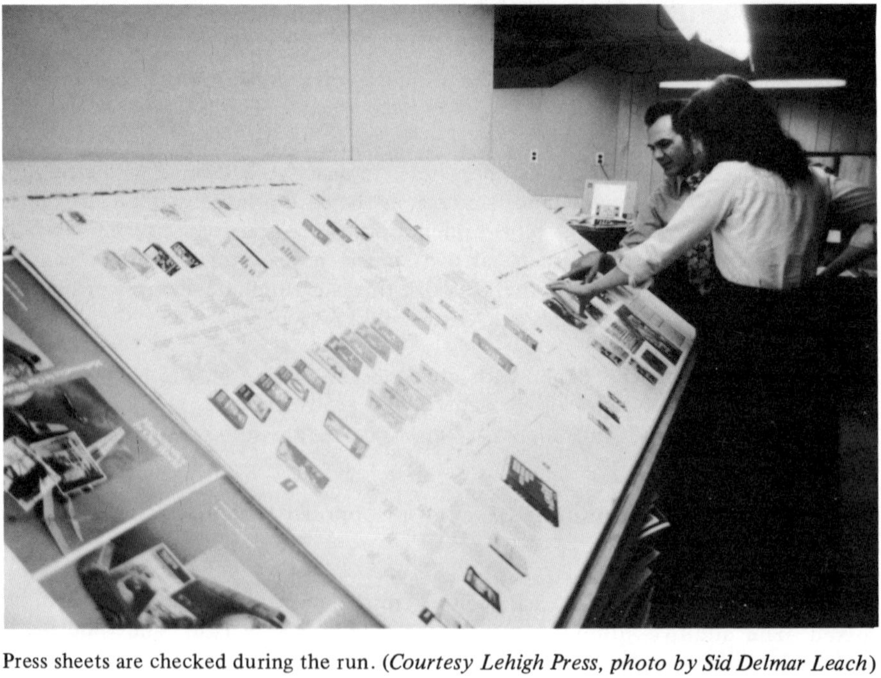

Press sheets are checked during the run. (*Courtesy Lehigh Press, photo by Sid Delmar Leach*)

In printing inks, the subtractive primary colors magenta, yellow, and cyan are printed together with black to produce the full range of colors. *See also* additive color, process color, and subtractive color.

print. A paper photograph made from a film negative.

printability. The properties of all materials and components used in the printing process to produce an acceptable product. The more compatible the components the better the printing quality.

printer. 1. One of the process color negatives used to make a plate for that particular printing color. The negatives themselves are black. The color comes from the ink on the press in areas of the plate where the negative has exposed the image. *See also* color separation. 2. A device such as a Teletype machine, or a line printer on a typesetting keyboard unit that produces typewriter copy, or hard copy, by electrical impulses. 3. The skilled employee of a printing firm who does all the fine tuning necessary to print a job. Seventy-four percent of all printing establishments in the U.S. consist of 20 or fewer employees, many being small, family owned and operated companies found in virtually every community throughout the country.

printer's device. *See* gauntlet.

printer's devil. *See* devil.

printer's error. An error made by the typographer or the printer for which the client does not pay. Abbreviated p.e.

printer's flower. *See* dingbat.

printer's measure. *See* type measurements.

printer's proof. *See* master proof.

printing. The same visible image reproduced in quantity. The different methods of printing, and the variations on each method sound somewhat confusing until the derivations and differences are explained. The following is a brief list of commercial printing methods and their definitions. Full discussions of each method are found under each separate entry in this dictionary.

Letterpress is printing from a raised surface. Hot-metal type is set and locked up in a form with engravings of illustrations. A direct impression is made from the inked form to the paper. A *cylinder press* or *flat-bed press* contains an impression cylinder carrying the paper, and a flat bed where type and plates are locked for printing. A rotary press has the printing plates curved around a cylinder.

Offset lithography makes use of planographic printing onto a blanket which in turn makes the impression onto the paper. The image on the plate is separated

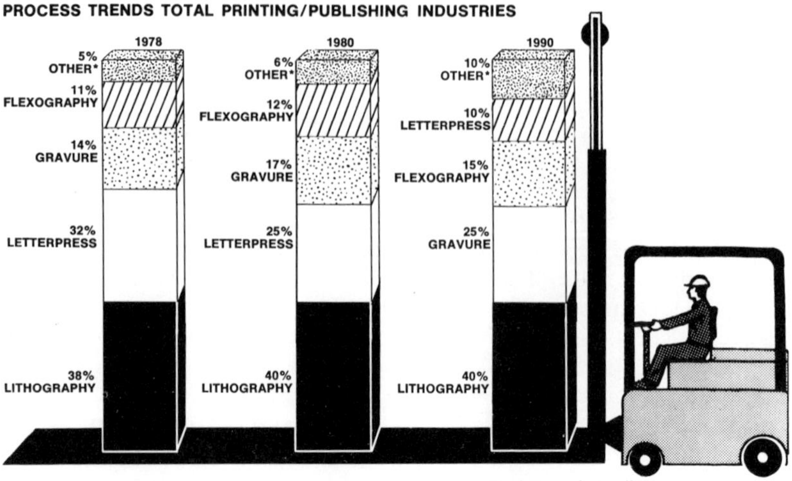

Process trends total printing/publishing industries. Estimates by Michael H. Bruno, Inland Printer Technology Editor. (*Courtesy Inland Printer/American Lithographer*)

from the nonimage area by a fountain solution that does not mix with ink. A *sheetfed press* feeds single sheets into the press, whereas a *web press* prints from a continuous roll of paper. A *blanket-to-blanket perfecting press* prints on both sides of the paper at once.

Gravure printing is done from a surface that is etched with wells which contain the dots for the impression. Ink is applied to the surface and scraped off with a doctor blade leaving only the ink below the surface. *Rotogravure* prints on a web of paper. Gravure can also be printed *sheet-fed.*

Screen process is printing with a silk screen. The image is stenciled on the screen, then ink is squeegeed through onto the printing surface.

An *engraving* is a print made from an intaglio plate prepared by cutting below the surface. The die is inked and wiped, leaving ink below the surface. Paper is laid on the die, and the press forces the paper into the cavities of the die where the ink is transferred to the surface of the paper.

Flexography, flexible letterpress, like letterpress, is printing from a raised surface although plates are made out of flexible plastic or photopolymer plates exposed to film.

Letterset, also called *Dry Offset* and *Indirect Letterpress* has a low-relief plate that uses a blanket to transfer the image to paper.

Direct Lithography is printing with the lithographic process directly onto paper.

Driography is waterless lithography in which the use of silicone and metal eliminates the need for water.

Thermography is an engraved effect achieved by fusing powder to ink on already printed sheets in a heating unit.

Impactless printing includes *Ink Jet* and *Electrostatic* printing. In *ink-jet* printing, thousands of tiny droplets of ink from a nozzle form dots of ink on paper passing under the nozzles.

Electrostatic printing uses static electricity, or electrical disturbances. The image is converted into electrical charges that attract oppositely charged particles of pigment.

Mimeograph refers to duplicating with the use of a stencil attached to a cylinder that presses ink through the stencil and onto duplicating paper passing beneath the impression cylinder.

The three mainstays of printing are letterpress, offset, and gravure, though letterpress is becoming obsolete.

printing abroad. *See* manufacturing clause.

printing depth. The minimum amount of etched relief needed in a photoengraving or duplicate plates for printing. The copy to be printed is all type high.

printing, first. Some experts suggest that playing cards were the first printed product in Europe, and that the widespread use of "games of hazard," as they were called in the 14th century, started an interest in learning for the many uneducated peasants there, creating the demand for a printed product.

printing ink. *See* ink.

printing plate. *See* plate.

printing press. The machine that transfers lettering and images from an inked surface onto paper or other printing surface in various ways. *See also* belt press, cylinder press, flatbed press, offset lithography, perfecting press, platen press, and rotary press.

printing trade customs. *See* Appendix Four.

printmaking. 1. A fine-arts term meaning the reproducing of original works by printing methods. 2. Loosely used to refer to making a photographic print.

printout. 1. A printed output with typewriter characters, as opposed to a typeface, produced by a line printer in a computer phototypesetting operation. The printout is used for proofreading and often contains computer coding. 2. The output of any word processor or computer that prints data.

process blue. *See* cyan.

process camera. A large, sturdy camera equipped with a vacuum back for holding the contact screen tightly against the film, a color-corrected lens, and a white light source, usually xenon lights. The process camera is designed for making halftones, color separations, and copies. *See also* color separation and gallery camera.

process-coated paper. *See* machine coated.

process color. A method of reproducing an illustration in the full, original hues by overprinting halftones for each of the subtractive primary colors—yellow, magenta, and cyan—as well as for black, which gives better tone control. Filters are used to subtract colors from the original, allowing only one primary color to pass through at a time. The red filter separation produces the cyan printer, or negative, from which a plate is made; the green filter produces the magenta printer; and the blue filter produces the yellow printer. One color is printed over another with transparent inks to produce the additive colors that in turn create an optical illusion of the full range of colors. Process color printing requires more skill than flat color printing which is done from specially mixed inks. *See also* additive color and subtractive color.

process color selector guide. Charts with vertical and horizontal columns showing all different combinations of percentages of the process colors in intermediate mixtures. Such a guide is available from most four-color printers, and is used to select exact color desired on a four-color job.

process inks. The magenta, cyan, and yellow inks used to produce process colors. These inks are suitable for process work because they are finely ground and are transparent. The inks are each applied to one of the four-color plates and when all are printed on the sheet they produce an optical illusion of the full-color original. *See also* color separation.

process lens. A highly corrected photographic lens for line, halftone, and color photography.

process lettering. Assembly of photodisplay lettering by hand that is enlarged or reduced to fit a layout. The fonts are usually available in only one size. The lettering artist retouches or modifies the display type before it is used. Also called photo lettering.

processor. The unit that develops and fixes positive or negative film used in typesetting or photographic stages in platemaking. The processor controls humidity, temperature, and the lightness and darkness of the page.

process plates. Halftone color plates for a four-color printing. Each plate is made from a negative that has been screened at an angle to reproduce the dots in an image of one of the process colors. When printed in register, the full range of colors is produced.

process red. *See* magenta.

process yellow. A transparent canary-colored ink that acts as a filter. When printed with cyan and magenta, the three colors together allow red, blue, and green to show through and create an optical illusion of the full range of colors.

production. Getting things printed or produced, or overseeing the traffic flow of jobs in a plant.

program. The complete set of instructions and operation routine required for a phototypesetting unit. The most versatile systems require the most sophisticated programs. With the cathode ray tube digital type systems, it is possible to produce literally anything in type. All that need developing are the programs necessary to tell the machine what to do. Also called software.

progressive proofs or **progs.** A set of proofs on paper showing every possible color combination of the four process colors, individually and progressively combined, proofed in the proper color sequence with inks used for the press run. The specific effect of any two combinations can be determined, and corrections can be formulated for the platemaker. The sequence of a normal set of progs is: yellow, red, yellow-red, blue, yellow-blue, red-blue, yellow-red-blue, black, yellow-black, red-black, blue-black, yellow-red-black, yellow-blue-black, red-blue-black, and yellow-red-blue-black. The progressive order of plates is yellow, magenta, cyan and black. Sometimes more colors are used. In gravure, the black plate is sometimes omitted. Progs are used to determine density and the effect of each color on the other colors. Also called bastard progs.

projection. The negative or positive made by exposure in a camera, as opposed to contacting emulsion to emulsion in a vacuum frame.

projection platemaking. Enlarging copy photographed on a small film format, for example 35 mm, back to plate size. The advantage is miniaturized storage of information. Also called microstripping. *See also* automated imposition.

proof. A sheet of printed copy that is checked against the original and on which corrections are marked. *See also* blueprints, engraver's proof, etch proof, foundry proof, galley proof, line printer, master proof, page proof, photoprint, plate proof, progressive proofs, and repro.

proofing. There is a difference between proofing a job and actually printing it. A proofing press is a relatively small, slow-speed, hand-operated or power-operated press designed primarily for pulling a dozen or so proofs of each job. A printing press is designed to operate automatically at high speeds and print large quantities.

Typeproofs pulled at the proofing press are called galley proofs or rough proofs. These are for checking to see that the job has been correctly set. Before the proof is sent to the client it is proofread in the shop, and corrections are indicated on the marked set. Several duplicate sets as well as the marked set are sent to the client for proofreading. The corrections made on the various proofs are transferred to the marked set. All corrections are marked either p.e. or a.a. P.e's are printer's errors and will be corrected free of charge by the typographer; a.a.'s are the author's alterations and will be charged to the client. A.a's include editor's or designer's changes.

The master proof is returned to the typographer who makes all the corrections indicated, and a new proof called a reproduction proof, or repro, can be pulled on a special coated paper. The repro proofs are used by the designer or compositor in the preparation of mechanicals. The mechanicals will be photographed and made into a printing plate for eventual reproduction.

Proofing for color work is either done by prepress proofs or press proofs. Prepress proofs show the colors from the separation by various methods, but they are not as accurate as press proofs pulled on paper either on a small proofing press or on the production press right before the press run. In a web offset four-color proof press, each color unit is one-tenth the size of the units on a conventional offset press. Also called proving. *See also* color key and Cromalin.

proof press. A small, hand-operated press used for pulling proofs.

Proofpress. (*Courtesy Lehigh Press, photo by Sid Delmar Leach*)

proofread. To read for corrections and mark the master set of proofs. One type correction may necessitate resetting a whole paragraph, so where there has been a type correction, the entire paragraph should be proofread. The typesetter makes corrections from galleys, so any corrections made on a paste-up dummy must also be made on the galleys from which the typesetter will work.

proofreader. The person who reads the typeset material to be sure it has been set properly. The proofreader also checks corrected proofs to ensure all corrections have been made.

proofreader's marks. A set of symbols used to communicate to the typographer and printer what corrections are necessary. These symbols are standard throughout the industry in this country, having evolved over many years. They should be used by every copyeditor, designer, or other person marking proofs.

proportion scale or **proportion wheel.** An instrument on which art is scaled for reduction or enlargement by the use of percentage shown on the wheel when the size of the original and the size of the desired piece are aligned. Once one dimension is calculated, the percentage may be used to read off the other dimension which also appears aligned on the wheel.

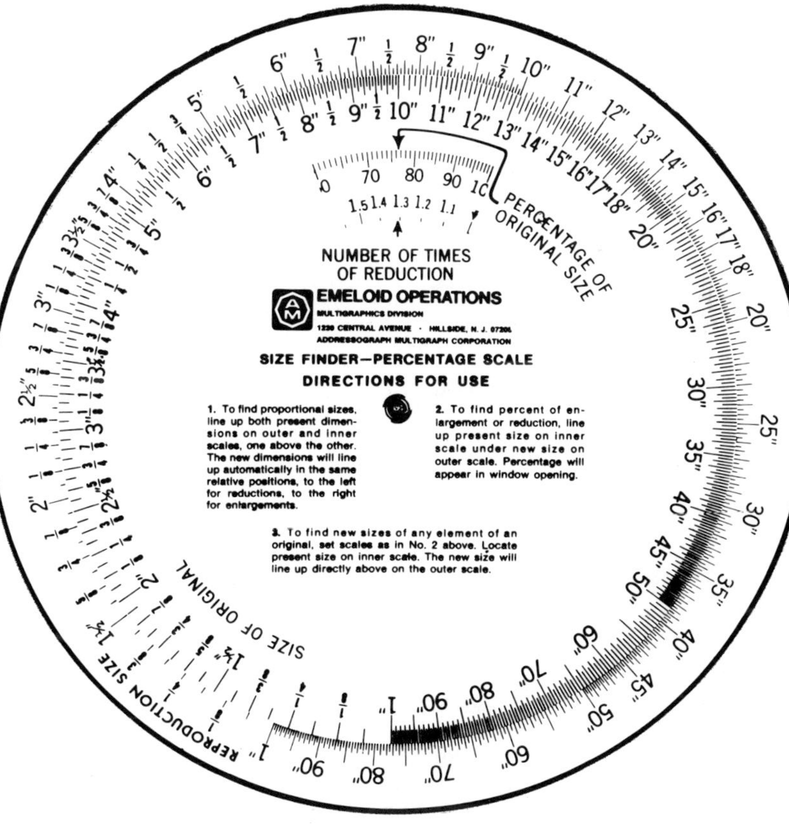

Proportion scale.

Proofreader's marks

	Delete
	Delete and closeup
l/s	L e t t e r spac e
#	Insert space(more space)
h #	Insert hair space
^	Insert character
!	Insert exclamation point
/=/	Insert hyphen
(	Opening parenthesis
)	Closing parenthesis
[	Opening bracket
]	Closing bracket
{	Brace
(/)	Parentheses
3/m or 1/m	Dash
1/n	Nut dash
1/m	l-em dash
2/m	2-em dash
e/	Correct letter or word marked
k (x) or x	Replace broken or imperfect type
⊥ or	Push down space or lead that prints
stet	Let it stand – (all ~~matter~~ above dots)
(.)	Period or full point
^,	Comma
(;)	Semicolon

Proofreader's marks (*cont'd*)

- (:) Colon
- ’/ Apostrophe or single quote
- “/ Open quotes
- ”/ Close quotes
- ?/ Question mark
- !/ Exclamation point
- ff‿i Use ligatures
- 3 Use inferior figure or letter
- a Use superior letter
- */ Asterisk
- & Ampersand
- . . . . Leaders
- / Virgule; separatrix; solidus
- ñ Tilde
- ç Cedilla or French c
- â Circumflex accent or doghouse
- é Accent acute — è Accent grave
- ü Umlaut or diaeresis

- rom Set in roman type
- ital *Set in* italic *type*
- lf Set in **light face** type
- bf Set in bold face
- bf **Set in** bold face **type**
- wf Wrong **font**

Proofreader's marks (*cont'd*)

lc	Set in LOWER CASE or ~~LOWER CASE~~
caps	SET IN capital letters
c+lc	Lower case with Initial Caps
sc	SET IN SMALL CAPITALS
c + sc	Set in caps and small caps
bld ital	Set in boldface italic
wr. ld	Wrong lead
solid	Means not leaded
leaded	Additional space between lines
lead	Insert lead between lines
𝒮 ld	Take out lead
tr. lead	Transfer lead
⁀	Close up en tirely; take out space
‿	Less space between words
#	Insert space
] [	Center
]	Move to right
[	Move to left
⊔	Lower letters or words
⊓	Raise letters or words
=	Align horizontally
‖	Align vertically
⌐ or ¶	Begin a paragraph

Proofreader's marks (*cont'd*)

no ¶	No paragraph. Run in
flush ¶	No paragraph indention
tr.	Transpose letters in a word
tr.	Transpose enclosed matter
X	Broken type
tr.	Rearrange words of order numbers in
run over	Run over to next line. (A two-letter division should be avoided.)
run back	Run back to preceding line. (This division is incorrect.)
hang in	Hanging indention. This style should have all lines after the first marked for the desired indention
□	Em quad space or indention
□ □ or 2	Indent two ems
□□□	Indent the number of em quads shown
⌐	Line break; start a new line
End or 30	End of copy or
(G?)	Question of grammar
(F?)	Question of fact
Qy au or ?	Query to author
Qy Ed or ?	Query to editor
~~Qy au~~	Query ~~to~~ author answered
init	Set large initial

Proofreader's marks (*cont'd*)

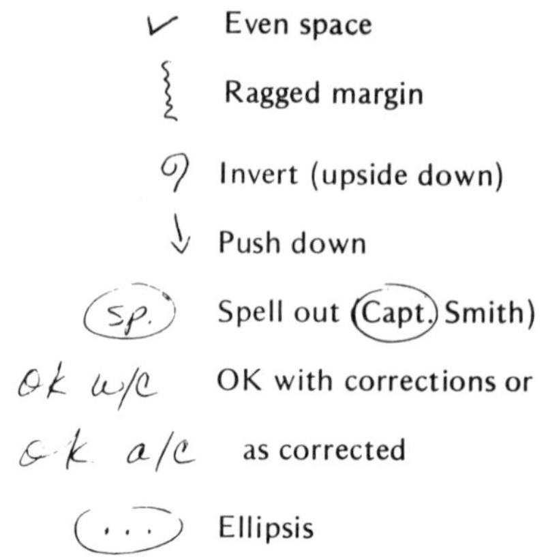

prove. 1. To pull a proof. *See also* proofing. 2. To verify a computer program.

p's and q's. Printer's jargon used to remind a novice to be careful in redistributing the type because p's and q's look so much alike when viewed upside down and backward. Thus, the term, "mind your p's and q's."

PSE. *See* paper surface efficiency.

p.u. *See* pick up.

publication date. The date booksellers are authorized by the publisher to begin selling a book to the public.

public domain. The realm comprised of property rights that belong to the community at large. It refers to material that was either never copyrighted or on which the copyright has expired. Thus it belongs in the public domain and may be used by anyone.

pull. 1. To make a print, by transferring ink to paper, as in printing. 2. To make a proof.

pulp. Cellulose fiber converted from raw wood, used in the papermaking process. *See also* papermaking.

punched tape. *See* paper tape.

punched kraft jackets. Protective dust jackets made of kraft paper. They cover a book during shipping from the bindery. A hole is punched in the spine so that the title can be read.

punching. *See* slot punching.

punch register. *See* pin register.

put to bed. Ready to go to press. *See also* bed.

pyroxylin. Liquid material used to reinforce or coat paper book-covering materials, or to coat index tabs. Pyroxylin makes a weak covering material and is falling into disfavor with publishers and binders.

Q

quad. A space used in setting type. An em quad is the square of the size of type being used, i.e., a 10 pt. quad is 10 pt. high and 10 pt. wide. An en quad is half the width of the em quad. So, in 10 pt. type, the en quad would be 5 pt. wide. An en quad is also called a nut to avoid confusion with em. A quad which is $\frac{1}{3}$ the size of the em quad is called 3-to-the-em, likewise a quad $\frac{1}{4}$ the em quad is 4-to-the-em. There are also $1\frac{1}{2}$-em, 2-em, and 3-em quads.

Originally a quad was a block of metal type less than type high used for indentions, to fill out lines, and to fill out space at the ends of paragraphs.

quad center. Centered type, in computer typesetting language.

quadding. Inserting quads, or larger than normal wordspaces in order to justify the line or position it flush right, left or center.

QUAD LEFT

QUAD RIGHT

QUAD CENTER

Quadding.

quad left. A term meaning flush left in computer typesetting language.

quad middle. To put text on either side with space in the center.

quad right. Flush right, in computer typesetting language.

quality. Perhaps the one area in the graphic arts where there is the most argument regarding quality is that of typesetting. One expert settles the argument thus: "Quality is both a tangible and an intangible. It certainly represents the level of the visual image, but it also represents the cultural and economic background of the purchaser. Quality is a state of mind, an opinion. We can recognize broken characters and bad base alignment as evidence of poor quality, but other aspects, such as image clarity, spacing, kerning and design are really one person's opinion versus another's . . . And what I consider quality, will differ with the next person. Thus, you must select your typesetting method to meet the requirements of your market."[7]

Quality in all areas of the graphic arts is a combination of guessing and psychological warfare. The highest quality requires the most handwork. Some clients may be satisfied with a clean job, while others may be more finicky. Only experience enables a client to be able to get the best quality out of his supplier economically.

quality control. Random sampling of the printed product in order to check the quality.

quality paperback. Paperbacks that are sold in bookstores and through other normal bookselling channels, but not on newsstands or in supermarkets, as are mass market paperbacks.

quaint characters. *See* ligature.

quarto. Originally, a book made from sheets that have been folded twice, each sheet forming four leaves, or eight pages. Loosely used now to describe a book measuring 9" x 12." *See also* folio.

query. A question written on a manuscript or proof addressed to the author, editor, or someone working on the manuscript. When answered, the query should be crossed out with a large X, which designates that the query has been handled. Abbreviated qy.

quick printing. Copying, duplicating, and offset printing on paper up to 11" x 17", often provided by "while you wait" service. Large printing presses are not used. This segment of commercial graphic arts was virtually unheard of in 1970 but has now taken hold so that there are some 10,000 quick-printing establishments throughout the country. Also called instant printing.

quire. Twenty-five sheets or 1/20th of a 500-sheet ream. Formerly, a quire was considered to be 24 sheets.

quotation. A passage authored by another who is usually credited. Lengthy quotations are often set as extracts, i.e., they are indented, and/or set in a different typeface from the text. *See also* fair use doctrine.

[7]Frank J. Romano, "More Than Meets the Eye," *Book Production Industry,* May, 1976, p. 70.

R

rag content. An ingredient sometimes used in paper making. Rags and cotton are used to make fine pulps for the permanent strong bond paper and cover stock called rag papers. Twenty-five percent rag is common in fine papers for stationery. One hundred percent is rare.

Rag fibers were once thought to render greater permanence than wood fibers. However, it has been found that very old papers have lasted because they were made by an acid-free process. For real permanence, acid-free paper, whether rag or wood pulp, must be specified. Also called cotton fiber paper.

ragged left. A column of type, flush right, with the left side unjustified.

This copy is set ragged left.
Ragged left copy is very hard
to read. The eye is trained to
go back to the same point
from which it started original-
ly when it returns to the
beginning of a new line. Rag-
ged left copy is sometimes
used for captions.

Ragged left.

ragged right. A column of type, flush left, with the right side unjustified.

This copy is set ragged right.
Ragged right copy looks the
same as flush left copy. It is
called ragged right copy,
however, because the typeset-
ter can tell his machine to set
the copy ragged right without
having to make the quad left
command at the end of every
line.

Ragged right.

rag papers. *See* rag content.

railroad board. Colored paper used primarily to print tickets.

raised printing. An expensive looking printing raised from the page such as that on formal invitations. *See also* embossing, engraving, and thermography.

Rapidograph. A ruling pen used by illustrators and pasteup artists to draw rules by hand. They are available in the different thicknesses of hairline rules.

In order to write, the point of the pen must be separated from the straight edge by at least the thickness of a piece of paper or tape. It must be held vertically, flat side to the ruler. It must be filled, not dipped so that no ink gets on the outside of the point.

rare books. 1. Collector's items printed in limited editions, or first editions of very old books. 2. Books from the incunabula (strictly speaking only books printed before 1501) and the early centuries of printing in Europe, circa 15th, 16th, and 17th centuries.

RC paper. Resin-coated paper. Photo-sensitive paper base film on which phototypesetters set type. It can be pasted down for camera work. RC paper does not have as heavy a base as the repro paper used for pulling repro proofs from letterpress type.

reader. 1. A device that can convert data in one form to another form by a set of signals. For example, OCR readers, magnetic tape readers, punched tape readers in typesetting, and marked sensing readers for magnetic inks. 2. A person who specializes in a field and is paid to read a manuscript to evaluate the content before the manuscript is edited.

readers's proof. *See* master proof.

ream. Five hundred sheets of paper. The weight per ream cut to a standard size for a particular grade of paper is that paper's basis weight and determines the paper price. *See also* basis weight.

recto. The right-hand page. The recto always bears the odd-numbered folios, whereas the verso, or left-hand page bears the even-numbered folios.

red. A paper-base material into which negatives are stripped in imposition for making printing plates.

reduce. To make an image smaller photographically. Reduction and enlargement are measured in percentage of the original. A photograph needed at ¼ the size of the original would be 25%. A proportion scale is used to determine the percentage needed based on the size of the original and the space needed to be filled. If one dimension is missing, a formula can be used to find the other dimension necessary in the reduction or enlargement.

$$\frac{\text{Width of original}}{\text{Height of original}} = \frac{\text{Width of enlargement}}{\text{Height of enlargement}}$$

reelbook. A collection of sample or swatches on a ring or reel that can be flipped through for the appropriate sample.

reference. A symbol or direction referring the reader to another part or passage in a publication.

reference marks. Numerals, letters, or symbols used at the point of reference and at the beginning of the corresponding note. When symbols are used, the order is

* † ‡ § || ¶ #

Reference marks.

reference matter. *See* end matter.

reflection copy. Any copy that is viewed and photographed by light reflecting from its surface such as photographs, paintings, and drawings, as opposed to transparent copy such as slides.

refractiveness. Light absorption in the surface of the paper causing halftones to appear darker than they should.

register. 1. Positioning two or more images over each other in exact position so the result is a single image. When process colors are imposed out of register, the result is fuzzy, with a line or shadow of color showing where it is not wanted. Poor register is caused by poor platemaking or paper that stretches. 2. Maintaining exactly the same margins from page to page, so that the type areas on both sides of the page are exactly backed up.

register marks. A device, usually a cross in a circle, applied to original copy and film before reproduction, and used to position negatives in perfect register or to perfectly register press plates for color printing. Also placed on mechanicals with overlays to ensure register. *See also* pin register.

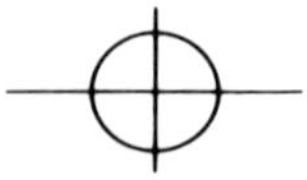

Register marks.

register pins. Stubby pins, usually on a metal base, used in a pin-register system to correspond to the size of register punch holes. *See also* pin register.

regular spacing. *See* spacing.

reinforced ends. Tape applied to the end papers to make a stronger book. Reinforcing can be either *concealed* or *exposed. Concealed* reinforcing is comprised of a strip of tape down the spine of the end papers and first and last signatures. The tape gets bound into the spine where the glue is. *Exposed* reinforcing makes use of an open joint so that one edge of the end paper sticks out at the spine and the tape is wrapped around underneath and attached to the end paper and the first signature.

relative humidity. The amount of water vapor present in the atmosphere, expressed as a percentage of the maximum amount of water vapor that could be present at the same temperature. Abbreviated RH, this factor affects the printing process, paper, and ink. The paper must be in balance with the relative humidity of the pressroom. If the edges of the paper absorb moisture they will become wavy. If they lose moisture, they will become tight. Both tight and wavy edges can cause wrinkles and misregister in printing.

relief photography. A flat photographic effect achieved by placing a continuous tone positive and negative on top of each other slightly out of register, resulting in a continuously gray area. The lateral motion produces a relief effect.

relief printing. Any printing method using a raised image area, such as a rubber stamp or letterpress. The raised surface is covered with ink and then prints this ink onto paper.

relief plate. A printing plate on which the image area is considerably higher, i.e., in relief, than the nonprinting area. The relief image carries the ink, as in letterpress printing, letterset, and flexography, as opposed to lithography which is planographic.

remainder. A book sold at a drastically reduced price because it is not selling but merely occupying space in the warehouse.

remake. To change the makeup of a page after it has been laid out and type elements are in place.

reprint. 1. To print a work after its original appearance without major changes. Plant costs are not incurred in a reprint, only manufacturing costs. 2. Part of a work reproduced and sold separately. Also called offprint.

repro. 1. Reproduction copy. Type set on photosensitive paper, which is really silver emulsion backed by paper base, made for pasting onto mechanicals to be photographed. Repro is sometimes referred to as film because it is exposed to light and also goes through a developer, a fixer, a wash tank, etc. 2. A clean, sharp proof of a page, made on coated paper. The repro proof can be photographed for reproduction. Illustrations, as well as type can be shown on a repro proof. With a letterpress form, the repro proof is pulled on a proving press. Phototype can be set on repro paper, and film negatives can be contacted onto repro paper. Letterpress repros will smudge, but photographic repros do not use ink and so will not smudge once the image is fixed on the photo-sensitive paper.

repro camera. A camera that produces repro copy from film, reduces or enlarges, and copies halftones. A repro camera is similar to a photostat machine.

reprographics. Something written or drawn, and reproduced.

reprography. Copying, duplicating, or other reproduction by means not identified as normal printing.

repro proof. Reproduction proof. *See* repro.

rescreening. Shooting camera copy that has already been screened, and using it at a different size. The copy has to be rescreened or else the dots will either close up, in reduction, or become visible to the eye, in enlargement. If the copy screen angle and the original camera screen angle are congruent, a moiré pattern will result. The copy must be rotated 30 degrees so the dots fall between one another. Also, if the camera screen lines-per-inch is equal to that of the copy screen, the moiré pattern can be even further eliminated. Lines-per-inch can be found on screened copy with the use of a screen determiner.

A graphic arts camera only sees black and white, or in the case of halftones, the halftone dots. Other techniques used to trick the camera into seeing continuous tones of gray for rescreening a halftone are setting the camera out of focus, diffusing the image, and using special rescreen filters. Some suppliers are more expert than others in handling jobs where rescreening is required.

resin. An organic substance used in printing inks and paper as a binder.

resist. A substance that inhibits the action of the acid in etching a plate. *See also* etch.

restricted bleeds. Bleeds in only part of a book restricted to a certain number of pages and to certain forms. The placement of bleeds in a book or magazine determine the size of paper used and how the sheets will be printed.

retouching. The correcting of imperfections by the use of an airbrush, pen, pencil, or dyes, on a photograph or other artwork before it is reproduced. It is best not to retouch with fluorescent white or colors because they cause hot spots which must then be corrected by the platemaker.

retrieval system. In computer typesetting equipment, a memory tape or disk which is kept after the job is finished. If a job is put on a retrieval system, sizes, faces, or measure of the text can be revised without rekeyboarding. Actual text changes must still be rekeyboarded because the words must be typed in. A client must clarify at the beginning of a job whether or not he wants a job to go into a retrieval system or not. It costs more, but can save money on the line changes or later editions.

reversal film. Special contact film which preserves the values of the original, i.e., a positive remains positive and a negative remains negative.

reverse copy. Wrong reading copy when printed.

reverse leading. Typesetting up the page as well as down. The film actually reverses direction so that copy can be placed in a desired position on the film. Reverse leading is useful when copy goes around the page like a frame or box or where it is difficult to align elements that are different sizes.

reverse out. An image or type in white surrounded by a solid block of color or black. White paper appears as the color of the type. *See also* reverse print and reverse type.

Reverse type.

reverse plate. A printing plate made from a film positive instead of a film negative. The result is that the tonal values are exactly opposite from the original copy. Blacks are white, and whites are black.

reverse print. A page on which the letters do not print, but allow the color of the paper to show through. This can be done by making the printing plate from a film positive so that a solid area is produced on the printing plate for the background. In printing, the background area carries the ink and will print solid.

reverse type. Type that drops out of the background so that it appears as the color of the paper.

revise. An alteration in any stage of composition.

revised proof or **revise pages.** A proof made after corrections have been made showing everything that has been changed.

rice paper. A sheet with ivory-like texture made from the pith of a tree. Rice paper is nonfibrous, and so not really paper.

right-angle fold. Folds that are 90° to each other in the binding process.

right-reading. An image which reads correctly from left to right, as opposed to a wrong reading image, which reads from right to left. Right-reading film, emulsion down, is the same as wrong-reading, emulsion up.

ring binder. A form of loose-leaf binding in which two or more rings pass through punched holes at the edge of the paper.

ripple finish. A wavy or rippled look on paper finished with an embossing process. *See also* pebbling.

river of white. Undesirable streak of white running through several lines of type due to poor wordspacing. A river of white disrupts the even appearance of a page. Where there are no rivers, the eye will travel right across the page.

**Rivers of white are
unsightly blank
areas created by
bad word or letter
spacing. The eye
tends to drift around
in the white rather
than move from
word to word.**

River of White

roll-out. Hand-rolled ink on glass or paper for sampling or to determine a characteristic of the ink.

rom. *See* proofreader's marks.

Roman. A class of type with upright letterforms, as opposed to italic, script, gothic, or text. Roman was originally an upright letterform with serifs derived from the original Roman stone-cut letterforms. It is used for most ordinary reading matter. The three roman-style divisions are old style, transitional, and modern. *See also* serifs and typeface styles.

rosette image. An image formed in four color printing used to check register. In perfect four color register, the four color dots do not touch.

Roman type.

rotary press. A printing press in which the plates are curved around a cylinder as opposed to lying flat. Rotary presses are used in offset, gravure, flexography, and collotype. Letterpress can also be done on a rotary press, as opposed to a flatbed or cylinder press in which the paper is wrapped around a cylinder, while the plate lies flat. *See also* cylinder press and platen press.

rotogravure. Web-fed gravure printing done on high-speed rotary presses. Most often used for economical long-run or medium jobs such as magazines, packaging, and Sunday supplements of newspapers. *See also* gravure.

rough. A sketch, giving general layout with size and position of elements in the design. A rough is made to give the general idea rather than finished details.

rough front. An old-style method of leaving the outside margin of a bound trade book untrimmed giving it a rough edge to simulate hand folding. If the edge and foot as well are left untrimmed it is called rough front and foot. Abbreviated RF and RFF.

rough proof. An in-house proof pulled from proofing press or plate, without makeready, for identification, or to show what the material being proofed looks like.

round-backing or **rounding.** The part of the bindery process in which the signatures are rounded at the spine. Clamps hold the book block together as an arm rocks back and forth to position the signatures in a curve to fit a rounded spine covering. The larger the book, the more difficult it is to get a good round. Rounding and backing builds a hinge into the book that makes it stay in its cover twice as long as a flatback book.

rout. To mechanically cut away or deepen the non-printing areas that have been etched in a printing plate or the printing areas in an engraving so they will not make a mark during printing. A router is a high speed hand-guided engraver's tool, much like a drill.

rubber type. An indication of a type size for a width in which that size of type a mold of the original plate and used mainly in flexography and in box and carton printing on uneven surfaces or in low-quality paperback printing. *See also* flexography.

rubber type. An indication of a type size for a width in which that size of type cannot be set. This is known as cheating on a layout.

rub-off type. *See* pressure-sensitive lettering.

Rubylith film. A separable two-ply acetate film with a clear-film base, used as a mask over artwork to be printed in flat color. The areas to be colored are outlined with a sharp knife, cutting only through the ruby layer, which is opaque to the blue light needed to expose the plate. Separate acetate masks are prepared including register marks for each color to be printed, and the ruby film is then stripped into a sheet of goldenrod or red, used as the flat for exposing a plate which will print that particular color. Many strippers now have more precision methods than this and prefer that designers and artists do not provide rubylith overlays for color work.

rule. A black line, available in various point sizes, called weights, and used as a box or a border, or in the form of a fancy design. The finest rule that can be produced in typesetting is called the hairline rule, less than ½-pt. *See also* tapered rules.

Rules.

runaround. Type with measures adjusted to fit around an illustration or another design element on the page. The measures for the type area are adjusted during typesetting. A runaround increases the cost of typesetting.

runnability. The ability of the paper to run smoothly through the press. Defective paper which causes either press or converting problems while passing through the equipment indicates poor runnability. Because of the use of water and tacky inks in offset printing, a paper used should be free of buckles, curl, loose dirt, have adequate water resistance, the same relative humidity as the pressroom, be trimmed square and accurate in size, have the proper paper-ink relationship, and be in good mechanical condition, i.e., free of holes, tears, spots, rope marks, slack or tight edges, etc.

run back. To move material from the beginning of a line to the end of the line above it. Abbreviated rb.

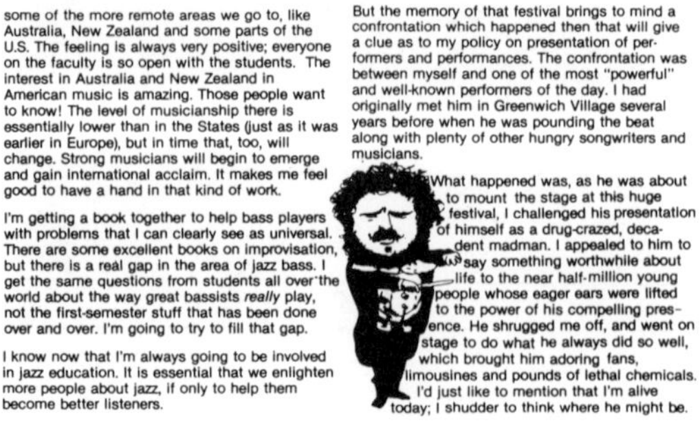

some of the more remote areas we go to, like Australia, New Zealand and some parts of the U.S. The feeling is always very positive; everyone on the faculty is so open with the students. The interest in Australia and New Zealand in American music is amazing. Those people want to know! The level of musicianship there is essentially lower than in the States (just as it was earlier in Europe), but in time that, too, will change. Strong musicians will begin to emerge and gain international acclaim. It makes me feel good to have a hand in that kind of work.

I'm getting a book together to help bass players with problems that I can clearly see as universal. There are some excellent books on improvisation, but there is a real gap in the area of jazz bass. I get the same questions from students all over the world about the way great bassists *really* play, not the first-semester stuff that has been done over and over. I'm going to try to fill that gap.

I know now that I'm always going to be involved in jazz education. It is essential that we enlighten more people about jazz, if only to help them become better listeners.

But the memory of that festival brings to mind a confrontation which happened then that will give a clue as to my policy on presentation of performers and performances. The confrontation was between myself and one of the most "powerful" and well-known performers of the day. I had originally met him in Greenwich Village several years before when he was pounding the beat along with plenty of other hungry songwriters and musicians.

What happened was, as he was about to mount the stage at this huge festival, I challenged his presentation of himself as a drug-crazed, decadent madman. I appealed to him to say something worthwhile about life to the near half-million young people whose eager ears were lifted to the power of his compelling presence. He shrugged me off, and went on stage to do what he always did so well, which brought him adoring fans, limousines and pounds of lethal chemicals. I'd just like to mention that I'm alive today; I shudder to think where he might be.

Runaround. (***Courtesy Not Just Jazz***)

run down. To move material from the end of a line of type to the beginning of the next line.

run in. To merge a paragraph with the preceding one, or to insert copy into the text without making a new paragraph. Indicated by a wavy line connecting one line to the next.

A Run-in Head runs right into the copy to which it calls attention. It is usually set in a different face or weight than the copy into which it runs. Run-in heads save some space in very tight copy.

Run-in head.

running foot. Similar to a running head, only at the bottom of the page. A running foot is more commonplace in magazines than in books. Also called footline.

running head. A headline repeated at the top of each page, containing the title, or divisions of the work, such as chapter titles, or date of issue. In book work the book title appears on the left, the chapter title on the right.

runover. **1.** The lines after the first line of a flush-and-hang entry. **2.** The continuation of a heading on a second line. Also called stacked. **3.** A large amount of material which has been reset.

runover copy. Copy in the back section of a newspaper or magazine, continued from a story in the main editorial section.

S

saddle stitch or **saddle wire.** A method of binding in which wire staples are inserted through the fold at the spine and clinched in the center of the center spread. The folded sheets ride on a saddle while this type of work is being done. The pages lie flat when the publication is opened, but a publication cannot be bound this way if it is more than ⅛-in. thick.

safelight. A red light used in a darkroom to provide enough light for work. The red light does not affect photographic materials as they are blind to it.

salt print. An old wet-bath process for proofing halftones in a a brown shade, used for position only. Now loosely refers to other methods of copying halftones for position only, but in truth the salt print is a better quality print than those to which the term now loosely refers. *See also* Warren print.

sample pages. Representative pages typeset according to specifications and layout to show what a job will look like, or to show the promised quality of the finished product. Publishers usually check sample pages before composition begins.

sans serif. A class of type without the serif, or cross-strokes of the main part of a letter, having plain lines of uniform thickness. Also known as block letter, and gothic. *See also* typeface styles.

saturation. Strength or amount of the color present in a hue. *See also* color tree.

sausage. Galley of type which the pasteup artist may cut to fit the layout. So called because the galley is made of lengthy running text that looks like a sausage.

sawtooth edge. A symmetry of halftone dots broken into the appearance of the teeth of a saw. It is caused by the edge of a halftone crossing a line at a certain angle.

sc. *See* small caps.

scale. The proportion between the size of an original piece of art and its reproduction to fit a layout. Scale is measured in percentages of enlargement or reduction and is marked F for focus. One hundred percent is indicated SS. Scale can be found either on a proportion wheel or geometrically with the dimensions. Illustrations enlarge or reduce along their diagonals and the diagonal line can be used on a layout to determine scale as well.

scanner. **1.** An electronic device that recognizes the presence or absence of data on the surface of continuous tone or halftone copy. The scanner stores the information in a computer, then creates halftone copy, and resizes and crops the copy for full page makeup. The scanner reads halftones as line work, requiring only a simple binary computer program: black/on; white/off. The digitized information can be transmitted via telephone lines or satellite then fed into a CRT phototypesetter that combines photos and text to create pages with all elements in place. **2.** A device that makes color separations with or without a laser. The advantage of a scanner for photographic enlargements is that it can enlarge up to 1600%, whereas a camera can only enlarge to 400%. Color previewers can be attached to a scanner so that re-assembled separations can be displayed on a color cathode ray tube for inspection and analysis before film is even exposed. **3.** In phototypesetting, a scanner electronically reads copy which has been typed and coded on special sensitive paper, and translates the copy into a paper or

Color scanner can finish the entire operation of color separations in less than 20 minutes. (*Courtesy Kingsport Press*)

magnetic tape that drives the phototypesetting machine. The scanner stops and signals when there is something indistinguishable to it. *See also* color scanner, laser, and optical character recognition.

Optical Character Recognition Scanner reads manuscript for correct coding and keyboarding. (*Courtesy Autologic Incorporated*)

scant. Somewhat less than the measurement stated in a spine bulk. Represented by a minus sign after the fraction. For example ½–.

scoring. 1. To mechanically indent paper, to make tearing easier. Sometimes a solid line is stamped as well. The fibers of the paper are bruised with a sharp steel rule. 2. Creasing heavyweight paper to facilitate folding. If heavyweight paper such as cover stock is not scored, it will fold unevenly, especially if folded across the grain. Also called creasing.

Scotchprint. Trade name for translucent, plastic, matte-finish proofing material which may be used for making contact negatives, as camera copy, or for converting letterpress plates to film. Manufactured by 3M.

scratchboard. Clay-coated cardboard that can be scratched with a stylus for wood-engraving effects, reverse effects, or highlight effects. The scratchboard may be covered with india ink and then scratched, to show white.

scratch resistance. Resistance of ink on a printed surface to normal abrasions and wear.

screen. 1. A cross-ruled glass plate or piece of film or plastic placed in front of the lens of a camera or in contact with film in a contact frame. The screen is used to break up continuous-tone copy into dots that will carry the ink in reproduction. Screens are designated by the number of ruled lines per inch they contain, from 50 lines per inch to 500 lines per inch. The greater the number of lines per inch, the finer the printing will be. The size of the dots in an area determines the darkness of the copy. The number of dots determines amount of detail. Coarse screens, for example 50 to 55, are used for newspapers, while 100 linescreens and up are used on coated papers. 2. A pattern of dots or lines applied over line copy to obtain an illusion of tone. These screened tints are designated by percentages of black. They are available as art supplies, or can be made by the compositor or printer. *See also* Benday process and Zip-A-Tone.

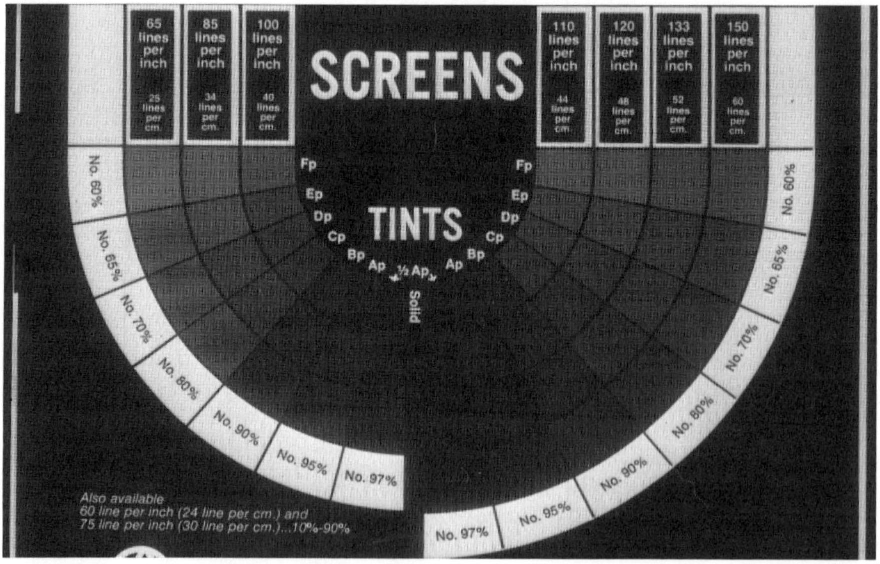

Screen tints. (*Courtesy Beta Screen Corporation*)

screen angles. In color reproduction, continuous-tone copy is shot at a different angle for each of the primary colors into which the full color is broken down with the corresponding filter. Different angles of the screen are necessary so that the dots do not pile up on top of each other causing the undesirable moiré pattern. If all the angles were exactly the same a pile of purple and black dots would result. The four screens are often angled at 105° for cyan, 90° for yellow, 75° for magenta, and 45° for black.

screen determiner or **screen finder.** A lined piece of plastic or film which, when placed over a halftone, indicates by a star pattern, the number of lines per inch in the screen used when shooting that particular halftone.

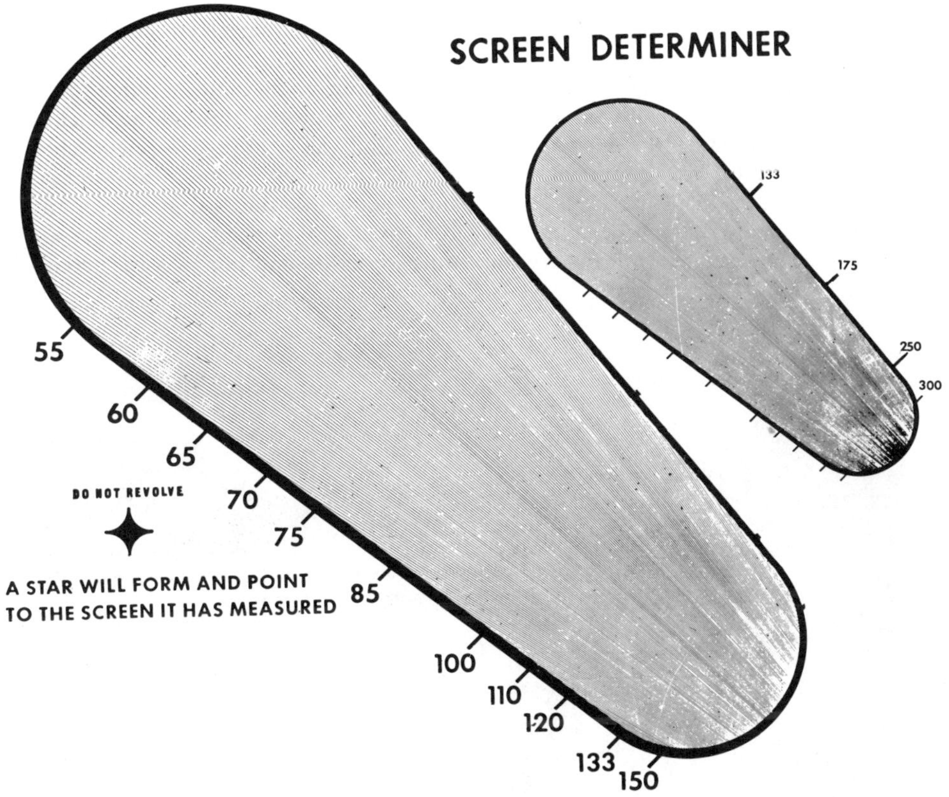

Screen determiner. (*Courtesy Halliday Lithograph*)

screened enlargements. A photographic enlargement of a screened positive or negative, used for a graphic effect, similar to line conversions.

screened negative. *See* halftone.

screened positive. A positive reproduction of continuous-tone copy.

screened print. A print made from a halftone negative, the negative having been made from copy which was screened photographically.

screened tint. *See* screen para no. 2.

screenless printing. A lithographic process for use with continuous-tone films. It is as yet impractical because of the inconsistency of the plates.

screen mask. An adhesive positive screen mask that can be rubbed onto artwork for effects of dark or light areas, special patterns, or any structure such as gauze, gravel, wood grain, or foliage that is superimposed on the photo. Even negative and positive pictures can be combined into a total graphic screen structure.

screen printing or **screen process printing.** A printing method in which ink is manually or mechanically forced by means of a squeegee through a stenciled fabric that contains the image, made from film, and through a fine-meshed screen. This method is extremely good for decals, posters, or point-of-purchase displays that require a thick layer of paint, ink and/or fluorescent ink on any material. Inks for screen printing have the consistency of thick paint. They are short inks in order to print sharp and squeegee easily and not clog the screen.

Screen printing. (*Courtesy Autoscreen. Photo by Sid Delmar Leach*)

Very small type does not reproduce well in screen process printing. However, screen printing is excellent for handling rich, solid colors. Formerly called silk-screen printing.

Screen printing. (*Courtesy Kingsport Press*)

screen ruling. The number of lines per inch on a contact or glass halftone screen, or the number of dots per inch on the halftone.

scribed lines. Lines scratched into the emulsion of negative film. They will print as black rules.

script. A class of type designed to look like handwriting, either formal or informal, and available in different weights. Commonly used in announcements, invitations, and stationery. Also called cursive. *See also* typeface styles.

scuff resistance. A characteristic of inks, used for packages, which must stay bright and appealing in spite of shipping and handling.

secondary colors. Orange, purple, and green that result from the mixtures of the primary colors red, yellow, and blue.

second-generation type. Electromechanical typesetting devices that photograph type carried on film fonts. The devices are run by punched or magnetic tapes that carry computerized instructions. These phototype units are faster than first-generation typesetters, which adapted hot-metal line-casting principles to film, but they are not as fast as third-generation computer-driven digitized typesetters. Second-generation type came about because of newspaper publishers' concern for more efficient, less expensive prepress and editorial operations that led to development of photographic composition and video display terminals. *See also* computer typesetting, generations of type, and phototypesetting.

self-cover. A cover made of the same paper as the text pages of a booklet or brochure. A self-cover saves the extra costs of producing and binding a cover, if the cover doesn't have to be particularly strong.

self-ends. End papers made out of the first page of the first signature and the last page of the last signature, both of which are attached to the covers of the book.

self-mailer. A printed piece, usually for promotion purposes, designed to be folded and mailed without an envelope.

self-sealing envelopes. *See* envelope styles.

semimonthly. Twice a month.

separation. *See* color separation.

separation negative. *See* color separation.

sepia print. A brownish ozalid transfer process of image to paper proof. Used for old-fashioned effects or for copying very old photographs.

series of type. *See* type series.

serifs. The short cross-lines at the end of the main strokes of letterforms. Originally, the beginning or finishing strokes of the pen. Gothic and sans serif faces do not have serifs.

Serifs come from the letterforms cut into granite by early Roman stone masons. The horizontal and vertical lines were cut with iron chisels. Where strokes did not intersect, the tool left a rugged appearance at the end of the line. A cut made with the tool straightened the unevenness, and the cut was called a serif. *See also* typeface styles.

serigraphy. The production of fine art prints by pressing pigments through a stenciled silk screen. *See also* screen printing and stencil printing.

serrated edges. Roughly cut edges of paper. Newspapers are one example. The cutting is done on the press during folding. Since serrated edges are not trimmed at the bindery, they are cheaper than trimmed edges.

set. The horizontal dimension of type measured in units on the composing machine and described as condensed, extended, thin, or fat. *See also* set width.

set-off. The undesirable transfer of ink, not set in time, from one printed sheet to the back of the next sheet as it is being delivered. Formerly called offset, not to be confused with offset printing.

set solid. Lines of type set without leading.

setting of ink. The first phase of ink drying, after which the sheets can be handled without smudging.

setup time. The time required to load a program and load the input and output devices in a typesetting operation.

set width. The width of an individual character plus a normal amount of space on either side, measured in units. Letterspacing can be adjusted on a photounit. In metal type, the set is the width of the body upon which the type character is cast. *See also* unit.

sewing. *See* side-sewing and Smyth sewn.

sewn soft cover. A method of binding in which saddle-sewn signatures are fastened to each other and to a paper cover by sewing.

shade. The alteration of a color by adding black or a complementary color. *See also* color tree and tint.

shading tint. A pattern of tiny dots or lines that gives the effect of shading. The drawing may be made on a stipple board having raised dots; the dots may be stippled by hand; a screened tint may be adhered or applied as an overlay; or a screened tint may be made by the compositor or printer. *See also* Benday and Zip-a-Tone.

shadow. 1. The relatively dark parts of a photograph as opposed to the highlights and middle tones. The dark areas in a halftone are represented by the largest dots. 2. In display type, the image of a shadow behind the main letter, giving the letter a depth dimension. Direction of shadows on type are designated by their positions relative to the hands on the face of a clock. For example, a 45° shadow below the letter would be read as 4:30, while a 45° shadow above the letter would be 1:30.

sharpen. A decrease in the size of the halftone dots as opposed to thickening or dot spread. More small dots, i.e., those produced from a finer screen, will result in sharper detail in the picture.

sheet. Piece of paper that feeds into an offset press upon which the printing impression is made.

sheeter. A rotary unit over which the web of paper passes to be cut into individual sheets.

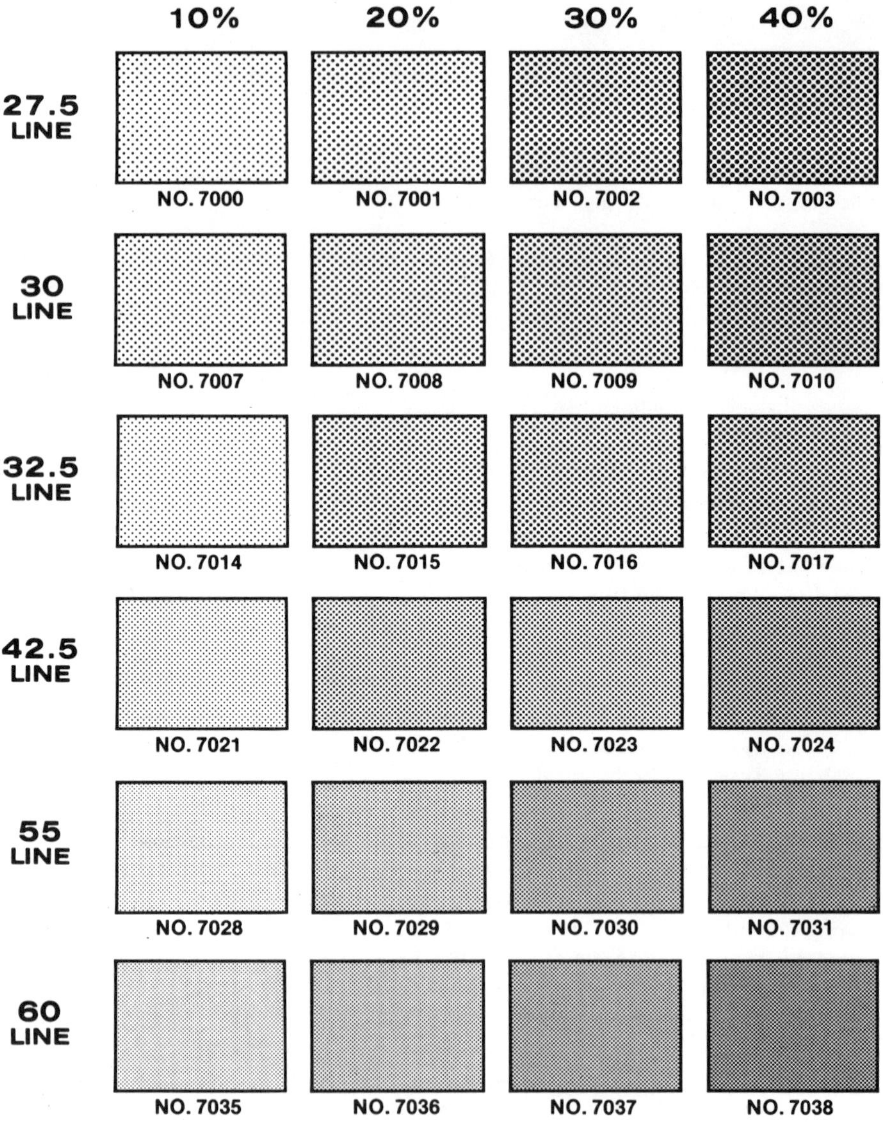

Typical shading tints available in adhesive shading films or overlays. (*Courtesy Graphic Products Corporation, manufacturer of Formatt and Formaline*)

sheet-fed. A press that prints on sheets of paper, as opposed to a web-press which prints on paper coming off a roll. There are some advantages to sheet-fed offset over web offset. Although there is a shift from sheet-fed to web offset for books and medium- and long-run periodicals, sheet-fed remains dominant

Sheetfed press. (*Courtesy New Horizons Color Corporation, reprinted by permission of Printing Views Magazine*)

for the printing of labels, specialty work, and for small commercial jobs. Sheet-fed has faster makeready, and less paper spoilage even though the overall cost of a roll of paper is cheaper than the sheets. There is more versatility as to the kind of paper stock that can be run on sheet-fed including pressure-sensitive, tissue, board, etc., which means that sheet-fed presses are geared to more diverse work such as long- and short-run posters, labels, dress patterns, mechanical drawings, magazine inserts, and folding cartons. The web press is faster, but on short and medium runs, this is not a factor if sheet-fed makeready is quicker and paper stock is conserved. Sheet-fed printing requires fast-drying inks since the paper cannot go through a drying unit as does a web. The web press has in-line folders, gluers, and perforators which add to speed and economy, but these attachments are being added in-line to many sheet-fed presses to equalize the web's advantages.

For quality jobs requiring a fifth or sixth color, or spot varnishing, a sheet-fed press is required. There is also more precise backing up and cutting on sheet-fed for more perfect alignment from page to page.

In spite of these points, many experts predict a dim future for sheet-fed presses because of the high volume that can be handled on the web press.

sheeting. Cutting rolls of paper or book covering materials into sheets.

sheet size. The dimension of the size of paper required on a sheet-fed press in order to produce the desired trim size of a publication. Sheet size is also determined by type of binding and whether or not there are bleeds on the pages. The supplier calculates the size, although he can give the client a sheet size calculator to help determine what is needed for a job. The supplier should always verify sheet size, however, as the client can easily make a mistake.

sheetwise. A method of printing in which each sheet is printed first on one side with one form and then on the other side with a different form. Guides and gripper remain the same. In work-and-turn and work-and-tumble the same form is used for both sides. *See also* work-and-tumble and work-and-turn.

shilling mark. *See* solidus.

shingling. Graduating the margins on a saddle-wire bound publication so there is more space on gutter margins of the outside pages of the book than on the gutter margin of the inside pages. Shingling is done so that the outer pages will have the same outside margins as the inside pages. The graduated margins are necessary because the outside pages have to wrap around a greater thickness in the gutter. *See also* graduated margins.

shoot. The term comes from the gun camera, built around 1882, during the brief vogue for "detective cameras." These cameras looked exactly like guns, and were designed for the amateur photographer who wished to disguise the fact that a picture was being taken. Cameras were hidden in flowers and hats, camouflaged as neckties, and even concealed in walking-stick handles. The gun camera is photographic memorabilia, but it is still a common event for a photographer to "shoot a picture."

shooting copy. 1. Photographing copy for reproduction. 2. The camera-ready copy itself.

short ink. An ink that cuts off cleanly, allowing small type and halftones to be clearly and crisply printed. However, a short ink has less ability than long ink to resist dampening solution on the offset press. Short inks have a tendency to pile on the rollers, plate, or blanket. *See also* ink.

short run. A printing quantity of about 10,000 copies or less, usually done on a sheet-fed press as opposed to a web press, which is more suitable for long runs. Plates for short runs are made differently from those for long runs which demand a longer life for the plate.

shoulder. 1. Space on the body of a piece of metal type to allow for ascenders or descenders. The shoulder provides the minimum space required to separate successive lines. Point size is based on the entire block of type from ascender to the bottom of the shoulder. *See* type for illustration. 2. In phototype, the space between the bottom of the descender and the line designating the point size. Type is designed slightly smaller than its point size, i.e., the x-height plus the ascender is 2/3 the type size. The descender is less than 1/3 the type size to allow for the shoulder.

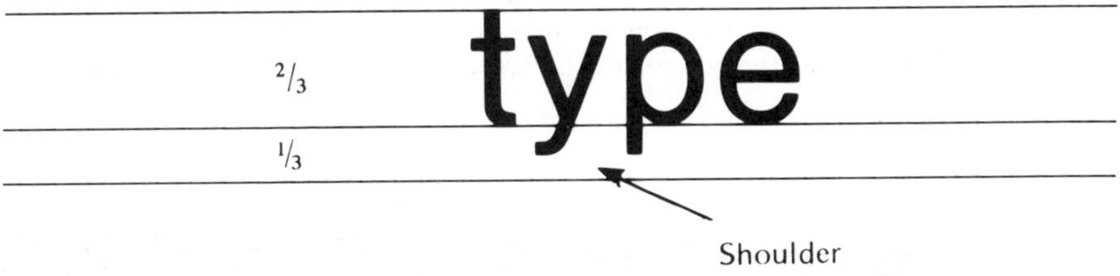

Shoulder.

show. The amount of material extending from the spine onto the front and back covers of a book which has a three-piece binding.

show-through. A condition in printing in which printed matter on one side of the page can be seen through the back of the page under normal lighting. Show-through is caused by too heavy an impression or penetration of inks and can be avoided by printing on a more opaque paper.

shrink wrap. Cellophane wrapping done by machine at the bindery. Shrink wrapping helps a book hold its shape and cuts down on damage during shipping.

sic. A notation in a quote showing that an error was in the original. In recent years publishers have tended to correct obvious misspellings in quotes rather than use sic.

sidebar. A short article related to a long article and separated visually, such as with a box and its own headline.

side head. A headline set at the side of a page or column, either flush with the margin of the type page, or run into the paragraph to which it belongs.

Side Head

A side-head is often set in the margin to call attention to a new subject or to break up the page. Side heads are attractive in lay-outs with a lot of white space. For example, this paragraph has a side head next to it.

Side head.

side sewing. The strongest binding method there is, used often in children's books, reference sets, library editions, and family bibles. The thread passes through holes drilled in the sides of the signatures. Reinforcements are often added. The signatures can be opened only to the stitching, however, and will not lie flat. Thus effective gutter spreads are prevented. Also called Singer sewing. *See also* binding.

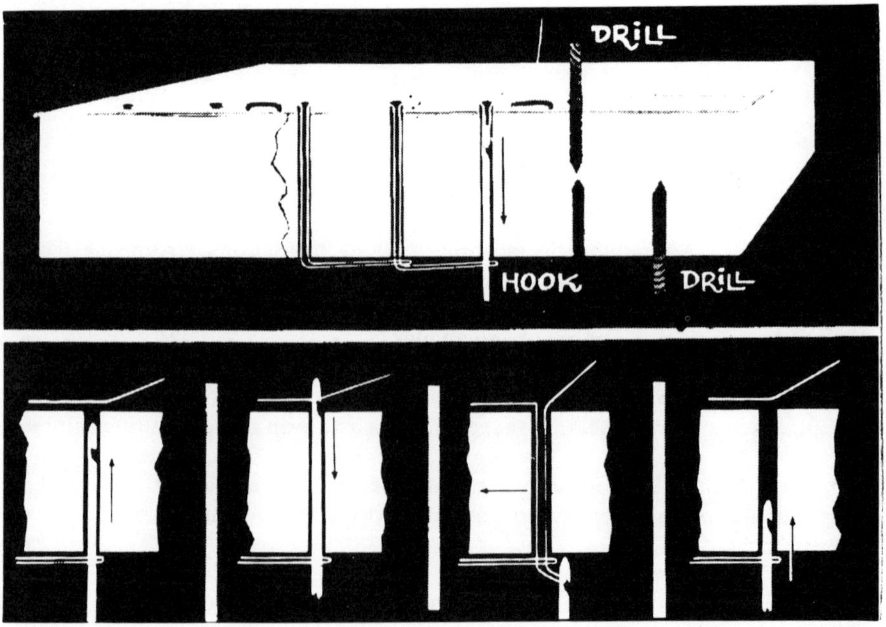

Side sewing, the strongest method of binding there is. (*Courtesy Kingsport Press*)

side wire. Binding books, catalogs or magazines by means of wire staples inserted through the binding edges of the pages and clinched at the back. Pages do not open flat, and gutter spreads are difficult to create so that they look like spreads. *See also* binding.

signature. 1. The printed sheet once it has been folded and is ready to be sewn. Signatures are made of multiples of four pages, usually 16 or 32 pages. They are called signatures because originally they were folded by hand, and the folder had to initial his or her own work in case an error in the work was found. 2. The advertiser's name in an advertisement.

Signatures being collated onto a conveyor belt. (*Courtesy Kingsport Press*)

silhouette halftone or **silo.** A halftone in which the main image is shown with the background area cut out by the removal of all the dots which would ordinarily print. Abbreviated silo. Not to be confused with dropout halftone.

silkscreen printing. *See* screen printing.

silver emulsion. The light-sensitive coating on film that darkens when light hits it, thus creating an image. When the film is developed, the unexposed silver is washed away, preventing any further exposure.

silverprint. *See* blueline.

Singer sewing. *See* binding and side-sewing.

Silhouette halftone.

sinkage. The point at which the text page begins when an unusually wide head margin is used. Sinkage is measured in picas.

six. *See* thin spaced.

sixteen. Slang for a 16-page form. *See also* page forms.

size of type. Originally the size of the slug on which the type characters were set. Now refers to the height of type from ascender to the bottom of the shoulder, or from base to base in unleaded type.

sizing, 1. The substances such as gelatins and resins added to paper to produce a smooth surface that resists moisture and receives ink. **2.** The process of suitably bonding or stamping foil to the binding material of a book. **3.** Calculating the dimensions of an illustration for reduction or enlargement using a proportion wheel or formula. *See also* scale.

sizing test. A paper test for the penetration of a liquid into or through the paper, an important consideration for the ink image which should penetrate a certain amount but not too much. A sizing test is also important in the making of labels to which an adhesive is applied.

skid. A movable wooden platform that holds piles of cut sheets of paper, books ready to be cartoned, or any similar bindery components.

skid lift. Any mechanical device which raises or lowers the skid.

slant or **slash**. *See* solidus.

sleeping giant. Nickname for the gravure industry. So called because of needed innovations in order for the industry to compete economically with offset lithography, although the quality obtained by gravure is useful for a number of markets. *See also* gravure.

slip case. A protective box into which books are placed with their spines visible. The boxes are manufactured outside the bindery and the books are inserted into the slip cases by hand at the bindery.

slip sheeting. Inserting blank sheets of absorbent paper between printed sheets coming off the press in order to prevent ink from setting off onto the back of the subsequent sheet coming off the press.

slipsnake. An artificial stone used to delete unwanted areas on an offset printing plate by rubbing away the emulsion. This is called stoning out.

slitting. Cutting sheets or webs into page-size strips by means of cutting wheels on the press. Slitting saves a later cutting operation.

slot punching. Rectangular as opposed to round punching holes such as those used for mechanical binding of loose-leaf sheets. *See also* comb binding.

slug. 1. A strip of metal used for spacing. Slugs are usually 6, 12, or 24 p., whereas leads are 1, 2 or 3 p. thick. *See also* furniture. 2. A line of type cast in one solid piece on Linotype or Ludlow hot-metal machines. 3. A heading used to inform the reader of the topic of a story or the department of the magazine. Also called department slug.

slurring. A printing error caused by slippage of paper, plate, blanket, or a combination, most often when printing halftones and solids on smooth coated paper. Slurring causes halftones and reverse lettering to fill in. Also called drag.

small capitals. Capital letters that are the x-height of a typeface, therefore not as tall as the regular capital letters. Abbreviated s.c. and indicated with two underlines. LOOKS LIKE THIS.

smash. A bindery process used to compress air out of the printed sheets if necessary to fit the bulking dummy or the size of the binding that has been prepared. Smashing gets the air out of the folds before the trim.

smoothness. A consideration in desirable paper. Smoothness is more important in letterpress and gravure than in offset. As smoothness decreases, solids and halftones get sandy and rough, but type is not much affected.

Smyth sewn. A strong method of binding in which signatures of a book are sewn together by a continuous piece of thread on a sewing machine. The machine sews thread through each signature at the binding edge with the threads passing continuously through the entire book. The thread passes from the inside of the signature to the binding edge, and the pages will lie open flat. This book is Smyth sewn. *See also* binding.

soft contouring. A photographic effect achieved by light diffraction which causes the image to have washed-out, unsharp contours and outlines.

soft cover. A paper, or other nonboard cover on a publication, usually adhesive bound.

soft dot. A condition in which the halation, or fringe around the dot is strong and almost equals the strength of the dot itself, as opposed to a hard dot which is very sharp with barely noticable fringes.

software. The programming, procedures, and coding used in computer typesetting systems, or in any computer system, as opposed to the hardware, i.e., electronic circuits or equipment.

solid. 1. Type that is set with no extra space, or leading, between the lines, except for that allowed by the shoulder area where the ascender or descender of the type would fall. Designated in type specifications with the same number on either side of the solidus, for example, 10/10 or 12/12. When type is set solid there is a danger that ascenders and descenders may touch. 2. Printing areas which are completely covered with ink, or areas printed with 100% of a given color.

solidus. A slant line used between parts of a fraction; to separate lines of poetry when quoted in a run-in fashion, etc. Looks like /. Also called shilling mark, slant, slash, and virgule.

solvent. A liquid that dissolves or suspends the pigment in the ink. Used to clean the ink fountains on a press or to wet up gravure inks.

sort. 1. The piece of metal which is type high and has a character on one end. The shoulder of the sort is the nonprinting area. 2. Pi characters, or special characters not in the font.

spacebands. The wedges used on linecasting machines to justify lines of type or to create word-spacing before the line is cast.

spaces. Small pieces of metal used in handset type for proper spacing of a line.

spacing. The lateral space between letters, words, sentences, columns or paragraph indentions, as opposed to leading, or vertical spacing between lines. The basic unit of measure is the em quad, or square of the type size being used. *French spacing* refers to the same band of space used after the period of a sentence as is used between other words in the text. *Regular spacing,* somewhat confusedly, calls for the band of space used between the words plus extra space. Spaces smaller than an em quad are, in sequence, en quads, 3-to-em, 4-to-em, and 5-to-em. A hairspace is about 1/2-pt. thick.

Letterspacing calls for the use of thin spaces between letters and is usually used for display type to make it more readable. Lower-case letters are rarely letterspaced except when necessary to fill out a line. Letterspacing is measured in units; an arbitrary number of units comprising an em quad. The most common unit system uses an 18-unit quad. Letterspacing would be + or – a unit or units.

This line is spaced with em quads

This line is spaced with en quads

This line is spaced with 3-to-the-em-spaces

This line is spaced with 4-to-the-em-spaces

Spacing.

spec. To specify type size and face and other details of a layout and design in graphic reproduction.

specimen book. A loose-leaf notebook containing samples of type, color swatches or any product of a graphic arts supplier. Suppliers will give specimen books to their clients free of charge. *See also* swatchbook.

spectacolor. A variation of hi-fi color in which preprinted ads are made, but with spectacolor the point where the paper is cut is critical to the sense of the ad. *See also* hi-fi color.

spelling. Before printing there was no consistency of spelling or punctuation. Medieval scribes ran words and sentences together at the whim of the individual. The early printer invented spaces, commas, periods, etc., as signals to the reader. Much of the printer's language also became part of our everyday conversation, such as upper case and lower case. *See also* p's and q's.

spine. The backbone of a publication which is visible when the publication is shelved. The title usually reads across the short dimension or from top to bottom, but this varies from publisher to publisher according to style.

spine-bulk. The thickness in inches of the spine of a book not including the thickness of the boards. The spine-bulk is determined by the amount the pages bulk per inch. It is a measurement given to the printer and binder for manufacturing. *See also* bulk.

spiral binding. A method of binding in which a continuous wire is threaded through holes punched in the binding edge of the pages.

spirit duplicator. An office duplicating machine. Aniline-dye carbon paper is placed against a sheet of coated master paper. The message is typed or drawn with a hard pencil or a ballpoint pen, producing a reversed copy on the back of the sheet, transferring some of the dye carbon from the carbon paper to the master. Copies are printed directly from this master. The paper to be printed is slightly moistened with an alcohol base solvent that picks up a thin layer of the dye from the reverse carbon on the master.

split fountain. Dividing the ink fountain on the press so that the left side prints one color and the right side prints a different color; or achieving a rainbow effect by splitting the fountain with narrow dividers. Because of the oscillation of the rollers on the press a third color can be produced where two colors meet. Since the ink rollers ink only certain pages in the form this way, there are limits as to which pages can be run with which colors.

split run. **1.** Printing two different mailing pieces two-up on a press, then cutting and mailing them separately. **2.** Two or more advertisements of the same size in the same position in different copies of a publication used as a testing procedure for separate ads or different versions of the same ad in regional editions of a national magazine.

spotting. Eliminating white dots on a photograph or negative by painting or opaquing them out with water-soluble, light-blocking opaque applied with a fine camel's hair brush.

spot varnish. To apply varnish in selective spots according to image areas. Spot varnishing is done from a plate or silk screen. *See also* varnishing.

spray. **1.** Substance such as corn starch applied to sheets coming off the press to prevent them from set-off of ink onto the subsequent sheet. **2.** Cans of pressurized fixative for drawings or strike-on type. Used sparingly it gives good protection against rub-off.

spread. **1.** To thicken a printed image. In particular to thicken letters. A spread can be accomplished by holding film out of emulsion-to-emulsion contact by the use of a layer of clear film which permits the light to spread as it passes through the layers. Or it can be done by underexposing the repro type so that less of the background is reflected and the letters appear to spread. Not to be confused with enlargements in which the inner openings of letters such as "o" would become larger rather than smaller as in a spread. **2.** The enlarging or thickening of printed areas caused by such things as the bleeding or lateral creep of ink, a poorly made plate, or running too much ink. **3.** Any two facing pages when a publication is lying open. A spread made of material that jumps the gutter and made of one unit is called a double truck or double-page spread.

square halftone. Any rectangular halftone with edges perpendicular to one another. Originally so called because the edges of the plate could be machine-cut on a finishing machine.

square serif. An easily recognizable typeface style that has serifs the same weight or heavier than the main letter strokes. Memphis is an example, also called Egyptian. *See also* typeface styles.

ABCDEFGHIJKLMNOPQRSTUVWXYZ ab cdefghijklmnopqrstuvwxyz 1234567890 - .,';$!%&)(':?/_ A specimen book is a cold thing—lifeless. In itself it has no beauty. It is merely a tool with which the artist helps bring out the ideas in his creative mind. *Without the artist the specimen book* of type faces is not much good. No matter what beauty there may be in the shape of a letter,

Square serif.

squeegee. A rubber blade used in silk-screen printing to push the ink through the mesh and stencil onto the paper. *See also* screen printing.

s. s. Abbreviation for same size in designating enlargements or reductions of illustrations.

stable base film. Film manufactured with quality control so that the emulsion does not vary from box to box and from year to year. Thus, the density of type or illustrations exposed to it will remain the same. Unstable base film is much cheaper and varies from box to box, so needs in-house control. Many printers use unstable film for economic reasons, but they make sure the density is controlled in their camera departments.

stabilization paper. Processed photopaper used for output of good-quality photorepros. Not to be confused with photosensitive papers that are chemically wet-processed in a tray or processor. Stabilization processed materials are sensitive to ultraviolet light and have a lifespan of only about 6 weeks. There are also problems with matching densities from batch to batch, and they tend to stretch so are useful only on jobs to be printed within a short period of time and requiring no corrections.

staining. Decorative coloring of the edges of the pages of a book. *See also* gilding.

stamping. Making an impression with a heavy, routed, relief die, made of copper or brass. The die is either inked or pressed with heat and pressure through a metallic foil that unrolls like a ribbon. Blind stamping uses no ink or foil, so the die alone leaves the impression of the letters. Stamping is commonly used on the binding of a book or for box printing.

standard book number. *See* International Standard Book Number.

standard colors. Standard red, yellow, green, blue, etc. chosen by the American National Standards Institute for publication printing. These colors for standard proofing inks are formulated using Borden Chemical Company manufactured pigments. Color proofs should be viewed under standard viewing conditions; 5000° Kelvin when viewing original and proof; 7500° Kelvin when viewing proofs against press run.

standard viewing conditions. Accurate color evaluation is an essential part of any successful printing business. From original artwork through the press run, color judgements must be made with accuracy and consistency. Misjudgments at any phase of the process can necessitate remakes and increase waste of time and materials. However, more than a good eye is required for accurate color evaluation, for the eye, no matter how well trained, can be overwhelmed by the many factors that contribute to the apparent color of an image.

The two major factors that influence color judgements are: the amount and quality of light illuminating the image, and the color of the background against which the image is viewed.

The color of the light is the most important factor affecting the appearance of an image. Correlated color temperature can best be described by imagining a large furnace with a small opening in one side. If the furnace is heated uniformly to a high enough temperature, the small opening will first appear red, then yellow, and then whiter, as the temperature rises. The correlated color temperature of a light is the temperature in Kelvins of the furnace when the color of the hole visually matches the color of the light.

The color-rendering index is a number that defines the ability of a light to make colors appear as they would when illuminated by daylight of the same correlated color temperature. An index of 100 represents a perfect simulation of daylight.

The brightness of the illumination affects the apparent purity of colors and the amount of detail visible in shadows. In general, the brighter the illumination, the more saturated colors appear, and the greater the amount of detail that may be seen in shadow areas.

Finally, the geometry of the illumination also affects the apparent color and contrast of an image. Whether the illumination is coming from a small source or a large diffuse one, the angle at which the light strikes the image and the angle of view all affect the appearance.

The surround is the area that appears in the field of view of a person doing an evaluation. If the surround has a definite color, it affects visual evaluation in two ways. First, any light that strikes the surround and is reflected onto the image will change the color of the viewing illumination. Secondly, the eye tends to adapt to the color of the surround, so a colored surround will bias the judgement of color.

Light sources in the surround can bias color judgments in much the same way as a colored surround does. If lights other than the main viewing lights illuminate an image they may alter the color of the illumination. If these lights are in the field of view of a person evaluating color, his eyes tend to adapt to the color of the lights, which will cause color judgments to be biased.

Knowing that these many factors contribute to the appearance of an image, the American National Standards Institute (ANSI) has established viewing standards, which, if carefully followed, will improve the accuracy and consistency of color evaluation.

The standard specifies that light with a correlated color temperature of 5000° Kelvin be used for *color quality evaluations and comparisons.* An example of color quality evaluation is when an original is selected for use in a job. Color quality comparisons are made when images from different processes are compared, such as when a press sheet is compared with an original. 5000° Kelvin illumination was chosen for this purpose because it appears very white. Also 5000° Kelvin is an average color of daylight and has an almost equal energy output at all visible wavelengths. The color-rendering index should be from 90 to 100.

Light with a correlated color temperature of 7500° Kelvin is specified for *color uniformity evaluations;* i.e., those in which two reproductions from the same process are compared. The main use of this lighting is comparison of sheets from a press run. 7500° Kelvin illumination was chosen for this purpose because it is bluer than 5000° Kelvin, making comparison of the yellow printer easier. The color-rendering index should be from 90 to 100.

Viewing areas should be protected from any lights which are not known to conform to the standard lighting specifications. The surround should be painted neutral gray. Images should always be positioned to minimize glare. When viewing transparencies there should be an illuminated area at least 2 inches wide on at least three sides of the transparency. However, the area of this illuminated border should not exceed four times the area of the transparency.[8]

standing initial. *See* stick-up initial.

standing type. Hot metal type that has been set and is ready for printing, as opposed to printing from an electrotype or sterotype made from that type. KTS, or keep type standing, means to hold the madeup pages for subsequent printing. The opposite of this is kill.

stapling. *See* saddle-stitch or saddle-wire and side wire.

start-up sheets. Waste sheets from the beginning of the press run before the ink is settled to the right color balance. Start-up sheets should not be used in the final product.

stat. *See* Photostat.

steel engraving. An intaglio printing process used to print fine stationery, business cards, stock certificates, and engraved bank notes. The plate is made by manually cutting away the printing areas on the metal plate. Intricate designs are machine engraved. The surface of the plate is inked, wiped clean, and the printing is done by pressing the paper into the fine grooves that hold the ink, thus giving a raised effect to the ink on the paper.

stencil printing. Forcing ink through openings in order to obtain an image. The idea may have originated from observations of insects eating holes through leaves. Polynesians forced dyes through openings of the leaves onto bark cloth. Intricate designs became possible when coarsely woven silk fabric was used to hold the stencil pieces in place. Also called silk-screen, serigraphy, and screen process printing. The accepted term for modern stencil printing is screen printing. *See also* screen printing.

step-and-repeat. A method of making multiple exposures of the same printing image onto a plate by stepping it to the position determined by a layout, thus eliminating the necessity of stripping negatives to a flat. The step-and-repeat machine is a photo-mechanical process. For example, 16 repetitions of the same image could be printed on one 16 page form all at once. The method requires a good-quality plate with high-exposure speed.

stereotype. A duplicate letterpress plate made by forcing papier-mâche' into the face of the type matter and drying it by baking. This is called a mat or matrix. This mold is then filled with metal to form the duplicate plate. Stereotyping is used mostly in newspaper printing where copy consists mostly of line art and coarse-screened halftones for printing at high speeds.

[8]*Standard Lighting For the Graphic Arts,* Macbeth, A division of Kollmorgen Corporation.

Step-and-repeat machine. (*Courtesy Lehigh Press. Photo by Sid Delmar Leach*)

stet. From the Latin *stare,* "to stand," hence, let it stand. A proofreader's mark indicating copy should appear as it originally was before any correction was marked. Usually the copy to be stetted is marked with a row of dots underlining it. *See also* proofreader's marks.

stick. *See* composing stick.

sticking. Set-off of ink from one sheet to the back of the next sheet to the point where the sheets actually stick together.

Stick-up initial. A letter larger than the text which aligns at the bottom of the first line of text. A stick-up initial sticks up into the white space above the line. It is often used to begin a chapter, or for decoration. Also called standing initial. *See also* initial.

stiffness test. A paper test that measures what it takes to bend a piece of paper.

still. A prescreened halftone that has been shot dot for dot and has to be developed by hand so that it can be watched while the dot is developed with precision. If it is underdeveloped the dots will show, if overdeveloped, they will run together. *See also* dot for dot.

stipple. To use small dots to create light and shade. Stipple board has a pattern of raised dots on its surface. A line drawn across stipple board is dotted or stippled, not solid. *See also* shading tints.

stitching. *See* binding, sidesewing, and Smyth sewn.

stock. 1. The beaten and refined pulp that is ready to be made into a sheet of paper. It is the combination of fiber, size, fillers, and alum which determines the characteristics of the paper and its use. *See also* papermaking. 2. Any material used to receive a printed impression. Also called substrate.

stock cut or **stock photos.** Cuts of stock photos. Formerly called mat service. Photos available from stock houses. Stock photos depict common subjects that can be used in advertising articles, promotion, etc., where original photos are not necessary. Everything is available from animals to night skies. The photographer and the photo agency are usually credited.

stone. The machine metal surface, originally made of stone, on which letterpress forms are assembled and locked up prior to putting them on the press. Also called imposing stone.

stone out. To delete minor areas unwanted on an offset printing plate by using an abrasive stone.

stone proofs. A proof taken from the letterpress form after it is locked up but before it has gone to press. A stone proof is used only to check position as the quality is poor. The paper is simply laid over the form, and a block is placed over the paper and given a sharp rap so that the ink is transferred to paper. *See also* stone.

stopping out. **1.** Applying opaque to photographic negatives to prevent light from passing through the negative and creating an image on the plate. **2.** Protecting certain areas of deep-etched plates so that no ink will go on the protected areas. **3.** Using a special lacquer in dot etching to protect areas on positives.

storage. A device in phototypesetting equipment into which information can be keyboarded and later retrieved. This can be a memory tape, a disk, or a drum.

straddle head or **straddle rule.** A heading or a rule that is centered over more than one column.

Straddle Head

Sub-head Sub-head

Straddle head and rule.

straight matter. Body type, as opposed to display type, set in columns with little variation.

strength. The amount of saturation that a color has. *See also* color tree and saturation.

stress. The slant of a character.

stretch and shrink. Paper tends to stretch when it absorbs moisture, and to shrink when it loses moisture. The stretching and shrinking occurs mostly across the grain. On press, the paper should run in the direction of the least shrinkage. This affects grain direction when ordering paper. Paper for most offset presses should be ordered grain long.

stretch test. A paper test for the degree of elasticity a paper has as fibers re-align, stretch, and come back without bursting the paper.

strike-on composition. Type set by direct impression, as on a typewriter com-posing machine. *See also* cold type.

strike-through. 1. The penetration of the vehicle of the ink into a paper so that it shows through onto the other side of the sheet, likely to occur when printing on an absorbent stock. 2. An embossed impression of type in letterpress printing which can be seen on the opposite side of the sheet.

stripper. A makeup person who assembles and strips negative or positive film onto a flat for making printing plates.

stripping. 1. Preparing and positioning negatives or positives in relationship to each other for the making of a printing plate. The film is exposed to a photo-chemical printing plate. The plate ready film of an entire page is laid out accord-ing to imposition, masked according to specifications, and taped to goldenrod or red material used as a carrier when the film is exposed to the plate, emulsion to emulsion. 2. Assembling all the linework, text, and halftone film on a grid according to a layout in composition. From this working flat, a proof is taken which can be read for corrections. Many stripping steps are now being eliminated with greater reliance on paste-up.

stripping guide. Translucent layout tissue or grid used as a guide for stripping film mechanicals.

stroke. The vertical, horizontal, or oblique motion of the letterforms of a typeface.

stub. The guiding entries, words or numbers, in the first column of a table, usually aligned flush left.

Stripping. (*Courtesy Arcata Book Group*)

style. Rules of uniformity concerning punctuation, capitalization, hyphenation, spelling, and other details in writing. House style is set by a particular publishing house, and varies from house to house.

style sheet. A list of details of the editing and typography of a manuscript and how they are to be handled in matters of spelling, capitalization, punctuation, and the publisher's style. The style sheet is compiled by the editing supervisor or the copy editor. *See also* copy editing.

subhead. Any type of heading making a subdivision. A subhead is usually smaller than the main heading and helps to break up a column or a page.

subscript. *See* inferior figure.

substance. *See* basis weight or basic weight.

substrate. **1.** The material which is to be printed, i.e. paper, board, etc. **2.** The carrier, i.e., emulsion, or coating of film.

subtractive color. In the graphic arts, we deal not with light energy sources, which use the additive color theory, but with pigment filters and paper surfaces. Materials that are not sources of light operate under the subtractive theory of color and either transmit or reflect color.

An ink, a dye, a pigment, or a filter subtracts some of the colors from the white light projected through it. This is possible because white light is made of all the colors of the spectrum, and complementary colors act as filters for each other. In the subtractive color method of printing, yellow, magenta, and cyan are the primary colors because when printed, they act as filters.

For example, magenta inks filter out green and allow blue and red to come through. Cyan filters out red and lets blue and green come through. Yellow filters out blue, leaving red and green. When a yellow dot is overprinted with a cyan dot, the yellow filters out blue, while the cyan filters out red, allowing only green to reflect to the eye. Therefore, the subsequent combinations of yellow, cyan and magenta allow green, red, and blue to come through in turn. When green, red, and blue are combined in very small dots, an optical illusion is formed of all the colors of the spectrum.

suede coating. A finish on papers that is not mirror bright, but when rubbed with a finger is made shiny.

sulphate paper. Paper made from wood chips cooked under pressure in a solution of caustic soda and sodium sulphide. Sulphate paper is very strong but cannot be bleached as white as sulphite paper. Kraft paper is a sulfate paper. *See also* chemical pulp and papermaking.

sulphite pulp. Paper pulp made from wood chips cooked under pressure in a solution of bisulphite of lime. *See also* chemical pulp.

super. 1. Crash paper used as a lining for the spine of a hard-bound book. 2. A grade of coated paper. Abbreviated SC.

supercalendering. Putting the paper through a separate stack of shiny rollers, some of which move faster than others to make the paper smooth and glossy. Supercalendered paper is not as smooth as coated paper, but has the highest gloss that can be given to an uncoated paper. Supercalendering is done off the papermaking machine. *See also* calendering, finish, and papermaking.

superimposition. Enhancing or altering an image photographically by covering a portion of the negative then exposing another image into that area.

superior figure or **superscript.** A small numeral or letter that is printed above the x-height of a letter. It is often a mathematical symbol. Looks like ^{7}. *See also* proofreader's marks.

surface plates. A printing plate on which the image area is in the same plane with the nonprinting area, although the inked image may be minutely above the surface of the nonprinting area. Surface plates are available with or without light-sensitive coating on their surface. Uncoated plates may be coated in the shop or can be purchased for use with electrostatic facsimile transfer or other platemaking methods.

surface sized. *See* sizing.

surface strength. The ability of the paper surface to withstand the tack or pull of the ink and blanket.

surprint. To expose a second negative upon a previously exposed image of the first negative, usually printing type on a halftone background by double burning. *See also* double burn.

swash initials. A florid version of standard italic capital letters, usually used for ornamentation. Swash caps are often used with italic lowercase letters.

Swash letters.

swatchbook. 1. A sample book of color-matching systems, e.g., Pantone Matching System. The colors are numbered for identification, and in the printer's edition ink-mixing instructions are included. 2. Books containing samples of covering materials or paper.

swipe. An idea taken from an original source and modified enough for use without obtaining permission. Commonly used in illustration and layout.

synthetic papers. Papers, which, like plastic-coated stocks, have dimensional stability, grease, oil, and moisture resistance, durability, and require an ink that dries by oxidation rather than by absorption. *See also* pyroxylin.

T

tabbing. Bindery operation in which index tabs are laminated or adhered to the edge of the page for books such as dictionaries, bibles, and cookbooks, which are thumb-indexed. Tabbing is done by hand and is very costly. *See also* thumb cut.

tabloids. A publication in newspaper format, about half the size of a regular newspaper page.

tabular. Type set in columns or tablets. Some typesetters specialize in this type of work.

tack. The amount of an ink's internal cohesion between particles, or its stickiness. A tacky ink has high pulling power and can cause picking, or lifting of particles from the paper, and can reduce the ink's film-splitting ability and thus its effectiveness. A certain amount of tack is required in process inks for proper trapping. Tacky inks print sharp lines and halftones.

tag. A grade of paper which has good bending and folding qualities, good tearing and water resistance, and a surface adaptable to printing, stamping, or writing. Tag board is sometimes tinted and colored on one or both sides.

tail-piece. A small line ornament used at the end of a chapter.

tape. Punched paper ribbon or magnetic tape, produced by the keyboard unit of a typesetting system and used to activate either the unit that photographically sets the type, a unit that directly strikes-on type, or a computer that further processes the data to be used for phototypesetting input.

tape editing. The transferring of information, via a video display terminal, from one tape to another to produce a corrected tape for the phototypesetting unit.

tape merging. A method of editing and correcting tapes in phototypesetting systems.

tapered rule. A rule which is thicker in the middle than at the end. Usually used to graphically divide parts of a page where a complete box rule is not wanted.

Tapered rules. (*Courtesy Kingsport Press*)

tap-out. A method of ascertaining the true color of an ink by applying a spot of it to paper and tapping it out with the finger to the approximate thickness when printing. Also called draw-down. *See also* flat color.

teacher's edition. A textbook that does not have to meet the standards and specifications required in manufacturing textbooks.

tearsheet. A page from a magazine or newspaper containing a printed article, story, or advertisement.

teaser. *See* kicker.

tear test. **1.** A paper test to establish the tear strength of a paper. Bags, maps, currency, etc., all have different tear requirements. **2.** A method of determining the direction of the grain. Paper tears more easily with the grain than against it.

technifax. *See* T-print.

teletypesetting. Use of word-processing devices that permit communication over telephone lines for keyboarding at one location and actual setting of type at another. Letters, reports, copy or even pictures can be transmitted electronically to another location where they are recorded and printed out. This eliminates the use of pouch delivery, messengers, or the postal service.

tensile test. A paper test to ensure that the web of paper will not break during printing. Strength of paper depends on the nature of the fiber rather than the thickness of the paper. Papers subject to considerable tension require high tensile strength. *See also* stretch and shrink.

tertiary colors. Colors produced by mixing any two of the secondary colors to achieve orange-green, green-violet, or violet-orange.

text. The body matter of a page, as opposed to the headings.

textbook. A book meeting certain specification standards made for quantity distribution to schools or colleges.

text paper. A grade of paper such as antique, laid, or wove papers used for booklets, programs, announcements, and advertising printing, as opposed to book papers, or business papers. Text papers are noted for their interesting textures and attractive colors.

text type. A class of type that originates from the first cast types. Text type was an imitation of handlettering. Similar to German Fraktur. Also known as block letter. *See also* typeface styles. *See* black letter for illustration.

thermography. An engraved look achieved by a nonprinting method which is less expensive than steel-engraving with dies. A resinous powder is dusted over ink that is still wet on a sheet that has been printed by either offset or letterpress. A vacuum collects the excess dust from the nonprinted area. The sheet goes on a conveyor belt, and a heating unit causes the particles of powder to fuse with the ink, giving the letters a raised effect. The slow-drying ink can be gold, silver, copper, or any number of other colors. The back of a piece of thermography printing remains flat, whereas an engraved piece will be slightly debossed. The thermography finish is usually very shiny. Also called plateless engraving and imagic.

thickness. Paper thickness, or caliper, is measured in mils, or thousandths of an inch. The bulk of the paper determines the thickness of the book, and is expressed in numbers of pages per inch.

thicks and thins. The strokes of various thicknesses on letters. Some typefaces are designed with thicks and thins, while others, usually sans serif faces, keep the same thickness in the strokes.

thin spaced. A six-unit space based on the unit system of typesetting which counts 18 units to the em for purposes of justification and hyphenation of a line. Also called six. *See also* unit.

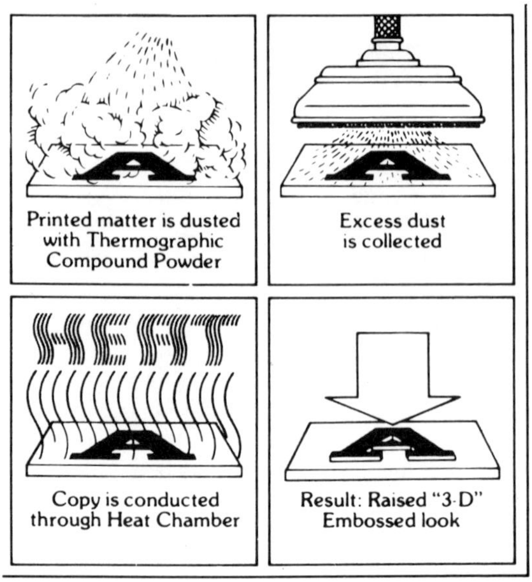

Thermography. (*Courtesy Van Son Holland Ink Corporation, Handbook of Helpful Press Hints*)

thirty. Written –30–, it means the end of a story in newspaper copy. Originally, telegraphers used it as a symbol for the end of a story being transmitted.

thirty-two. Slang for 32-page forms. *See also* page forms.

thirty-five mm film. The type of film used most often for color enlargements in publications. When enlarging up to poster size, 35 mm film cannot be used, because the colors break down. Rather, a 4 x 5 transparency should be used.

three-color process. Similar to four-color process except that the black plate is not used.

3M color key. *See* color key.

thumb cut. A half-moon notch cut out of the edge of a book to provide a step-like effect with which to open the book at a desired spot. A half-moon label is then adhered to the page to indicate whatever information is indexed. This is a hand operation at the bindery, since a person, rather than a machine must look up what in the book must be indexed, and mark that place in the pages. Thus it is very expensive. *See also* tabbing.

thumbnails. Miniature rough sketches or layouts.

tilting. A foundry type alphabet of capital letters which fills the full face of the piece of metal type, thus permitting the setting of caps with a minimum of leading. Tilting caps have no corresponding lowercase alphabet.

tint. **1.** A color obtained by adding white to a solid color. This is done photomechanically in printing by screening to obtain a reduction of the solid color. **2.** A piece of screened photographic film placed over an area of a flat to provide a gray tone. For process color, any shade on a color chart can be laid onto an area by applying the necessary combinations of tint screens. The screen angles must be positioned carefully to avoid moiré patterns. Also called screen. **3.** *See* shading tint.

tint block. **1.** A panel of color, either solid or screen. **2.** A solid or screened plate used to print a background color over which halftone art, or type of a darker color, will be surprinted.

tip-in. The hand operation at the bindery in which a leaf is pasted onto a page of a signature before binding. This occurs when a full-color page is required in a black-and-white signature. A tip-in is expensive and not as strong as wraps or placing inserts between signatures. End papers are tipped into the first and last signatures of a book.

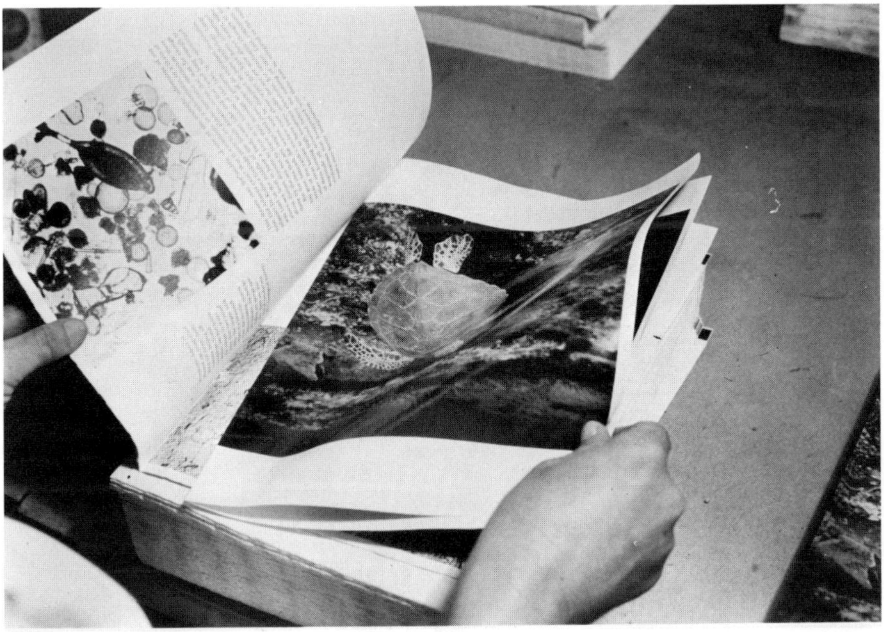

Tip-in of color insert is done by hand at the bindery. This is why a tip-in is so much more expensive than a wrap, which can be dropped between signatures by machine. (*Courtesy Kingsport Press*)

tissue. Lightweight, gauzy papers, weighing less than 18 lbs. used for tissue overlays, carbon copies of correspondence, or for overseas correspondence.

tissue overlay. A thin, translucent piece of paper placed over artwork for protection and to indicate color breaks or corrections for the cameraman and platemaker.

title page. The page that carries the title, author, and name of the publisher of the book. It is usually the third page, and counted among the roman numeraled front matter which precedes the text. Abbreviated TP.

to come. An indication that part of the job is not included with the material currently being worked on, but that the missing elements will be submitted before a specified deadline. Sometimes abbreviated TK.

tombstoning. Undesirable visual alignment of separate elements horizontally across a page so that they appear as one. For example, aligning three subheads in three adjacent columns. Tombstoning is to be avoided in layout.

tone. The range of grays between black and white. This range can vary a color from light to dark. *See also* color tree and value.

tone-line. Shooting continuous-tone copy as line copy by masking and special processing so that darks fill in, and highlights become whiter, thus losing detail.

Tone-line. (*Courtesy ProPiano and Not Just Jazz*)

Tone line illustration made from a black and white photograph. (*Courtesy Joel A. Levirne, Graphic Images, Ltd.*)

tonnage. Amount, in pounds, of paper used for a job. Tonnage is calculated by multiplying the M-weight times the number of sheets used and dividing by 1000.

tool. **1.** To shoot two halftones together and then separate them. If the halftones are not cut apart evenly, a ragged edge can cause a dirty tool-out, or a dirty effect in the final printing. **2.** To alter the surface of a printing plate with engraver's tools. For example, separating illustrations which were engraved on the same halftone plate.

tooth. A rough texture to some paper's finishes which permit the paper to take ink readily. Toothy paper is good for charcoal and pencil drawing, and watercolor painting. It can be used in letterpress or lithographic printing, but not gravure, because full contact between plate and paper is not possible, thus causing a snowflake effect.

top side. *See* felt side.

TP. *See* title page.

T-print. Technifax photoproof. The photosensitive paper is dimensionally stable and gives a photographic proof that comes close to press quality. Often requested when the client wants to see how the artwork provided will reproduce when printed. Erroneously called velox.

tr. *See* transpose.

trade book. A book intended for sale to the general public. Not to be confused with trade magazine.

trade magazine. A magazine either written for a profession or for a group, as opposed to a consumer magazine, which is written for the general public. Not to be confused with trade book.

trademark. A device or symbol that identifies the manufacturer of a product. The phrase "Reg. U.S. Pat. Off." is abbreviated ®, and refers to a trademark that has been registered in the U.S. Patent Office. Trademarks are usually more sophisticated in design than logos.

Transfer key. Trade name of prepress acetate color proof on one sheet, manufactured by 3M. Not to be confused with color key which has one sheet of acetate for each filter. *See also* Cromalin.

transfer type. Text and display type, ornaments, and borders carried on sheets for transferring onto the working surface. Transfer type is either pressure-sensitive and transferred by burnishing and then lifting the sheet, or self-adhesive cut-out letterforms with a protective backing.

transitional. A Roman type style that combines both old style and modern features. Serifs are bracketed, and those of the lower-case are oblique. The axis of the curves is vertical or inclined slightly to the left. Looks like Baskerville. *See also* roman.

translucent. Somewhat clear so that an image can be seen through a slightly opaque material.

transmission via satellite. Sending page data or page make-up from editorial or composition services to printing services via satellite. The publisher has the advantages of control, storage, retrieval, editing, and flexible scheduling, and material can be sent at the last minute.

As volume or schedule increases equipment becomes more expensive. Time-sharing allows clients to make use of a single video terminal connected to a big system via special communications lines or a satellite. A remote terminal can take instructions over phone lines. Information is input, edited and formated, then stored on floppy disk and later transmitted to the main system. It is predicted that telecommunications via orbiting satellite will eventually be cheaper than using the U.S. mail.

transparency. Positive colored photograph on transparent film, as opposed to a reflective color print. A transparency is viewed by transmitted light and can be used for color separations. Prints can also be made from transparencies.

transparency viewer. A box containing bulbs of 5000° Kelvin filtered through a diffuser, used for viewing transparency copy under the best possible light conditions, especially for color correcting four-color process printing against the original transparency. Also called light box.

transparent. Clear, so that an image is visible through it. Transparent copy must be viewed by passing light through it. For example, a color slide or negative.

transparent ink. Printing inks that blend together to produce a secondary color when they are printed one on top of the other. They do not conceal the color beneath them as do opaque, or flat color inks. Process color inks are transparent.

transpose. To change places with another word, letter, line or illustration. Abbreviated tr.

transposition. A typographic error in which letters or words are reversed. For example, hte for the, or adn for and. *See also* proofreader's marks.

trapping. 1. The ability of a printed ink to accept a succeeding or overprinted ink, making it possible to superimpose one color over another to create proper color balance. On a web press, the darkest tonal area should not exceed 260% trapping because the ink is wet. The colors first printed must be tackier than the subsequent inks so that the first ink helps pull the subsequent one off the plate or blanket. Ink tack should be adjusted for good trapping. 2. A slight overlapping where two colors meet, necessary to avoid a white line between the two color areas.

trim. To cut off and square the edges of paper before printing, or to cut and square a printed piece after printing. If illustrations bleed, up to 1/4 in. should be allowed for the trim.

trimetal plates. *See* bimetal plates.

trim marks. Marks placed on the copy, or on a mechanical or dummy, to indicate the edge of the page.

trim size. The size of the printed sheet after it has been trimmed. Allowance is made for the final trim during imposition. The jacket and cover of a book are usually 1/4 in. larger than the trim for overhang.

T-square. A wood, plastic, or metal instrument used for drawing horizontal lines and as a guide in drawing vertical and inclined lines. The head is held firmly against the left edge of the drawing board and slid along the edge.

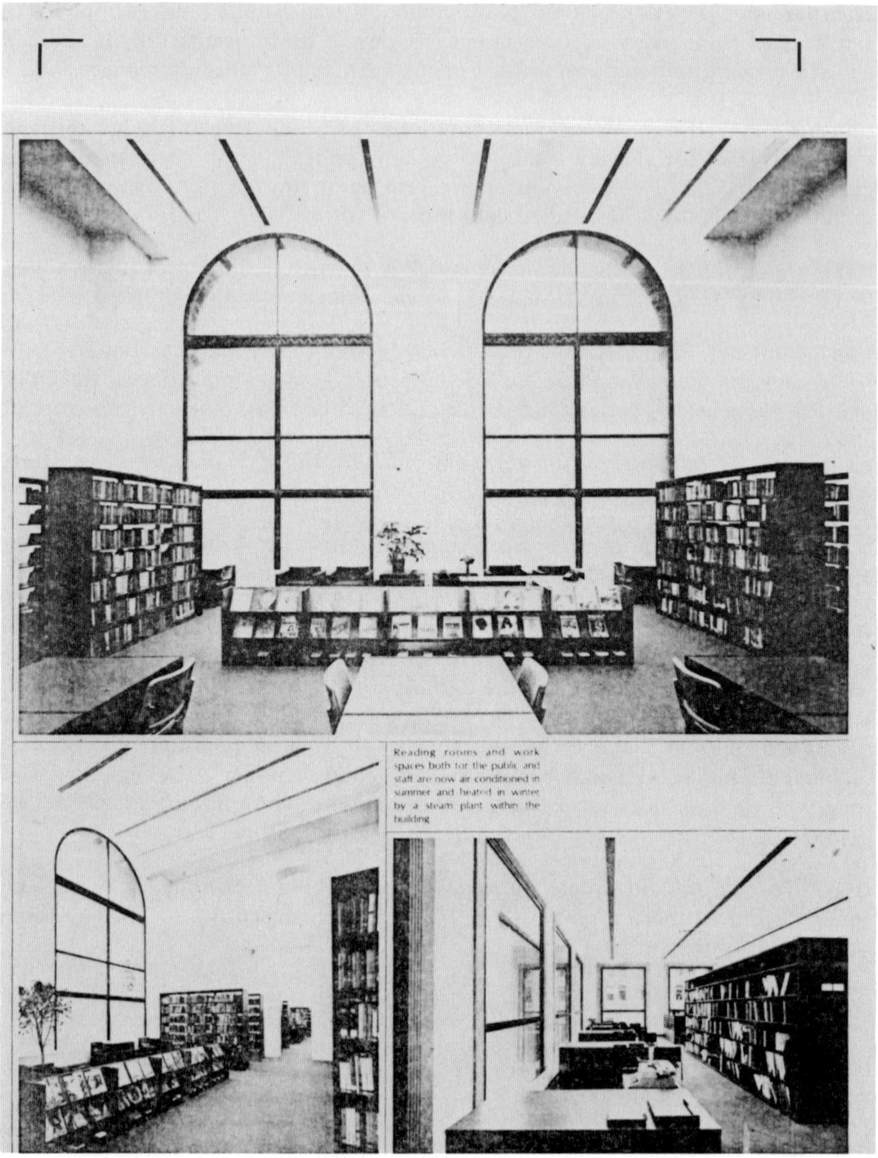

Trim marks.

turnover. Words transferred from the end of one line to the beginning of the next. Also called runover.

tweezer work. Stripping-in corrections that are only a word or a line and require delicate handling on the flat or mechanical.

two-ply. *See* ply.

two-tone paper. *See* duplex paper.

two-up. **1.** Printing two impressions of the same thing at one impression by using duplicate plates or a step-and-repeat machine. This is often more economic than printing the single image on smaller sheets of paper because duplicate plates cost less than double press time. Printing can be done three-up, four-up, etc. as well. **2.** Two books, usually joined together at the head, folded gathered, and sewn as one, then cut apart during trimming.

two-up book production. A method of printing material so that the folded signatures at the end of the line contain two books on a sheet instead of one. The signatures are folded, gathered, and covered as two books until cut in two. *See also* head-to-head come and go.

type. **1.** The characters produced either by direct impression such as with ink in letterpress or through a carbon ribbon in cold, or strike-on type, or by the photographic method on paper or acetate. Type is camera ready and can be pasted up on a mechanical. Type can be set by hand, by hot-metal casting, by photographic or electronic methods. **2.** The rectangular metal or wood block having a face shaped to produce an impression of a character or symbol. *See also* generations of type, phototypesetting, typeface styles.

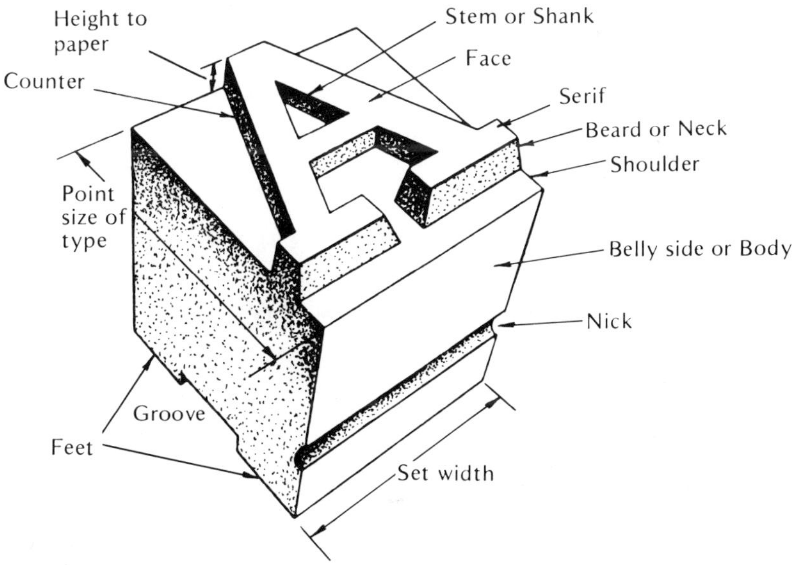

Hot metal type with names of each part. (Illustration by Andrew Steigmeier)

typecasting. Setting type by casting it in molten metal either as a complete line of type, or in individual characters.

typeface styles. A style applies to all designs with common stroke, stress, and serif. There are thousands of typeface designs, some styles are 400 years old, and some styles differ only very slightly from one another. But all alphabet variations can be categorized into seven classes of typeface styles. They are *roman; sans serif,* or *gothic; square serif,* or *egyptian; text,* or *black letter; script,* or *cursive; italic,* or *oblique* in the case of sans serif faces; and occasional. Any typesetter will supply his clients with type specimen books showing his selection of the various typeface styles he carries. No one book shows all of them.

The *roman* style is based on the characteristics of letterforms cut into granite by early Roman stone masons who used iron chisels to cut horizontal and vertical lines. The serif originated where the strokes did not intersect and the tool left a ragged edge. A cut would be made to straighten the unevenness, and this cut was called a serif. Today we call any type style that has stroke variation and a serif a roman typeface.

There are three subcategories of the roman typeface. *Oldstyle* roman has little stroke contrast, rather, strokes are strong and bold with no weak hair lines. It communicates a feeling of strength. *Modern* roman has massive thick strokes contrasted by thin hair lines and thin, straight serifs. It gives a feeling of ele-

Oldstyle Roman	— Garamond Medium
Transitional Roman	— Tiffany Medium
Text or Black Letter	— Old English
Script or Cursive	— *Original Script*
Italic or Oblique	— *Oracle Italic*
OCCASIONAL OR NOVELTY	**— ANTIQUE**
Modern Roman	— Baskerville Roman
Square Serif or Egyptian	**— Stymie Bold**
Sans Serif or Gothic	— Helios Medium

Typeface styles.

Text faces	*vs.*	display faces
Roman	*vs.*	*italic*
Lightface	*vs.*	**boldface**
Old style	*vs.*	Modern
Serif	*vs.*	sans serif
Condensed	*vs.*	**extended**
Solid	*vs.*	OUTLINE

Typeface styles.

gance. A few *transitional* typefaces combine characteristics of the two with greater stroke contrast than oldstyle but less than modern. A roman typeface is easy to read, and most ordinary reading matter such as books and magazines is set in a roman face.

Sans serif means without serif. It is made with uniform strokes and vertical stress, sometimes called block letter. These faces communicate a contemporary feeling but are fatiguing to read in body text. They are also called gothic, and should not be confused with the heavy massive architectural style.

Square serifs are formed with uniform strokes including serifs. Square serifs are often used in publications for younger readers because the letters are so easily recognizable.

Text, or *black letter* typefaces were designed to imitate the hand lettering of medieval scribes and were the first types cast. Text is used in formal situations such as wedding invitations. It is difficult to read, especially the upper case.

Script or *cursive* typefaces approximate the feeling of free-form handwriting Script faces are gradually replacing textfaces in contemporary invitations. They are also difficult to read but create a sweeping effect.

Italic is a slanting face used for emphasis and display. It matches all roman and sans serif faces.

Occasional or *novelty* forms are usually designed to meet specific needs and include faces that cannot be classed with the other six styles. There are no design constraints, and these designs are sometimes patented.

Other variations of a typeface style can be achieved with condensed or extended type, where the measure is stretched or narrowed. An outline face is one in which the body of the letter is dropped out. And there are differing weights of light, medium, and bold of most faces. A second-generation phototypesetting machine holds as many as 18 different typefaces at a time, and the CRT is virtually limitless, but this does not mean it is practical to mix typefaces. Font changes often require monitoring by the operator, who must make the changes manually. At keyboard stage, the photomachine may require over 10 commands to make the type changes, and this is time-consuming and costly. It is often also unesthetic to mix too many typefaces on a page, even though the advent of the CRT makes the possibilities of mixture infinite. *See also* graphics modifier and lettering.

type family. A range of various typeface designs that are all based on one style of the alphabet. This usually includes roman, italic, bold condensed, extended, and variances in weight from light to extra bold. Some families have more versions than others.

type founders. Those persons who hold the rights on the design of the type face. These designs are patented and cannot be duplicated without permission. Therefore, many similar typefaces have appeared by would-be copiers. Many typesetting systems have slightly different faces for this reason.

type gauge. A tool used for copy fitting, and measuring the number of lines set in a given type size. Type gauges are calibrated in points and picas on one edge and in inches on the other. Also called a line gauge.

type high. The height of metal type or engravings when mounted on wood or metal in order to make an impression. The height of metal type is 0.918 inch.

type mark. To indicate on the manuscript how the type is to be composed by the typesetter. *See also* specifications.

type measurements. *See* em, en, pica, and point.

type metal. An alloy of lead, tin, and antimony, and sometimes a trace of copper, used for casting type.

type page. The area of the page on which there is live matter, or copy. Outside the type page are the margins, running heads, and folios.

type series. One typeface design in its full size range from 6 pt. up to 72 pt., or up to 120 pt., depending on the typesetting equipment.

typesetter. 1. A person who sets type. 2. A device that actually creates the type from keyboarded instructions.

typesetting. The assembling by hand, linecasting machine, strike-on typewriter, or phototypesetter of typographic materials suitable for printing or for incorporating into a printing plate.

type sizes. Before the adoption of the point system, in about 1878, type sizes were known by distinguishing names, such as Great Primer for 18-pt. type.

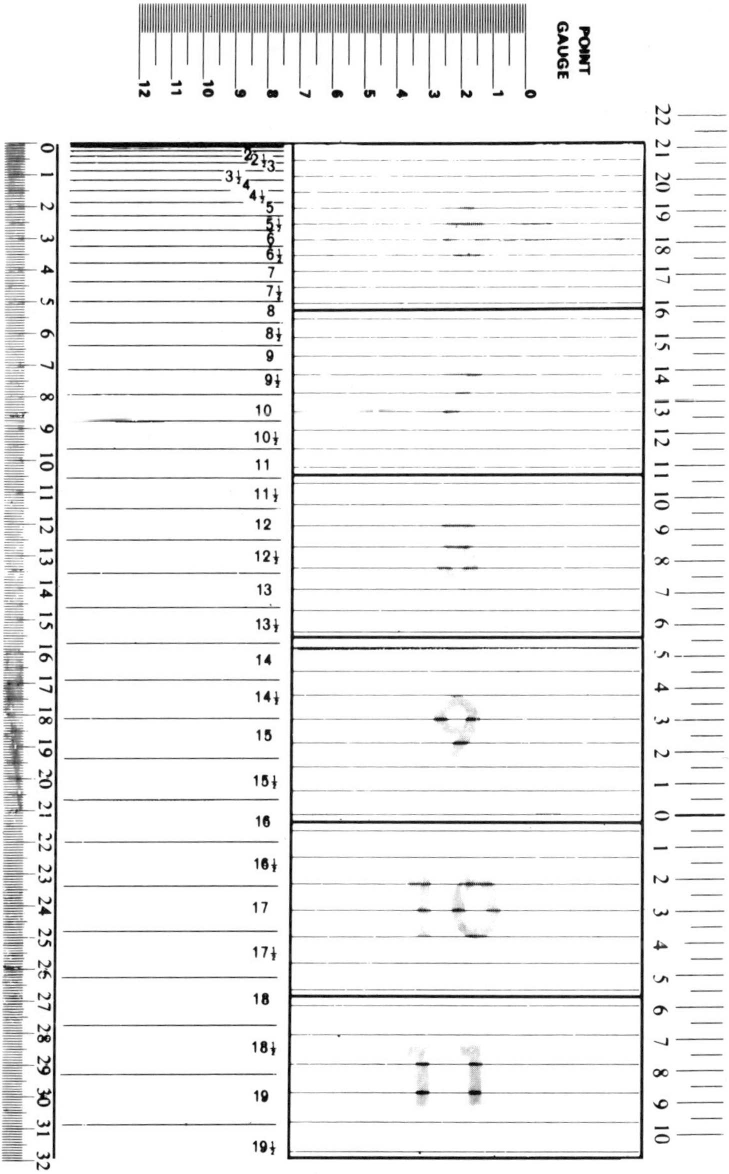

Type gauge.

FROM 6 8 10 12 14 18 24 30 36 48 60 72 POINT

Type series.

A complete list of these can be seen in any large dictionary under the entry "type". The sizes to which these names referred lacked uniformity among different type-founders, particularly in different countries. This confusion led to the popularity of the point system, which originated in France and was developed in the United States.

The designation of type sizes by points refers to the vertical size of the sort, or piece of metal it is set on and has no definite reference to the size of the typeface itself. All the different styles of 10-pt. faces, for instance, are approximately the same size, but there is considerable variation. The designation 10-pt., as referring to a particular typeface, means that it is ordinarily cast on a 10 pt. body. In Monotype and Linotype composition the size of the body often increased to enlarge the space between the lines without having to insert leads for that purpose. Thus a face ordinarily cast on a 10-pt. body may be cast on a 12-pt. body to give the appearance of 2 pt. leading; it is then referred to as 10 on 12. Although America and England use the pica system for measuring type, Europe uses the Didot system. Here is a comparison between the two systems of the more common type sizes:

Didot	Pica
4	4.3
5	5.4
6	6.4
7	7.5
8	8.6
9	9.7
10	10.7
11	11.8
12	12.9
14	15.0

type styles. *See* typeface styles.

typewriter. Called a writing machine in 1867 when it was first successful, it posed a threat to printers. The first writing machine hit paper from the back, pushing the sheet against a piece of carbon paper to form the impression. The writer could not see what had been produced until the paper was removed from the machine.

Printers were forced to use fonts that looked like the office machine, and there was great fear that much work done by the printer would be taken over by the new machine. Today's typewriter keyboard is an important part of every composition department, since the typewriter keyboard is used for all computer systems as opposed to the old Monotype and Linotype keyboards. *See also* cold type, copy fitting, and word processor.

typewriter composition. *See* cold type.

typo. Typographic error. Errors made in the copy either at the typewriter or at the keyboard stage of typesetting. Typos made by the compositor are p.e.'s and are not charged to the client.

typographer. A person, or a company of persons who set type. Also called typesetter.

typographic parameters. Markup translated into machine language for a computer-run typesetting system.

typographic revolution. The movement from hot-metal line casting typography to computer-operated phototype devices, the first, second, and third generations of typography. *See also* generations of type.

typography. The art and craft of setting type to be used in printing, whether by hand, mechanical device, or computer.

Typositor. *See* Photo Typositor.

U

u&lc. Specification for type that is to be set in upper- and lowercase letters. Also called caps and lower case. Abbreviated c&lc, u/lc, or ulc.

ultraviolet inks. "The ordinary light we see is composed of many different kinds of light. What we see is the visible spectrum. At either end of light's visible spectrum are other, invisible kinds of light radiation. Between visible purple and invisible X-rays lies an area of light called ultraviolet. Although we can't see it, ultraviolet light does have many effects. What we call sunburn is really an ultraviolet burn, because the sun's rays are rich in the ultraviolet component of light that reacts with skin pigments to cause reddening and discomfort.

Besides sunburn, ultraviolet light can cause many other chemical reactions. Manufacturers have developed inks which are chemically sensitive to ultraviolet light. When these specially-formulated, acrylic-based inks are exposed to ultraviolet light, their chemical configuration literally changes, through polymerization, from wet to dry instantly. So ultraviolet inks don't really dry; because they polymerize from a liquid state to a solid state, it's more accurate to say they set or cure."[9]

uncial. A style of type characterized by somewhat rounded capital letters found in Greek and Latin manuscripts from the 4th to the 8th centuries A.D.

LEADERship in the creation

Uncials.

uncoated paper. Machine-made paper that has no coating. Uncoated paper is not good for halftone printing.

underlay. A drawing by a layout artist, placed under a layout sheet and used for the structure of the layout.

[9]Harry Baldwin, from "Web and Ultraviolet: Two New Partners," *The Printing Salesman's Herald,* Book 34, Champion Papers, Hamilton, Ohio, p. 23.

unit. **1.** A piece of equipment used for typesetting or printing. The number of units and the number of webs must be known to determine the printing capacity of the web press. **2.** A subdivision of the em into vertical segments. The number of units varies from character to character and differs on various phototypesetting systems. One of the most common systems is 18-units-to-the-em. Other unit systems are 4, 9, 32, 36, 48, 54, and 64. A unit system is a counting method used by most phototypesetting systems and some strike-on typewriters to determine when a line of type is ready to be justified. The system measures the width of the individual characters and spaces being set in order to total the accumulated units. By adjusting the units of space between the letters, the type can be set with regular, loose, or tight letterspacing. *See also* kerning.

unjustified tape. A magnetic or paper tape which is keyboarded with no end-of-line decisions, allowing the keyboard operator to type as fast as possible. The tape is fed through a computer which adds the units and hyphenates or justifies the line according to the computer program. The justified tape is then used to operate the phototypesetting equipment. Also called idiot tape.

unjustified type. Lines of type set at different widths. They align at one side and are ragged at the other.

-up. Two-up, three-up, etc., refers to imposition of material to be shot or printed in duplicate form in order to take advantage of space on the negative or printing plate.

uppercase. The capital letters of a typeface. Originally so named because capital letters were kept in a box, or case, above the small letters.

upright. A book or catalog that is bound along its longest dimension, as opposed to oblong, which is bound on the short dimension.

UV inks. *See* ultraviolet inks.

V

vacuum frame. A glass-topped frame used for holding copy and reproduction material in contact during exposure by the action of vacuum pumps which expel air trapped between the two layers of emulsion or between film and plate. Also called contact frame.

value. Amount of gray, or how light or dark a color is based on tonal values from pure white through gradations of gray to black. *See also* color tree.

Vandyke. A brown blueprint. A photocopy used as a proof, having the image in dark brown. Vandykes can be used as printer's proofs before going to press. *See also* blueline.

varnish. **1.** Thin coating applied to the printed sheet for protection of appearance. It is applied in an even film in much the same manner as ink. Varnish can be overprinted or added directly into the ink. Too much varnish will cause the sheets to stick together. Sheets should be stacked in small amounts and winded after the varnish has had a chance to set. **2.** All, or part of the vehicle in ink.

varnishing. Finishing process done with ink rollers and blank plate on press, or with spray guns or blade coaters off press. Spot varnishing may also be done where a press plate is made to varnish only certain areas. Inks used to print the job must be compatible with the varnish. They must be lacquer resistant so as not to bleed through the varnish. The varnish maker needs to know the specifications required of the varnish such as chemical resistances, gloss requirements, scuff tests, etc.

VDT. *See* video display terminal.

vegetables. *See* printer's flowers.

vehicle. The liquid ingredient in ink. It is the varnish or oil carrier for the pigment and other ingredients, and is the binder of the pigment to the printed surface. Vehicle also determines such characteristics of the ink as viscosity, flow and consistency, and dictates how quickly an ink will dry. It is responsible for the degree of adhesion of the ink film to the paper. The type of vehicle used is determined by the type of printing process and drying system used. Some popular vehicles are linseed oil, petroleum oils, resin oils, and alcohol.

vellum. 1. A strong, toothy, cream-colored, relatively absorbent paper. The term originally referred only to a lambskin parchment. 2. A type of finish given woven book-covering materials. *See also* parchment.

Velox. Derived from the trade name for glossy photoprint papers, Velox Print, it refers to screened photoprints. The prints can be pasted up into the mechanical to enable the designer to see the illustrations in place, and make highlight or darkening corrections. Retouching and surprinting can be done on the velox, then the print can be copied dot for dot as a line illustration. When high quality is not necessary this can eliminate the necessity of stripping in the halftones at the printer. An alternative to shooting the velox is to give the printer the negative for stripping to size since it has already been screened. Different line screens are used.

verso. Left-hand side of a spread, as opposed to the recto or right-hand side. Verso refers to the reverse side of a printed sheet or of the particular recto in question. The verso always carries an even-numbered folio.

vertical publication. A trade magazine which is written for all persons in the same industry regardless of their specific job function. For example *Architectural Record, Medical World News.* A horizontal publication is written for all persons in a specific job function regardless of the industry.

video display terminal. 1. A device that displays lines of copy on a cathode ray tube, as type is keyboarded or a composed tape or disk is read from memory. It looks like a television screen and is a window into the typesetting system. The operator can edit and correct copy on the screen of the video display terminal by keyboarding in corrections. The newly produced tape or diskette activates the phototypesetting unit. An entire page can be displayed in systems designed to do page make-up with all elements in place, so that corrections can be made and changes viewed, before the type is actually set. This can greatly facilitate design, placement of footnotes, and running heads, sizing of photographs, etc. Makeup of an entire page at the composition stage with the aid of an electronic composing and viewing system is called pagination or photocomposing. Also called CRT by users of computers and word processors.

2. Another use for VDT is a recent development of a computerized, desk-top system that creates 35 mm color slides cheaper and faster than handmade slides. Color slides, complete with type and illustrations, bars, charts, and visual effects can be designed in minutes on a keyboard, viewed on the VDT, modified and recorded on a magnetic disk. The VDT eliminates the necessity for proof stage. Data is transmitted by phone to production facilities and slides are returned by mail or messenger.

Video display terminal. (*Courtesy Mergenthaler Linotype Company*)

vignette halftone. **1.** Photograph without definite boundary lines. The halftone is produced so that the edges fade softly into the whiteness of the unprinted paper. **2.** A small decorative design or illustration. **3.** The exposure of a halftone dot formed when light passes through each aperture in a cross-line halftone screen.

vinculum. In typesetting math, a straight, horizontal mark placed over two or more members of a compound quantity, equivalent to parentheses or brackets surrounding them.

VIP. A second-generation method of photocomposition which sets type from small fonts on film strips loaded into the machine. Light is passed through the font and onto light-sensitive paper or acetate upon which the type is set. The VIP sets type from about 30 to 100 characters per second, whereas hot metal linecasting machines can set only 5 characters per second, neither of them being near the speed of the cathode ray tube device which sets type electronically from 1,000 to 10,000 characters per second.

virgule. *See* solidus.

VIP. (*Courtesy Mergenthaler Linotype Company*)

viscosity. The properties of printing ink that make it resistant to flow. If an ink is heavy bodied it has a high viscosity. If it flows readily, it has a low viscosity. Offset inks usually have a high viscosity.

visual. *See* layout and comp.

visual display. A visual representation of computer output. This may be in the form of a video display terminal on which lines of type are shown on a cathode ray tube screen, or on a screen similar to those of digital electronic calculators. The purpose of the visual display is to allow the operator to make corrections. *See also* video display terminal.

visual space. Refers to the appearance of a size of type in which there are no ascenders or descenders, such as in some short heads. The actual, or mechanical size of the type is larger, measuring from top of ascender to bottom of the shoulder. *See also* cap height.

W

warm colors. Red, yellow, and orange, as opposed to blue, green, and violet which are cool colors.

Warren print. A photographic print similar to a photostat, but contacted with ammonia. A Warren print shows the image and can be pasted in place on a mechanical or dummy. Unlike the blue and yellow dylux proofs, the Warren print is reproducible, and when the mechanical with repro type is shot, the Warren shows the position of the image on the film so that the stripper will know where to place the halftone negative. A Warren print is not as good quality a print as a salt print.

wash drawing. An illustration done with black ink or paint diluted to various degrees of gray. Light, even tones are washed on illustration board with a brush, with darker tones obtained by successive layers of washes. A wash drawing must be reproduced as a halftone.

wash-up. The process of cleaning the press, rollers, plate and ink fountain when the color used on the press is changed.

waste sheets. *See* start-up sheets.

watermark. A translucent symbol or logo on paper, visible when the paper is held to light. The watermark identifies the brand or manufacturer. It is made by a raised pattern of wire soldered onto the dandy roll which helps distribute fibers during the manufacture of paper. *See also* papermaking.

water-soluble inks. Inks in which the pigments are soluble in water. Used in offset lithography, screen process printing, and gravure. Also called watercolor inks.

waxed paper. Paper which has either been dipped into a wax bath and immediately chilled, or passed through rollers which drive the wax into the paper.

wax engraving. A method of impressing lines of type in wax which can be used as a mold for electrotypes or duplicate letterpress plates. Often used for ruled forms.

wax pick test. A test to see how well ink will stay on the paper and not pull fibers off. Wax is melted and put on paper. The wax goes through the coating to the fibers. After it is hardened, it is pulled off. Papers for web presses have higher wax pick standards than do those for sheet-fed offset or letterpress.

web. A continuous ribbon of paper which unwinds from a roll and threads through the press. The web is cut into short lengths for delivery at the end of the press, or folded into signatures in-line. Any splice must be made properly or a parting situation will occur whereby the mill splice will separate due to the tension on the web. A web break can cause from 15 to 40 minutes down time on the press and can waste from 400 to 750 impressions during start up following the break. If the web weaves because of an elliptical or egg-shaped roll, it will bounce from side to side causing the tension to change likewise.

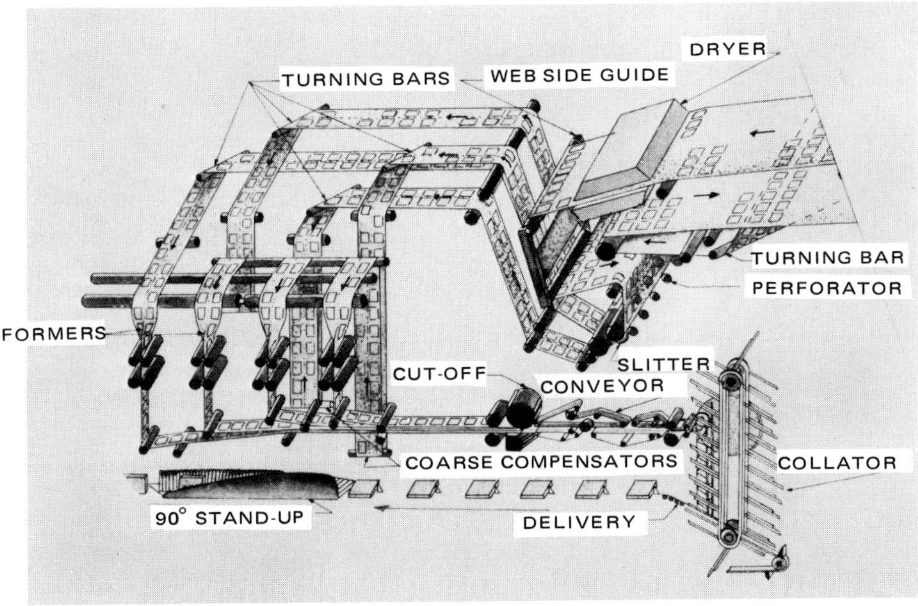

Web press for four color work. (*Courtesy Kingsport Press*)

web-fed. General term for all presses that print from a continuous roll of paper, as opposed to sheets, as in sheet-fed printing. Webs are used in offset press rotary letterpress, and rotogravure.

web offset. Offset printing that is done on a large press utilizing rolls of paper rather than sheets. Usually economical for medium and long runs, web offset accounts for well over half of all periodical printing in the U.S. at the expense of letterpress and gravure. The Printing Industries of America estimates that 60% of all commercial printing is produced on web offset. There has been a shift from sheet-fed to web presses for books and medium- and long-run periodicals.

Since, when running a web press there is more paper, more ink, more people involved, a worry in the past has been soft registration, poor color match, and it was once thought that good quality would not come off a web. Today's good controls have changed all that. However, a lot of makeready paper goes to waste until the press operator gets the best product the press can deliver.

web press. *See* web-fed.

web splicer. The automatic pasting device that splices a new web of paper onto an expiring roll without stopping the press. *See also* flying paster.

weight. 1. The weight of 500 sheets of paper of standard size for a particular grade. If an M follows the dimensions the weight is for a thousand sheets. *See also* basis weight or basic weight. 2. The degree of blackness of a typeface. The relative weights are: extra light, light, medium, semibold, bold, extrabold and ultrabold.

welding. A new method of binding with superior strength for quality binding which uses no glue, adhesives, or thread and holds faster than adhesive binding. Heat welds printed pages together and offers the prospect of cost reduction through elimination of materials such as glue, staples, thread, etc. However, special coated paper must be used, which can add 10% to the cost of paper, and binding machinery manufacturers will not make equipment limited to one kind of paper from a limited source.

wet printing. Printing one process color over another before the first color has dried, as in offset printing.

WF. Wrong font. A proofreader's mark indicating that letters of type fonts have been mixed.

where list. A list of qualifications stating that certain symbols equal certain entities for a given equation.

white. There is no color of white in printing. When you see white you are really seeing the color of the paper showing between dots of ink. *See also* halftone dot.

white print. *See* diazo.

white space. The portions of a layout that have neither copy nor illustrations. Also called air.

widow. 1. A short line of type ending a paragraph at the top of the page. It is corrected by re-adjusting spacing or by writing more words to fill out the line.

2. Loosely refers to any short line of a few characters at the end of a paragraph or the beginning of a page. Not to be confused with a short line leading to a display element or extract material.

width. Variations of letterforms such as condensed and extended.

window. A rectangular panel in a flat into which halftone negatives are stripped with tape for platemaking.

window envelopes. *See* envelope styles.

wire binding. *See* binding, saddle stitch or saddle wire, and side wire.

wire-o binding. A method of loose-leaf binding in which a continuous series of wire loops runs through punched slots along the binding side of a booklet.

wire side. The side of the sheet which has rested on the wire in paper manufacturing, opposite the felt, or top side. Also called the wrong side. The wire side has less fine lines on the surface and collects less loose paper dust or lint on the blanket of an offset press.

New machinery which squirts the pulp up between two wire screens instead of laying it down on the wire, creates paper with two wire sides. This will not be used however until publishers standardize their requirements for paper so that larger quantities can be made at one time. *See also* papermaking.

wire stitching. *See* saddle stitch or saddle wire, and side wire.

with the grain. Directional character of the paper created as the fibers flow along the wire on the papermaking machine. Paper folds more easily and tears straighter parallel to the grain.

woodcut. An illustration cut in lines of varying thickness on the grain side of a block of wood for the purpose of making prints. The block is inked with a roller and is pressed directly against the surface to be printed. Wood engravings were often used as illustrations for letterpress printing before the halftone became competitive.

wood pulp. *See* chemical pulp, and groundwood pulp.

wood type. Type made from wood, and set by hand usually for display sizes over 1-in., or 72 pt. Wood type is usually made from end-grain maple and the faces are cut by machine and trimmed by hand. It has been made obsolete by hand-set typositors which can set photodisplay type in sizes larger than 72 pt.

word division. The division of words at the end of a typeset line. Most printers and publishers use Webster's New International Dictionary as the standard.

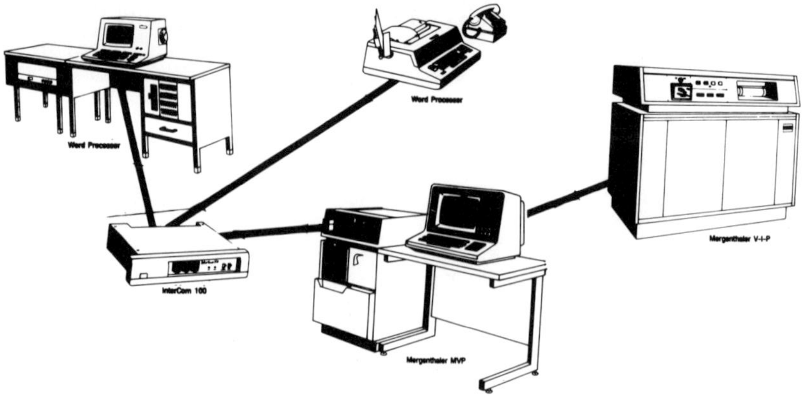

Word processing.

word processing. Sophisticated strike-on typewriter equipment connected to some magnetic recording medium; cassette or floppy disk in most cases. The major advantage is that of correction and editing. The magnetic tape or disk memory can be erased and reused. WP lets you play back the recorded medium and make changes, rerecording a new medium for output at the same time.

The result is an up-to-date recording and a hard copy or typewritten sheet. The print-out units fall into the strike-on category of typesetting, or cold type. Different word processors have different communication speeds. Word processing is 100% typing but adds the dimension of editing so one can change one's mind.

Some word-processing units use a video display so that you can edit more effectively. Some models can hyphenate, justify, and perform typesetting-like capabilities. Others allow clients to interface the recorded medium of a word processor to a phototypesetter. In that case, the typesetting firm would have to possess a device for reading the particular word-processing output and be able to translate the recorded code. The major problem in this area is the fact that there are over 100 models of word processing units and separate reading devices are required for each. *See also* interface.

word spacing. Inserting extra space between words in order to justify the line. All spaces are related in size to the em quad, the square of the type size being used. Too much wordspacing is frowned upon as bad typesetting. *See also* em. *See* spacing for illustration.

work and tumble. Printing both sides of a sheet by turning it over from gripper edge to back with the same side guide so that the printing plate doesn't have to be changed. Thus, each half of the sheet is backed up to the opposite half for proper page sequence when trimmed and folded. This is seldom used when register is important because changing the gripper edge means adjustments to the press. Also, extra paper must be allowed for gripper margins. on both sides of the sheet.

work and turn. Printing both sides of a sheet by turning it over left to right so that the same gripper edge is used. This provides better register than work and tumble and the printing plates do not have to be changed. Two copies of the pages are produced when the sheets are cut in half.

work for hire. Work done for a client who keeps the rights for the work. The free-lancer who does work for hire usually signs an agreement specifying that the work is "for hire" and that the free-lancer loses the rights to the work.

working title. A convenient title used while a book is in production until a title is settled upon for publishing.

woven. Any cloth binding material, as opposed to paper-based material.

wove paper. A soft, smooth paper having a uniform surface with no lines or marks. *See also* laid paper.

WP. *See* word processing.

wrap. To place color pages around signatures before sewing. Wrapping is far less expensive and stronger than other methods of placing color pages such as tipping, which requires hand work at the bindery. *See* insert for illustration.

wraparound plate. A flexible one-piece zinc, magnesium, copper, or synthetic relief plate wrapped around the cylinder on a rotary letterpress, much like an offset plate. Used for direct or indirect printing.

wrecked out. An internal instruction for the printer to bring the paper roll out of inventory so that it is ready for the print run.

wrinkles. 1. Creases in paper during printing caused by uneven absorption of moisture, inconsistent caliper, and sheets trimmed out-of-square. Wrinkles can smash type in letterpress or a blanket in offset, or cause stress on the sheet going through the press resulting in shutdown. 2. Uneven surface formed by inks during drying.

writing paper. A smooth paper with the surface sized to prevent absorption of ink into the fibers.

wrong font. An error in typesetting in which characters of different size or face become mixed in the wrong context. Abbreviated wf. *See also* proofreader's marks.

wrong-reading. A mirror image, or an image that reads in the reverse. Wrong-reading film emulsion up is the same as right-reading emulsion down.

X

xenon lights. Used instead of the old carbon arc lights to illuminate the copyboard on a gallery camera.

Xerography. Dry (*xerox*) writing (*graphos*). Derived from the trade name Xerox. Now loosely used to refer to other forms of electrostatic copying although the correct term for that is photocopying. *See also* electrostatic printing.

x-height. The height of the main body of the lower-case letter without ascenders or descenders.

x-line. The line that marks the tops of lowercase letters, not including ascenders. Also called mean line.

Z

zinc etching. Line or halftone etchings made on zinc for letterpress printing. *See also* engraving and linecut.

Zip-a-Tone. Trade name for a series of black-and-white screen patterns such as dots, lines, stipples, etc., imprinted on plastic sheets. Used by designers as an overlay on artwork to achieve an illusion of tone. Overlays such as Zip-a-Tone have replaced the old Benday tints. *See also* shading tint.

Appendix One

ARTICLES OF THE CODE OF FAIR PRACTICE[10]

Relations

Between Aritst & Buyer

1

"Dealings between an artist* or the artist's agent and a client should be conducted only through an authorized buyer

2

Orders to an artist or agent should be in writing and should include the specific rights which are being transferred, the price, delivery date, and a summarized description of the work. In the case of publications, the acceptance of a manuscript by the artist constitutes an order

3

All changes or additions not due to the fault of the artist or agent should be billed to the purchaser as an additional and separate charge

4

There should be no charges to the purchaser, other than those authorized expenses, for revisions or retakes made necessary by errors on the part of the artist or the artist's agent

5

Alterations should not be made without consulting the artist. Where alterations or retakes are necessary and time permits and where the artist's usual standard of quality has been maintained, the artist should be given the opportunity of making such changes.

[10] Reprinted by permission of the Joint Ethics Committee of New York which is composed of members from the Society of Illustrators, Inc., The Art Directors Club, Inc., The Artists Guild, Inc., American Society of Magazine Photographers, Inc., Society of Photographer and Artist Representatives, Inc. and the Graphic Artists Guild, Inc. appointed by the directing bodies of each organization, but serving jointly in furtherance of the purposes for which the Committee was founded.

6

The artist should notify the buyer of an anticipated delay in delivery. Should the artist fail to keep his contract through unreasonable delay in delivery, or non-conformance with agreed specifications, it should be considered a breach of contract by the artist and should release the buyer from responsibility

7

Work stopped by a buyer after it has been started should be delivered immediately and billed on the basis of the time and effort expended and expenses incurred

8

An artist should not be asked to work on speculation. However, work originating with the artist may be marketed on its merit. Such work remains the property of the artist unless purchased and paid for

9

Art contests for commercial purposes are not approved because of their speculative and exploitative character

10

There should be no secret rebates, discounts, gifts, or bonuses requested by or given to buyers by the artist or the artist's agent

11

Artwork ownership and copyright ownership is initially vested in the hands of the creator

12

Original artwork remains the property of the artist unless it is specifically purchased and paid for as distinct from the purchase of any reproduction rights**

13

In cases of copyright transfers, only specified rights are transferred in any transaction, all unspecified rights remaining vested in the creator**

14

If the purchase price of artwork is based specifically upon limited use and later this material is used more extensively than originally planned, the artist is to receive adequate additional remuneration

15

Commissioned artwork is not to be considered as "done for hire"**

16

If comprehensives, preliminary work, exploratory work, or additional photographs from an assignment are subsequently published as finished art the price should be increased to the satisfaction of artist and buyer

17

If exploratory work, comprehensives, or photographs are bought from an artist with the intention or possibility that another artist will be assigned to do the finished work, this should be made clear at the time of placing the order

18

The publisher of any reproduction of artwork is to publish the artist's copyright notice if the artist so requests and has not executed a written and signed transfer of copyright ownership**

19

The right to place the artist's signature upon artwork is subject to agreement between artist and buyer

20

The should be no plagiarism of any creative artwork

21

If an artist is specifically requested to produce any artwork during unreasonable working hours, fair additional remuneration should be allowed

22

An artist entering into an agreement with an agent or studio for exclusive representation should not accept an order from, nor permit the artist's work to be shown by any other agent or studio. Any agreement which is not intended to be exclusive should set forth in writing the exact restrictions agreed upon between the two parties

23

All artwork or photography submitted as samples to a buyer by artists' agents or studio representatives should bear the name of the artist or artists responsible for the creation

24

No agent, studio, or production company should continue to show the work of an artist as samples after the termination of the association

25

After termination of an association between artist and agent, the agent should be entitled to a commission on accounts which the agent has secured, for a period of time not exceeding six months (unless otherwise specified by contract)

26

Examples of an artist's work furnished to an agent or submitted to a prospective purchaser shall remain the property of the artist, should not be duplicated without the artist's consent, and should be returned to the artist promptly in good condition

27

Interpretation of the Code shall be in the hands of the Joint Ethics Committee and is subject to changes and additions at the discretion of the parent organizations through their appointed representatives on the Committee"

*The word artist should be understood to include creative people in the field of visual communications such as graphics, photography, film, and television

**Artwork ownership, copyright ownership, and ownership and rights transfers after January 1, 1978 are to be in compliance with the Federal Copyright Revision Act of 1976

Appendix Two

COMMUNICATING WITH YOUR PRINTER[11]

"**Editors consider themselves,** and are so considered by the world, as communicators. Yet in one vital situation facing virtually all editors this important skill seems to desert them: dealing with their printers. By printers I don't mean just the people who run the presses, but rather all the people who do the mechanical work that makes a magazine happen after the editor has given birth to his brainchild of the month, week or day.

Quite frankly, the precise reasons for this failure, this sudden lapse of professional communications skills, escapes me. But I do have some thoughts on the matter, and how to change it.

One consideration, it seems to me, is one of class. With many editors I've had the opportunity to observe at first hand, it seems that having finally been bedecked with the ermine of this office, the recipient promptly forgets what it's like to get his hands dirty. He forgets the long hours of paste-up, the last minute make-up, the occasional confrontation with some headline machine or another he very probably had as a fledgling journalist. As editor he quite properly delegates such work. But he frequently seems to forget the skill involved in such operations, and the satisfaction. If you haven't wielded a razor-blade knife recently to do a little camera-ready paste-up, or leaned over a light table for a few hours lately, try it.

Another consideration is one of simple ignorance. Many editors never learned the rudiments of the printing and composition operation. This is akin to a lawyer not learning how to present a case to a jury. You can get by without it for a long time, but eventually the lack of such information is going to catch up with you. I had an editor (senior to me in years and experience) tell me the four colors used in printing are "black, white, red, yellow. . . and what is the last one?"

[11] Jay Holtzman, "Communicating With Your Printer," *Inside Stuff,* American Business Press Editorial Newsletter, New York.

I'm not suggesting that every editor be able to compose and print his magazine. But I am more than suggesting that ignorance in this area will make your life tougher, your relations with the printers stormy and your over-all image somewhat shabby.

Yet another consideration is one of deadlines and the observance thereof. Psychologists refer to the childish belief that the world revolves around us individually as "illusion of central position." Well, editors seem to have this illusion in full measure when it comes to the scheduling of their magazines.

At Chilton, we have more than 20 magazines being printed by our plant. Work is scheduled so that it can be moved through the whole system as rapidly and efficiently as possible.

When one editor sends 50 sheets of manuscript two days after his deadline he backs up the system for everyone. When the same editor still hasn't received his copy back a week later, he complains, "What's the problem, it was only 50 sheets?" And so it is. Times twenty.

Printers live by schedules even more than editors. It is the nature of the game. Downtime on equipment costs money. From the printer's point of view, printing magazines is a manufacturing process. He's got to make his nut, too, and seeing his presses idle and costing him money because editors have blown their schedules tends to make him testy and maybe a little hard to live with. Even as you and I.

There are a whole set of problems in dealing with printers but there are also a whole set of simple solutions to getting along with them.

First, treat printers like human beings. Respect them as you would a fellow professional. Printers and composition men for the most part may not be college-educated, they don't wear flannel suits to the office and frequently they have dirty hands. Thank goodness. They are as highly trained in their specialized field as editors are in theirs. In many cases, more highly trained. In my experience, they are at least as concerned about putting out a quality product as editors. Respect this and use this to your advantage.

Second, learn the process. This will help you every day of your working life. If you know only the rough outlines of the composition and printing process, you can begin to anticipate problems and avoid them. You may even learn how to save money on production, get more editorial color at little extra cost, get the best reproduction for those cirtical charts, or a whole lot of other things you will wish you had known before. Several years ago ABP produced and distributed to members the ABP Reference Guide for Business and Production Management which will tell you more than you ever wanted to know about printing and production. The two volume set probably resides in your production department. Your printer, too, is a great source of information.

Third, avoid an adversary relationship. It seems to me that many editors and printers get a lot of emotional sparks flying. The fault is usually on both sides. But if you can avoid an adversary relationship and instead foster one built on the mutual cooperation of fellow professionals with the same goal, you got 90 percent of the problem licked.

Fourth, respect schedules. Chances are you enforce your own deadlines on your staff writers. Extend the courtesy to the next step in the production process. There's always a reason to be late—your printer will have plenty of those, too, so why give him one more very legitimate reason for your book coming out two weeks late?

That's it in a nutshell. To my way of thinking, there's nothing esoteric or complicated about dealing with your printer. One hand washes the other and everyone has something to gain."

Appendix Three

GUIDELINES

Definitions, Practices, and Usages Commonly Employed in the Book Manufacturing Industry[12]

I. GENERAL PROVISIONS

1. **WRITTEN ORDERS.** All orders, instructions and changes therein shall† (sic) be in writing; printing orders shall specify the quantity of each title to be printed at one run; binding orders, the quantity of each title to be bound at one time. Manufacturer has the right to reject, within 10 days after receipt, without liability, any acceptance of quotation by customer. Neither party is bound by oral agreements or representations which are contrary to the provisions of a written contract or of the terms and conditions which follow. Regularly entered orders cannot be cancelled except on terms that will compensate the book manufacturer against any expenses incurred for any materials purchased, services performed or unrecovered production time.

2. **CUSTOMER'S PROPERTY.** Manufacturer shall† not be responsible for any loss of, deterioration of, or damage to the property of customer, unless caused by his negligence or failure to exercise ordinary care in safeguarding or handling the property.

3. **DAMAGES DUE TO DELAY OR LOSS.** Manufacturer shall† not be responsible for damages due to delay or loss, when such is caused by act of God, public enemy, or by fire, strikes, labor trouble, riots or unavoidable accident or causes.

4. **INSURANCE.** It is the responsibility of the customer to carry adequate insurance on material supplied and owned by him. Insurance shall be carried by the manufacturer on the value of the labor and materials

[12] Book Manufacturers' Institute, Inc., New York, 1969.

supplied by him during the progress of the work and until such time as the work is delivered or billed, whichever occurs first.

5. **MANUFACTURER'S LIEN.** In consideration of the acceptance of any order, the customer hereby pledges with and grants to the manufacturer a security interest in and lien* (sic) upon all chattels and property of the customer at any time in the possession or custody of the manufacturer, and which security interest and lien shall secure payment* of all amounts due and owing to manufacturer and unpaid for all work, labor and services, and materials theretofore or thereafter done, performed and furnished whether arising from completed books already delivered or billed, or from work done and labor and materials furnished in connection with property. The extension of credit or the acceptance of notes, trade acceptances or guarantee of payment,* whether or not the amount claimed was incurred in connection with such chattels and property or otherwise, shall not affect such security interest and lien.

   Manufacturer's security interest and lien* may be enforced under and in accordance with applicable laws and statutes governing the enforcement of security interests and liens on personal property, or in the absence thereof by public sale of the chattels and property upon 10 days written notice of sale to customer or customer's successor in interest and advertising the sale in a newspaper of general circulation in the city in which manufacturer's principal office if located, which notice customer agrees shall be reasonable notice of such sale.

   Manufacturer shall have the right at manufacturer's discretion, and the customer authorizes manufacturer, to file (and, in jurisdictions where permitted, to sign and file without customer's signature) such financing statements under the Uniform Commercial Code as may be required to assure perfection of manufacturer's security interest and lien* and customer agrees to execute any documents necessary therefor. Where local law requires the filing of a mechanic's lien or chattel mortgage customer agrees to sign all necessary documents to create and protect such lien or mortgage.*

6. **EXPERIMENTAL WORK.** If performed at the customer's request, experimental work on sketches, art work, positives, plates, presswork or binding, etc. shall be charged* for at manufacturer's current rate for such work.

II. COMPOSITION AND PLATEMAKING

1. **CALCULATING MANUSCRIPT.** The manufacturer shall not be responsible for inaccuracies in estimating probable number of pages a given manuscript will make, whether such estimate is from original manuscript or from a cast-off made from first galleys of the type.

2. **PRICE QUOTATIONS FROM MANUSCRIPT.** Price* quotations made from manuscript pages shall be based upon matter originally submitted for estimate.

3. **COMPOSITION FROM MANUSCRIPT.** Manufacturer's responsibility shall be limited to a careful composition from manuscript. In no case after proofs have been okayed by customer or his representative shall manufacturer be liable for any error in composition, except errors which occur after return of such okayed proofs. In case of errors thereafter occuring, such liability shall be limited to correcting type, plates, sheets or books.

4. **EDITING OF MANUSCRIPT.** Manufacturer shall not be responsible for editorial inconsistencies in manuscript.

5. **STANDING MATTER.** Composition materials remain the property of the manufacturer and there is no obligation on his part to sell or transfer it to the customer. Payment by the customer for the composition represents payment for an intermediate operation necessary for the production of printed material and title to the composition materials remains with the manufacturer.

6. **MATS AND MOLDS.** Mats and molds for printing plates are the disposable property of the book manufacturer unless the customer has specifically purchased them.

7. **RETURN OF PROOFS, ALTERATIONS AND DELAYS.** The publisher agrees to return promptly all specifications, proofs, dummies, sketches, blueprints, copies, etc. in compliance with schedule. Alterations in, or delay in accepting or returning sketches or proofs, will excuse manufacturer from all responsibility for delay resulting therefrom. All "Author's Alterations" (changes from original copy and/or specifications) which necessitates additional work will be charged* for at manufacturer's regular rate.

   Mechanicals supplied to manufacturer by customer as guide to make-up of pages and for camera work, must include precise and exact instructions for the positioning of illustrations. Any changes* in such positioning by customer subsequent to camera work represent author's alterations to be charged to customer at manufacturer's regular rates for the additional work done.

8. **COLOR PROOFING.** Because of the difference in equipment, paper and conditions between the color proofing and the pressroom operations, a reasonable variation in color between color proofs and the completed job shall constitute an acceptable delivery.

9. **PROPERTY RIGHTS FOR MACHINE-READABLE TAPES OR RECORDING DEVICES AND FOR THE FILM OR TYPE PRODUCED THEREFROM.**
   a) Any program specifically designed to activate a computerized output shall remain the property of the program originator.
   b) Any machine-readable tape, either paper or magnetic, punched cards or any other such data processing device from which type set material can be produced, shall be the property of the customer when such devices are furnished by the customer as original manuscript. The manufacturer rightfully assumes that backup files are maintained, and disclaims any responsibility for accidental damage or destruction of these devices, but will exercise care and diligence in the processing work.
   c) Any tape, either paper or magnetic, punched cards or any such devices used to prepare original typewritten or other conventional copy for typesetting, shall be the property of the manufacturer who produced them or obtained them under a subcontract.
   d) Any intermediate tapes, either paper or magnetic, produced from sources (a) and (b) above, but containing also the typographic programming for the job, are the property of the manufacturer who produced them or obtained them under a subcontract.
   e) Film produced from such tapes are subject to the practices reported in Section IV, No. 1 of this booklet.
   f) Conventional hot-metal type produced from such tapes will be the property of the manufacturer.
   g) Customer's property will be held without charge* for 60 days after final film or proofs have been delivered. If customer wishes manufacturer to hold longer, he should notify the manufacturer officially in writing before the end of the 60-day period and satisfactory terms for storage* can be arranged. If no such official notice is received, the manufacturer is free to destroy the information on the tape or to kill the type metal.
   h) It is understood that the information on the intermediate tapes will receive the same confidential treatment accorded conventional manuscripts, and manufacturer will not release it in any full or abbreviated form to anyone without written consent of the original customer.

III. LETTERPRESS PRESSWORK

1. **PLATES.** All plates furnished manufacturer shall be in proper condition for use without proofing, washing or repairing.

2. **PAPER.** Paper, properly identified, supplied by the customer, shall be delivered to the manufacturer approximately 15 days, and no later than

7 days, before it is required for presswork, such date or dates to be determined by the manufacturer. Paper delivered earlier than 30 days before presswork date and excess paper remaining 30 days* after presswork is completed shall be considered as requiring Warehousing* and will be subject to Warehousing provisions. (See Warehousing, Section VIII).

3. **OVER-RUNS OR UNDER-RUNS.** The printer shall be allowed a tolerance of ten percent for over or under-count, and the over or under-count shall be charged* for or deducted on a proportionate basis of the presswork running price.* By agreement, under-delivery beyond ten percent may be made up at the time of subsequent printings.

4. **PRESS OKAY.** Presses standing awaiting okay of customer will be charged* for at manufacturer's current rates for the time so consumed.

5. **COLOR PROOFING.** Because of the difference in equipment, paper and condition between the color proofing and the pressroom operations, a reasonable variation in color between color proofs and the completed job shall constitute an acceptable delivery.

IV. OFFSET PRESSWORK

1. **OFFSET PRELIMINARY WORK.** Final platemaking positives and negatives are the property of the publisher. Worker negatives and/or positives not used in platemaking shall remain the property of the manufacturer. All positives or negatives stored in the manufacturer's plant are stored at the publisher's risk and any loss or damage thereto caused by fire, water, leakage, breakage, theft, negligence, insects, rodents, deterioration, or any cause beyond the manufacturer's control shall not make the manufacturer liable for the value thereof.

2. **RETURN OF PROOFS, ALTERATIONS AND DELAYS.** The making of alterations or delays in returning specifications, proofs, dummies, sketches, etc. will excuse the manufacturer from responsibility for delayed deliveries resulting therefrom.

3. **REPRODUCTION PROOFS.** When manufacturer submits reproduction proofs to customer in multiple set for offset printing, it will be the customer's responsibility to furnish the manufacturer a suitable set for proper camera work, enabling manufacturer to reproduce acceptable work. Alterations and delays will be charged* for at manufacturer's existing rates.

4. **COLOR PROOFING.** Because of the difference in equipment, paper

and conditions between color proofing and pressroom operations, a reasonable variation in color between the color proofs and the completed jobs will constitute an acceptable delivery.

5. **OFFSET PLATES.** All offset press plates shall remain the property of the manufacturer.

6. **MATERIALS.** Paper, cloth and other materials furnished by the customer shall be properly identified and delivered to the manufacturer approximately 15 days, but no later than 7 days, before press date. Paper delivered earlier than 30 days before press date and any paper remaining 30* days after completion of presswork will require Warehousing* and will be subject to Warehousing provisions (See Section VIII).

   All such paper, cloth or other material furnished to the manufacturer shall be of proper quality and specifications for the individual manufacturer's requirements. Additional cost due to delays, spoilage or impaired production on account of improper packing or quality shall be charged* to the customer.

7. **OVER-RUNS OR UNDER-RUNS.** The manufacturer shall be allowed a tolerance* of ten percent for over or under-count, and the over or under-count shall be charged* for or deducted on a proportionate basis of manufacturer's presswork running price. By agreement, under-delivery beyond ten percent may be made up at the time of subsequent printings.

8. **PRESS DELAYS.** Press delays as a result of awaiting customer OK will be charged* for at manufacturer's existing rates for the time used.

9. **SKETCHES AND DUMMIES.** Sketches, copy, dummies, and all preparatory work created or furnished by the manufacturer shall remain its exclusive property and no use of same shall be made nor any ideas obtained therefrom be used, except upon compensation to be determined by the owner.

10. **APPROVAL OF PROOFS.** The manufacturer is not responsible for errors if work is completed as per customer's OK. Customer will return one sheet of proofs consolidating any and all changes, properly initialed, and indicating "OK" or "OK with changes". Manufacturer is not responsible for errors if the customer has not ordered or has refused to accept blues (Ozalids, silver prints or other types of proofs), or has failed to return blues with indication of any changes to be made or has instructed manufacturer to proceed with printing without submission of blues to customer.

11. **PRESS PROOFS.** A charge* at manufacturer's current rate will be made for press proofs, unless the customer is present when the plate is made ready on the press, so that no press time is lost. Presses standing awaiting OK of customer will be charged* for at manufacturer's current rate for the time so consumed.

V. WEB PAPER PRACTICES

A. PACKAGING INFORMATION

1. All roll stock shall be properly packaged so as to meet the individual book manufacturer's specifications and indicate at least the following:

   a. Type of core
   b. Core size (I.D.)
   c. Roll width
   d. Roll diameter (min.-max.)
   e. Direction of unwind (wire or felt)
   f. Type of moisture barrier (wrapper)
   g. Other

2. All roll stock shall be properly packaged so to protect ends and sides while in transit, in storage and in normal stock handling. In transit damage claims should be initiated by the consignee against the carrier. Paper supplier to be notified of such action. Roll wrappers or labels should be marked with identifying information desired by book manufacturers such as:

   a. Name of type of paper
   b. Basis weight
   c. Roll width
   d. Net weight
   e. Gross weight
   f. Publisher's name for whom furnished and order numbers
   g. Mill order numbers
   h. Roll numbers and position on paper machine
   i. *Yardage
   j. Title of book or job number
   k. Direction of unwind

   *To be computed from data taken during mill run.

B. MILL SPLICES.

1. Mill splices should be made from a type of tape or adhesive as required by book manufacturer. Splicing to be done according to specifications furnished by the book manufacturer.

2. Rolls of basis weights 50 lb. or more, 42″ or less in diameter should have no more than two mill splices, never within one inch of each other or two inches from the core or 1″ from outside diameter of the rolls.

3. Additional splices per roll are permitted if the roll fits any or all of the categories listed below:

   a. Basis weights 35 lb. to 49lb.
   b. Basis weights under 35 lb.
   c. Diameters over 42″ under 50″
   d. Diameters over 50″
   e. Supercalendered papers

   (value 1 additional splice per category to be cumulative)

C. ROLLS FOR SHEETERS.

1. The customer and the book manufacturer shall indicate on the order when rolls are to be used for off-press or on-press sheeting as distinguished from rolls intended for web printing. The type of press should also be indicated.

2. R.H. Factor will be indicated if desired.

3. Types and number of splices will be determined between the paper manufacturer and book manufacturer.

D. BASIS WEIGHT.

Paper is not to average over the basis weight specified.

VI. SHEET PAPER PRACTICES

A. PACKAGING.

1. Skids of sheet paper shall be properly packaged so as to protect while in transit, in storage and in handling. Damage claims should be initiated by the consignee against the carrier. Paper supplier is to be notified of action.

2. Load wrappers or labels will identify:

   a. Net weight
   b. Number of sheets on skids
   c. Mill order numbers
   d. Grain directions
   e. Basis weight
   f. Type of paper
   g. Name of publisher for whom it is furnished.
   h. Title of book or job no. and publisher's order no.
   i. Sheet size

VII. EDITION BINDING

1. **MATERIAL SUPPLIED BY CUSTOMER.** All materials such as sheets, covers, jackets, inserts, etc. shall be imposed for manufacturer's equipment and ready for use, delivered FOB manufacturer's receiving platform and properly identified.

   All printed sheets provided by the customer shall contain a set of collating marks acceptable to the manufacturer.

   All materials furnished by the customer or others shall be delivered to the manufacturer approximately 15 days, and no later than 7 days, before they are needed for binding, such dates to be determined by manufacturer. Any materials delivered earlier than 30 days before such dates and any excess materials remaining 30 days* after binding is completed shall be considered as requiring Warehousing* and will be subject to Warehousing provisions.* (See Warehousing, Section VIII).

2. **COUNT.** Manufacturer shall not be required to hand-count sheets or other material supplied by the customer or his agent. The basis of count of sheets shall be the gathered record made as soon after receipt as practicable. All such furnished sheets or other material should include the customer's or his agent's count for comparison purposes.

3. **BALANCE OF EDITIONS.** Folding, gathering, and sewing, stitching, or wiring on all sheets may be completed and billed on completion by the manufacturer.

4. **DELIVERY OF BOOKS.** (a) Delivery to a common carrier, to customer's warehouse door, to manufacturer's warehouse or in an area regularly serviced or specified by the binder, if held subject to customer's disposition, shall constitute complete delivery. (b) All sales, unless otherwise specified, shall be deemed FOB* main warehouse or storage facilities of manufacturer. (c) Delivery shall be taken by the customer upon completion of binding or the agreed-upon completion date, whichever is later. Undelivered books remaining after such date shall be considered as requiring Warehousing and will be subject to Warehousing conditions. (See Section VIII).

5. **DEFECTIVE WORK.** The manufacturer will not be responsible or liable in any way for defects in paper nor, in case of binding, for printing when done by another. Where printing is done by others, a binder has no obligation to perform any proofreading operations, is not responsible for editorial continuity, and has the right to rely upon printed folios as representing proper sequence of pages. If such a book contains no folios and each signature is identified by a printed collating reference or

printed signature identification, the binder has the right to place full reliance upon such identifications and their positioning on the printed sheets as final guides to the folding, gathering, and sewing. In the case of defective books, where responsibility attaches, manufacturer's liability shall be limited to correcting and repairing such books. Where such correcting and repairing are not practicable, liability shall be limited to the cost of paper, when furnished by the customer, presswork and binding in such books. However, the manufacturer's responsibility for paper and presswork shall only start once the manufacturer has exceeded normal spoilage allowances. Where a special examination for defects is desired, a separate and distinct agreement must be made.

6. **OVER-RUNS AND UNDER-RUNS.** Manufacturer shall be allowed a tolerance* of ten percent over or under the quantity ordered.

7. **EXPERIMENTAL WORK.** All experimental work performed at the customer's request (sample cases and stamping dies) will be charged* at current rates.

VIII. WAREHOUSING

Warehousing as performed by the book manufacturer shall be the care and keep of materials furnished by him, or purchases by the manufacturer for the exclusive use of a publisher, for processing in the manufacture of book and the care and keep of the finished product (or partly finished, if so ordered, e.g., art work, film, letterpress plates, stamping dies, press sheets, signatures, gathered or sewn books, any type of cover material, carton, etc.). It shall be distinguished from the care and keep of such property during manufacture, which for the purposes of definition shall be called Manufacturing Storage.

As part of the service of book manufacturing, the manufacturer shall allow as part of Manufacturing Storage a period of allowable material storage before manufacturing begins. This shall be approximately 15 days*, with a maximum of 30 days*. Manufacturing Storage shall terminate upon completion of binding. Materials and products required to be held by the manufacturer beyond the allowable period of Manufacturing Storage shall require the service of Warehousing* and shall entitle the manufacturer to compensation* in addition to normal charges for manufacture, for this added service.

Practices and customs applying to the Warehousing Service shall be those which by general application govern the Warehousing Industry, modified only as required by the particular requirements of the Book

Manufacturing Industry. Therefore, materials and products being Warehoused are subject to the following:

a. An In and Out charge* as they become liable for Warehousing at Manufacturer's current rates.
b. A Warehousing charge* per month at manufacturer's current rates.
c. Charges* in (a) and (b) to be made in advance.

Charges* shall be on a per hundred-weight unit basis but may be converted to such expressions in terms of books or loads as may be convenient.

IX. TERMS

1. Paper supplied by manufacturer shall be billed* when received by him.

2. Composition and plates shall be billed* when completed. Interim billings on extensive or delayed jobs may be arranged.

3. Presswork and binding shall each be billed* upon completion, whether actually delivered or held in stock by the manufacturer subject to the disposition of the customer.

4. Billings* for folding, and/or plating and/or gathering and/or sewing on all sheets shall be made on completion.

5. All charges* for Warehousing are to be billed in advance. In and Out and one month's storage at the start of Warehousing and storage monthly in advance thereafter.

6. All extra work order performed for customer, not specifically covered in original or supplemental quotations, is to be billed* at the manufacturer's rate for such work.

7. Shipments of customer's property, other than bound books on customer's order, are subject to handling, packaging and shipping charges.*

8. Promises of production or delivery by specified dates appearing either in customer's orders or manufacturer's production schedules supplied to customer, are based on circumstances existing at the time of the making of such promises. Any delay(s) from any cause whatever in meeting such promises shall not constitute default or breach of contract and customer shall not have any right to refuse any late deliveries or claim any damages from such delay.

Appendix Four

PRINTING TRADE CUSTOMS[13]

1. **QUOTATION.** A quotation not accepted within thirty (30) days is subject to review.

2. **ORDERS.** Orders regularly entered, verbal or written, cannot be cancelled except upon terms that will compensate printer against loss.

3. **EXPERIMENTAL WORK.** Experimental work performed at customer's request, such as sketches, drawings, composition, plates, presswork and materials will be charged for at current rates and may not be used without consent of the printer.

4. **PREPARATORY WORK.** Sketches, copy, dummies and all preparatory work created or furnished by the printer, shall remain his exclusive property and no use of same shall be made, nor any ideas obtained therefrom be used, except upon compensation to be determined by the printer.

5. **CONDITION OF COPY.** Estimates for typesetting are based on the receipt of original copy or manuscript clearly typed, double-spaced on 8–1/2" x 11" uncoated stock, one side only. Condition of copy which deviates from this standard is subject to re-estimating and pricing review by printer at time of submission of copy, unless otherwise specified in estimate.

6. **PREPARATORY MATERIALS.** Art work, type, plates, negatives, positives and other items when supplied by the printer shall remain his exclusive property unless otherwise agreed in writing.

7. **ALTERATIONS.** Alterations represent work performed in addition to the original specifications. Such additional work shall be charged at current rates and be supported with documentation upon request.

[13] Originally formally promulgated, Annual Convention, United Typothetae of America, 1922. Revised and updated and repromulgated, Annual Convention, Printing Industries of America, Inc., 1945 & 1974.

8. **PROOFS.** Proofs shall be submitted with original copy. Corrections are to be made on "master set", returned marked "O.K." or "O.K. with corrections" and signed by customer. If revised proofs are desired, request must be made when proofs are returned. Printer regrets any errors that may occur through production undetected, but cannot be held responsible for errors if the work is printed per customer's O.K. or if changes are communicated verbally. Printer shall not be responsible for errors if the customer has not ordered or has refused to accept proofs or has failed to return proofs with indication of changes or has instructed printer to proceed without submission of proofs.

9. **PRESS PROOFS.** Unless specifically provided in printer's quotation, press proofs will be charged for at current rates. An inspection sheet of any form can be submitted for customer approval, at no charge, provided customer is available at the press during the time of makeready. Any changes, corrections or lost press time due to customer's change of mind or delay will be charged for at current rates.

10. **COLOR PROOFING.** Because of differences in equipment, paper, inks and other conditions between color proofing and production pressroom operations, a reasonable variation in color between color proofs and the completed job shall constitute acceptable delivery. Special inks and proofing stocks will be forwarded to customer's suppliers upon request at current rates.

11. **OVER RUNS OR UNDER RUNS.** Over runs or under runs not to exceed 10% on quantities ordered up to 10,000 copies and/or the percentage agreed upon over or under quantities ordered above 10,000 copies shall constitute acceptable delivery. Printer will bill for actual quantity delivered within this tolerance. If customer requires guaranteed "no less than" delivery, percentage tolerance of overage must be doubled.

12. **CUSTOMER'S PROPERTY.** The printer will maintain fire, extended coverage, vandalism, malicious mischief and sprinkler leakage insurance on all property belonging to the customer, while such property is in the printer's possession; printer's liability for such property shall not exceed the amount recoverable from such insurance.

13. **DELIVERY.** Unless otherwise specified, the price quoted is for a single shipment, without storage, F.O.B. local customer's place of business or F.O.B. printer's platform for out-of-town customers. Proposals are based on continuous and uninterrupted delivery of complete order, unless specifications distinctly state otherwise. Charges related to delivery from customer to printer, or from customer's supplier to printer are not included in any quotations unless specified. Special priority pickup or delivery service will be provided at current rates upon customer's request. Materials delivered from customer or his suppliers are verified with delivery ticket as to cartons,

packages or items shown only. The accuracy of quantities indicated on such tickets cannot be verified and printer cannot accept liability for shortage based on supplier's tickets. Title for finished work shall pass to the customer upon delivery, to carrier at shipping point or upon mailing of invoices for finished work, whichever occurs first.

14. **PRODUCTION SCHEDULES.** Production schedules will be established and adhered to by customer and printer, provided that neither shall incur any liability or penalty for delays due to state of war, riot, civil disorder, fire, strikes, accidents, action of Government or civil authority and act of God or other causes beyond the control of customer or printer.

15. **CUSTOMER FURNISHED MATERIALS.** Paper stock, camera copy, film, color separations and other customer furnished materials shall be manufactured, packed and delivered to printer's specifications. Additional cost due to delays or impaired production caused by specification deficiencies shall be charged to the customer.

16. **TERMS.** Payment shall be net cash thirty (30) days from date of invoice unless otherwise provided in writing. Claims for defects, damages or shortages must be made by the customer in writing within a period of thirty (30) days after delivery. Failure to make such claim within the stated period shall constitute irrevocable acceptance and an admission that they fully comply with terms, conditions and specifications. Printer's liability shall be limited to stated selling price of any defective goods, and shall in no event include special or consequential damages, including profits (or profits lost). As security for payment of any sum due or to become due under terms of any Agreement, printer shall have the right, if necessary, to retain possession of and shall have a lien on all customer property in printer's possession including work in process and finished work. The extension of credit or the acceptance of notes, trade acceptances or guarantee of payment shall not affect such security interest and lien.

17. **INDEMNIFICATION.** The customer shall indemnify and hold harmless the printer from any and all loss, cost, expense and damages on account of any and all manner of claims, demands, actions and proceedings that may be instituted against the printer on grounds alleging that the said printing violates any copyright or any proprietary right of any person, or that it contains any matter that is libelous or scandalous, or invades any person's right to privacy or other personal rights, except to the extent that the printer has contributed to the matter. The customer agrees to, at the customer's own expense, promptly defend and continue the defense of any such claim, demand, action or proceeding that may be brought against the printer, provided that the printer shall promptly notify the customer with respect thereto, and provided further that the printer shall give to the customer such reasonable time as the exigencies of the situation may permit in which to undertake and continue the defense thereof.

Appendix Five

TRADE CUSTOMS OF THE TYPOGRAPHIC INDUSTRY[14]

ALTERATIONS. (*Any addition, change or modification of work in progress made by the customer in copy, style, or specifications originally submitted to the typographer.*) Alterations will be charged for at prevailing rates at the time of the alteration. When type selection and style are left to the best judgment of the typographer, charges will be made for the customer's alterations.

CHANCE ORDERS. (*Work produced without charge in speculation of an order.*) No work will be produced on the chance an order may be placed.

CHARGES FOR WORK. (*The basis upon which work will be performed.*) Charges for work may be at either the hourly rate, on a piece-work basis or total job price, as determined by the typographer at his discretion at either the time of making a quotation or invoicing the work.

COMPUTER PROGRAMS AND UNDERLYING MATERIALS. (*A computer program is a system, consisting of a series of instructions or statements in a form acceptable to a computer, prepared in order to achieve a certain result. Underlying materials are those production tools necessary to the development of the computer program.*) Computer programs, systems analyses and underlying materials developed by the typographer in order to produce work for a customer with the use of data processing machines or computers are the property of the typographer. No use shall be made of, or ideas taken from, such programs, analyses or materials without the express permission, and only upon payment of just compensation to the typographer.

CORRECTIONS. (*Changes in composition and other work performed by the typographer due to errors by the typographer.*) Corrections of errors will be made by the typographer without charge, but no financial liability is assumed for errors beyond making the corrections.

[14] Issued jointly by the International Typographic Composition Association (ITCA), and the Advertising Typographers Association of America (ATA). Trade Customs of the Typographic Industry were originally adopted in 1920, and were restated in 1921, 1922, 1940, 1944, 1947, 1960 and October, 1973.

CUSTOMER'S PROPERTY. (*All property, materials and/or supplies belonging to the customer which are delivered to the typographer for use in the production work.*) Customer's property delivered to the typographer for use in producing work is received by the typographer without any liability for loss or damage from causes beyond his control, such as Acts of God, fire, water, theft, or strikes. All such property, materials, and/or supplies used in producing the work will be considered dead six months after completion of the related work and disposed of, unless prior written instructions are given by the customer.

DELIVERY. (*Conveyance of work to points or receivers designated by the customer.*) Delivery is complete upon conveyance of the work to points, receivers (such as common carriers) designated by the customer, or upon deposit in the National Postal Service. The typographer assumes no responsibility after delivery.

ESTIMATE. (*A preliminary projection of cost which is not intended to be binding.*) Estimates are based upon prevailing wages, the anticipated hours of work and cost of materials and supplies necessary to produce work in accordance with preliminary copy, style and specifications, and are not binding upon the typographer.

EXPERIMENTAL WORK. (*Innovative attempts to create unique production tools, samples or style pages.*) Experimental work, performed at the request of customers will be charged for on the basis of prevailing rates.

HANDLING AND SHIPPING. (*The preparation of work for transportation and the conveyance or mailing of the work.*) Handling and shipping charges must be paid by the customer.

INPUT DATA STORAGE. (*Information which has been prepared in specialized form for utilization by data processing machines or computers.*) Punch cards, magnetic and paper tapes, disc packs, programs or other documents, materials or property relating to work either in progress or completed may be stored for 12 months by the typographer at the client's risk. Input data will be destroyed after such time, unless there is a specific written agreement.

LAYOUTS, STYLE PAGES, DUMMIES AND PASTE-UPS. (*Preliminary representations of work created as production tools or prototypes for the production of the work.*) Layouts, style pages, dummies, paste-ups or other specially-created production tools made or developed by a typographer at the order of a customer shall be charged for on the basis of prevailing rates. No use shall be made of, or ideas taken from such production tools or prototypes without the express permission and only upon payment of just compensation to the typographer.

LIEN. (*A right to hold the property of another pending the satisfaction of an outstanding obligation.*) All materials or property belonging to the customer, as well as work performed, may be retained by the typographer as security until all just claims against the customer have been satisfied.

METAL. (*Alloys composed of lead, tin and antimony which are commonly used in the manufacture of printers types, rules and spacing materials.*) All metal delivered to customers in the form of composition, made-up pages or forms shall remain the property of the typographer until the customer either returns or pays for the metal in accordance with the prevailing local customs. Made-up jobs must be returned intact to receive maximum credit. Linotype and Monotype metal, except when returned intact in made-up jobs, must be separated when returned to receive maximum credit. All mixed metal not in made-up form will only be credited at the scrap metal price. Metal which contains any brass, copper, zinc, or harmful chemicals will be classed as "junk" metal and will be credited as such.

ORDERS. (*Verbal or written requests for specific goods and/or services.*) Orders accepted by a typographer can only be cancelled on terms that provide for just compensation for work commenced and necessary work-related obligations entered into pursuant to the order. Verbal orders and instructions must be confirmed in writing prior to commencement of the work to be binding on the typographer. All orders are accepted subject to contingencies such as strikes, fires, vandalism, Acts of God, and other causes beyond the control of the typographer.

OUTSIDE PURCHASES. (*Any materials purchased by the typographer as necessary to produce work in accordance with a customer's order.*) All outside purchases will be charged for on the basis of cost.

OVERTIME. (*Work performed by employees in excess of the prevailing regular daily and/or weekly schedule of hours, or as provided by law.*) Overtime may be charged at the typographer's prevailing rates for overtime.

PRELIMINARY PROOFS. (*Reproductions of composition, illustrations, or other graphic representations.*) Preliminary proofs (also referred to as rough, customer or galley proofs) submitted to a customer for approval must be marked "OK" or "OK with Corrections or Alterations" (with such alterations and/or corrections indicated with standard proofreaders marks) and signed or initialed by the customer.

QUOTATIONS. (*A statement of price for which specified work will be performed.*) Quotations are based on the number of man hours at the prevailing scale of wages, and the cost of materials, supplies and services necessary to do the work. Quotations are based on copy, style, and other specifications and information originally submitted; and *any* change therein, including delivery requirements, automatically voids the quotation. Quotations are only valid for 30 days or as otherwise specified and must be in writing.

STANDING TYPE AND ELECTROTYPE FORMS, MECHANICAL ART AND FILM OR PAPER MAKEUP. (*Metal, film or paper assembled for reproduction into final plates, proofs, negatives or other graphic products.*) All metal, film or paper assembled for reproduction is considered dead seven days after reproduction and may be destroyed without notice unless written instructions are provided prior to the date of destruction. All such materials will be subject to storage or rental charges after sixty days.

TERMS. (*Conditions of Sale.*) Work may be billed either on the basis of work completed, or upon completion of the order at the discretion of the typographer. COD jobs must be paid for upon delivery of first proofs. The value of all metal furnished as type, borders, ornaments and other materials shipped wil be included in the COD charge.

TYPE. (*Letters, figures, symbols and ornaments individually cast from lead alloy.*) The value of type used for direct printing and for molding (except less than five wax molds) will be charged to the customer in addition to composition charges.

WORKING NEGATIVES AND POSITIVES. (*Original or intermediate images, on film or paper, of type composition, illustrations or other graphic representations used in the production of work.*) Working negatives or positives, made by or developed for the typographer for the production work, remain the property of the typographer.

Appendix Six

BINDERY USAGES OF THE TRADE[15]

1. **QUOTATION.** Unless otherwise stated, a quotation is an offer subject to acceptance for thirty (30) days. After thirty (30) days and until acceptance is received, the quotation is subject to change without notice. Work shall start within thirty (30) days after acceptance unless otherwise agreed to by the parties.

   Long-term contracts are subject to specific negotiations taking into consideration wage and all material increases over which the buyer has no control.

   All quotations are based on work performed on a straight-time basis. Any work or deliveries requiring over-time shall be billed at over-time rates.

   Any downtime caused by customer delays shall be billed at regular rates. This includes, but is not limited to, time lost due to delays in obtaining office copies or o.k. sheets. Any additional work requested or required by the customer such as, but not limited to, extra make ready, extra material handling and rescheduling problems shall be billed at regular rates.

2. **AGREEMENTS.** The customer shall furnish a written purchase order, line-up sheet and sample copy with the order. No verbal agreement or representation shall be binding unless confirmed in writing. In the event that the line-up sheets and sample copy are not provided the binder shall not be liable in the event there are lay-out errors on impositions.

3. **DELAYS.** The binder is not responsible for any delays caused by accident, fire, strikes, water, or for any other cause whatsoever beyond his control.

4. **MATERIAL.** Following the acceptance of binder's quotation, but before the commencement of actual production, the customer and the binder shall agree to the imposition.

   Printing sheets shall be furnished to the binder properly jogged, securely wrapped or skidded and otherwise protected against damage which would

[15] Binders Group, Printing Industries of Metropolitan New York, Inc., February, 1978.

prevent efficient bindery production (guide and gripper edges shall be marked).

In the event there is no agreement between the customer and the binder as to the imposition, or the material is not properly finished or marked, the binder may return the material to the customer at the customer's risk and expenses.

5. **CASES, WRAPPERS, SKIDS, PALLETS, etc.** Unless a separate agreement is entered into between the binder and customer to provide otherwise, all cases, boxes, wrappers, skids, pallets and other packing materials received from the customer in connection with work to be performed becomes the property of the said binder. If otherwise, a separate charge will be made by the binder for additional expenses incurred for the replacement, return or delivery of such items.

6. **DELIVERY.** Prices are quoted "f.o.b." unless otherwise agreed in truck-load lots. Any additional handling or wrapping required will be charged to the customer.

7. **CUSTOMER PROPERTY.** All customer property whether in storage or in production is at the customer's risk. Binder is not liable for any loss or damage caused by fire, water leakage, theft, negligence, insects, rodents or any other cause beyond his control.

   A monthly storage charge will be made for handling and securing customer's property held for more than thirty (30) days.

   Binders reserves the right within ten (10) days after a written request for disposition of over sheets or bound stock to deliver such material to the customer and charge any handling and trucking charges which may be incurred thereby.

8. **QUANTITIES.** A quotation covers only specified quantity stated to be bound or completed as in the initial order. If, however, the customer calls for a partial lot or non-production office copies, it is understood that the binder will add to the quoted price any increase in cost.

   Overruns or underruns are not to exceed ten (10%) percent of the bound or printed sheets furnished and shall constitute an acceptable delivery unless otherwise agreed. Any excess or deficiency shall be pro-rated at the per thousand (1,000) rate of the quoted price.

9. **COUNTS.** The binder makes no hand count on receipt of sheets or other materials unless a separate and distinct agreement is made, for which service and extra charges will be made. The basis of the count shall be the folding, gathering or other machine counts recorded as soon after production as is convenient.

10. **TERMS—NET CASH.** Interest will be charged on any past-due accounts.

The binder reserves the right to bill any part of the order which has been completed. Preliminary deliveries, set-up costs or any additional expenses incurred due to customer delays or other conditions beyond the binder's control may be billed at the prevailing rates.

11. **ARBITRATION.** All claims, demands, disputes, differences or controversies and misunderstandings arising under, out of, or in connection with or in relation to any agreement entered into between the binder and customer, shall be submitted to and be determined by arbitration before the proper parties of the American Arbitration Association. Decisions shall provide for reasonable attorneys fees for the binder of fifteen (15%) percent of the amount awarded.

12. **INDEMNIFICATION.** The customer shall indemnify and hold harmless the binder from any and all loss, cost, expense and damages on account of any and all manner of claims, demands, actions and proceedings that may be instituted against the binder on grounds alleging that the said job violates any copyright or any proprietary right of any person or that it contains any material that is libelous or scandalous, or invades any person's right to privacy or other personal rights. The customer agrees to at the customer's own expense, promptly defend and continue the defense of any such claim, demand, action or proceeding that may be brought against the binder provided that the binder shall timely notify the customer with respect thereto, and provided further that the binder shall give to the customer such reasonable time as the exigencies of the situation may permit in which to undertake and continue the defense thereof.

13. **LIMITED LIABILITY.** In no event shall the binder be liable to the customer, or any other party for loss of profit, loss of use, labor or material. Damages of any kind, including but not limited to, damages arising from the binder's negligence or his failure to perform under the contract or any of its terms, shall be limited to the contract price to the customer.

Appendix Seven

BIBLIOGRAPHY

BOOK PRODUCTION

Book Production Industry, Westport, Connecticut, monthly.

Latimer, Henry C.: *Preparing Art and Camera Copy for Printing*, McGraw-Hill Book Company, New York, 1977.

Lee, Marshall: *Bookmaking: The Illustrated Guide to Design/Production/Editing*, second edition, R.R. Bowker Company, New York, 1979.

The Literary Market Place, R.R. Bowker Company, New York, annual.

McMurtie, Douglas C.: *The Book, The Story of Printing and Bookmaking,* third edition, Oxford University Press, New York, 1943.

New England Printer and Publisher, Salem, New Hampshire, monthly.

Peters, Jean, ed.: *The Bookman's Glossary*, fifth edition, R.R. Bowker Company, New York, 1975.

Publisher's Weekly, R.R. Bowker Company, New York, weekly.

Stevenson, George A.: *Graphic Arts Encyclopedia*, second edition, McGraw-Hill Book Company, New York, 1979.

DESIGN AND ARTWORK

Biegeleisen, J. I.: *The ABC of Lettering*, fifth edition, revised, enlarged, Harper & Row, Publishers, Inc., New York, 1976.

Biegeleisen, J. I.: *Design and Print Your Own Posters*, Watson-Guptil Publications, New York, 1976.

Collier, Robert, *et al: Optical Holography*, Academic Press, Inc., New York, 1971.

Craig, James: *Production for the Graphics Designer*, Watson-Guptill Publications, New York, 1974.

Maurello, S. Ralph: *Commercial Art Techniques*, L. Amiel Publisher, New York,

Print: America's Graphic Design Magazine, New York, monthly.

Ridgway, John Livesy: *Scientific Illustration*, Stanford University Press, Stanford, California, 1938, reprint, 1978.

Silver, Gerald A.: *Modern Graphic Arts Paste-Up*, American Technical Society, Chicago, 1973.

Thomas, T. A.: *Technical Illustration*, third edition, McGraw-Hill Book Company, New York, 1979.

Wenyon, Michael: *Understanding Holography,* Arco Publishing Company, New York, 1979.

White, Jan V.: *Editing by Design; Word-and-Picture Communication For Editors and Designers*, R.R. Bowker Company, New York and London, 1974.

White, Jan V.: *Graphic Idea Notebook,* Watson-Guptil Publications, New York, 1980.

NEWSPAPERS AND MAGAZINES

Arnold, Edmund C. and Hillier Kreighbaum: *Handbook of Student Journalism*, New York University Press, New York, 1976.

Arnold, Edmund C.: *Modern Newspaper Design*, Harper & Row, Publishers, Inc., New York, 1969.

Ayer Directory of Publications, Ayer Press, Philadelphia, Pa., annual.

Editor and Publisher, New York, weekly.

PAPER

Pulp and Paper, Miller Freeman Publications, San Francisco, California, monthly.

PHOTOGRAPHY

Frobisch, Dieter and Lamprecht Hortmut: *Graphic Photo Design: Lab Techniques in Color and Black and White*, American Photographic Book Publishing Company, Inc., Garden City, New York, 1977.

Page, André: *A Dictionary of Photographic Terms,* The Technical Press Limited, London, 1966.

PRINTING

Adams, J. Michael and David D. Faux: *Printing and Technology: A Medium of Visual Communications*, Duxbury Press, North Scituate, Massachusetts, 1977.

Biegeleisen, J. I.: *Screen Printing*, Watson-Guptill Publications, New York, 1971.

Cogoli, John E.: *Photo Offset Fundamentals*, third edition, McKnight Publishing Company, Bloomington, Illinois, 1973.

Goodacre, Clive, ed.: *Penrose 78–79 International Review of the Graphic Arts*, Hastings House, Publishers, Inc., New York, 1978.

Haraess, Jack H.: *Paper and Printing Problems Guide*, second edition, Bergstrom Paper Company, Neenah, Wisconsin, 1978.

Melcher, Daniel and Nancy Larrick; *Printing and Promotion Handbook,* third edition, McGraw-Hill Book Company, New York, 1966.

Pocket Pal®: A Graphic Arts Production Handbook, eleventh edition, International Paper Company, New York, 1976.

TYPE

Biegeleisen, J. I.: *Art Director's Book of Type Faces*, third edition, Arco Publishing Company, New York, 1976.

Craig, James: *Phototypesetting*, Watson-Guptil Publications, New York, 1978.

Glossary of Automated Typesetting and Related Terms, second edition, Composition Information Services, Los Angeles, 1966.

Glossary of Computer Buzz Words, Profit Control Systems, Heidelberg Eastern, New York, 1980.

Graphic Arts Typebook: Machine Composition; vol. I, "Serif Faces"; vol. II, "Sand Serifs, Square Serifs, and Miscellaneous Faces," Reinhold Publishing Corporation, New York, 1965.

Karch, R. Randolf: *How to Recognize Type Faces*, Taplinger Publishing Company, Inc., New York, 1952.

Kleper, Michael L.: *Understanding Phototypesetting*, North American Publishing Company, Philadelphia, Pa., 1976.

WRITING, EDITING, AND PROOFREADING

Bernstein, Theodore M.: *Do's, Dont's, and Maybes of English Usage*, Times Books, New York, 1977.

Ferguson, Rowena: *Editing the Small Magazine*, second edition, Columbia University Press, New York, 1976.

Flesch, Rudolf: *The Art of Readable Writing*, twenty-fifth annual edition, revised and enlarged, Harper & Row, Publishers, Inc., New York, 1974.

Fowler, H. W., edited by Sir Ernest Towers: *A Dictionary of Modern English Usage*, Oxford University Press, New York, 1965.

Garst, Robert E. and Theodore Bernstein: *Headlines and Deadlines:* A Manual for Copy Editors, third edition, Columbia University Press, 1961.

Jordan, Lewis: *The New York Times Manual of Style and Usage*, Times Books, New York, 1976.

Kent, Ruth: *Language of Journalism: A Glossary of Print-Communication Terms*, Kent State University Press, Kent, Ohio, 1970.

Manual of Style, The University of Chicago Press, twelfth edition, Chicago and London, 1969.

Skillin, Marjorie E. and Robert M. Gay: *Words Into Type*, third edition, Appleton-Century-Crofts, Inc., New York, 1974.